P9-DGD-650

Jane Addams and the Liberal Tradition

The very best of everything to the Boyd Baileys

Dan Levine

Jane Addams in 1889, the year Hull House was founded.

PHOTOGRAPH COURTESY OF JANE ADDAMS' MEMORIAL COLLECTION, UNIVERSITY OF ILLINOIS LIBRARY AT CHICAGO CIRCLE CAMPUS.

JANE ADDAMS AND THE LIBERAL TRADITION

Daniel Levine

STATE HISTORICAL SOCIETY OF WISCONSIN

MADISON : MCMLXXI

FRONTISPIECE PORTRAIT

Jane Addams' Memorial Collection, University of Illinois, Chicago.

WOODCUT DECORATIONS

Susan Levine, Brunswick, Maine.

 Printed and bound in the United States of America by the Worzalla Publishing Company, Stevens Point, Wisconsin. Library of Congress Catalog Card Number: 70-634145. Standard Book Number: 87020-109-3.

CONTENTS

ACKNOWLEDGMENTS

As always, Ray A. Billington, Robert H. Wiebe, and Clarke Chambers were generous with their time and wisdom. They, as well as Louis Filler and Christopher Lasch, read the entire manuscript, and much to my profit. I am grateful also to the President and Trustees of Bowdoin College for making available to me a semester, free of other duties, in which to write the first draft of the manuscript. The Midwest History Research Grants Committee generously provided funds for research. None of these individuals or groups, however, shares any responsibility for errors of fact or interpretation the book may contain.

There are some people—and I am one of them—who think that the most practical and important thing about a man is still his view of the universe. We think that for a landlady considering a lodger it is important to know his income, but still more important to know his philosophy. We think that for a general about to fight an enemy it is important to know about the enemy's numbers, but still more important to know the enemy's philosophy. We think the question is not whether the theory of the cosmos affects matters, but whether in the long run anything else affects them.

G. K. Chesterton

INTRODUCTION

WHEN Jane Addams was born, Abraham Lincoln was running for the presidency. When she founded Hull House, Grover Cleveland was beginning his second term in office and the Sherman Antitrust Act was under consideration in Congress. When she died in 1935, the New Deal had moved beyond disaster relief to major reforms. Within a few months of her death, the National Labor Relations Act and the Social Security Act became law. She thus saw the great transformation of America from rural and agricultural to urban and industrial, from laissez-faire to general welfare state. It is the thesis of this book that she was an important moving force in this transition.

Miss Addams, as she was called by all but a few close associates, is by no means forgotten. She rates at least a sentence or two in any sixth-grade social studies book, and in any text in American history she is predictably one of the prominent reformers of the progressive years. Yet it is difficult from these brief descriptions to imagine the impact she had on her contemporaries. In newspaper features year after year she was voted the greatest woman in the United States, the greatest in the world, and, on one occasion, the greatest in history. She became, for two entire generations, not only a person, but a symbol for goodness: a symbol, perhaps, for the way in which the best traditional Christian impulses could be relevantly interpreted for a modern industrial society. Once a group of nurses arrived late at a hall to hear Jane Addams speak, and missed her remarks. At their pleading, she appeared briefly on the platform while the auditorium rang with cheers. Later she said that the whole affair had embarrassed her. She was glad that people agreed with her ideas, but she did not feel comfortable merely being gazed at.

For a symbol is not a human being. The adulation she received, and with which her memory is still honored by a generation now growing old, obscures rather than illuminates her importance. Jane Addams was not merely someone who loved the poor and did good, and to dismiss her thus is to bury her indeed. She must be taken rather more seriously than that by students of the American past: as an important force in changing the way Americans thought about themselves and their society. If one agrees with Chesterton that the most important thing about a man—and hence about men as citizens—is his view of the universe, then it is important to find out how and why his view of the universe has changed. It is here that Miss Addams exerted her lasting and her most important influence. Perhaps more than anyone else, she convinced Americans that the welfare ideology, and ultimately the welfare state, were both right and practical. Thus when Franklin Roosevelt decided that the power of the federal government might be used to alleviate suffering and cushion economic shock, the ground was prepared. Americans, with the spurs of depression drawing blood from their flanks, might have accepted anything from commissar to führer. What they got was a tentative beginning towards a meliorative welfare state, the first steps down the road which Jane Addams had been urging the nation to travel for more than forty years. To plot and guide these first steps, Roosevelt brought into his administration a long-time associate of Jane Addams as Secretary of the Interior, an ideological granddaughter of Jane Addams as Secretary of Labor, and a disciple of Jane Addams as general advisor and informal minister of welfare. Harold Ickes, Frances Perkins, and Harry Hopkins, together with many of their contemporaries, took the fundamental ideological position which Jane Addams had been advocating, and from it they worked out the beginning of what finally, in this last quarter of the twentieth century, may come to fruition.

Jane Addams was not an original thinker of major importance. One can find predecessors for almost every one of her ideas in the writings of English Fabians, German political economists, American pragmatists. Her importance was not as a manufacturer of ideas, but as their retailer. Though not original, she was extremely alert to currents of thought in the United States. In no one area did she possess enormous expertise; yet probably no reformer was so deeply involved in so many facets of reform. She was a well-informed activist and publicist in the causes of progresive education, housing reform, child-labor legislation, criminology, labor organizing, recreation, direct democracy, feminism, treatment of the immigrant, pacifism, and more. Virtually every major reform of the progressive years—with the significant exception of the antitrust movement—benefited to some degree from Jane Addams' participation. Her most important role in these causes was as a publicist and persuader. She effectively convinced Americans, both within and without legislative chambers, of the seriousness of the problems the nation faced, and of the need for change. Moreover she clearly pointed the direction these changes should take. And people listened to her—not only because her words seemed right, but also because she had put her words into action at Hull House. She knew what she was talking about.

In short, she asked those questions and gave those answers which most Americans from that day to this have found to be the right questions and the right answers. An examination of Jane Addams' thought can reveal much about the thought of the period. In a meaningful way, Jane Addams can act as a window on the age.

Subsidiary themes are implied by this major thesis. One is that if one looks for the origins of the welfare ideology in the United States, the place to begin is not with the New Deal, but with the progressive years. Recent scholarship has tended to scorn or belittle the efforts of the pre-World War I reformers. In looking back on these years, Miss Addams herself said that the experience of the war "makes it all seem so remote."[1] When one adds an experience like the New Deal, which shaped the thinking of most current scholars of American history, and yet another world war, the remoteness may increase manifold. Seeing how much the progressive years left for the New Deal to do, it is easy to scorn the earlier reformers for their limited vision and nearby goals. And seeing how much the New Deal left undone, a younger group of historians now belittles the second Roosevelt no less than the first. As a result, virtually all of twentieth-century American reform is in danger of being dismissed as essentially a sham.[2]

While this line of argument is producing some fruitful scholarship, particularly on the nature of the relationship between business regulators and the businesses regulated, its basic ideological presuppositions are ahistorical. In fact American reform in the twentieth century has been melioristic, not revolutionary. With all its gaps and shortcomings, it has been a relatively successful meliorism. Less successful, perhaps, than that of small homogeneous Scandinavian countries, but far more successful than revolutionary attempts in other industrialized countries. (Revolutionary upheavals in underdeveloped countries are still *in media res,* and impossible to evaluate, though they certainly are to some extent successful.)

Twentieth-century reform was in many ways a continuation of nineteenth- and even eighteenth-century trends—trends which were given a different cast by the necessities of industrialism. One way of looking at the history of social organization in the western world since at least the eighteenth century is as a history of increasing inclusiveness. Simply stated, this means that an increasing percentage of the population has become involved in making decisions about how society would function. One group after another either was granted influence, or insisted upon it. Here I am not talking merely about political power, though that is an important expression, but more broadly about the issue of who is noticed, who is influential, who *matters* in society. The successive reform bills in nineteenth-century England are symbols of this process in the political sphere, though scholars hasten to point out that merely extending the franchise did not necessarily alter the stratification of power in England. In 1832, 1867, and 1884 the franchise laws were altered, and each alteration allowed not only more people to vote, but more economic groups and interests to be influential: urban wealth, the urban middle class, agricultural workers, industrial workers. In France those who traditionally had held power were less willing to come to terms with groups seeking power, so the story was written in a series of revolutions. At the end of the eighteenth century, the upper reaches of the bourgeoisie gained influence, and throughout the nineteenth century first the petite bourgeoisie, then the industrial workers forced their way to a position where they could insist on being heard. In the Scandinavian countries well-organized groups of farmers broke the monopoly of power held by very narrow aristocracies, and the farmers were followed by the urban workers. In Germany the process was again different. A coalition was formed between the growing industrial bourgeoisie and the workers. This coalition successfully took power from a traditional landed aristocracy. But whether in England, France, Germany, or the Scandinavian countries the result of these differing processes has been the same: groups outside the decision-making portions of society have been brought within its compass.

In the United States the process has been more akin to the English story, though with important differences. One might look at the American Revolution itself as an attempt by the people who mattered in the colonies to exert their influence on the Empire, though perhaps it might be better to describe them as trying to maintain an influential position in the colonies against the empire. At any rate, the Jeffersonians were at least theoretically more inclusive than the Federalists. The Jacksonians in turn opened the door of social and political power to entrepreneurs of American business and to the western farmer, who in a real sense was the entrepreneur of American agriculture. Late in the century, as America became an industrial society, business entrepreneurs gained dominant political and economic power, and new outgroups struggled for power: the farmers, immigrants, and, most important, the new urban proletariat—part farmer, part immigrant, part city dweller in background. Women, too, asked that they no longer be treated as a dependent class. Even Negroes—always the last to receive what America has to offer—began to ask for notice, though their request was scarcely even acknowledged until after World War II. The struggle to readjust power relationships to an industrial-urban society has dominated the course of events in twentieth-century America. It is here that Jane Addams asked the fruitful questions and came to the relevant answers.

The pace of American industrialization and concomitant urbanization was simply too rapid for the social and political institutions to adjust. Someday soon perhaps a scholar will write a history of garbage in the United States. It would be a revealing study. Factories created cities which created garbage—which no one was prepared to deal with. Garbage is simply one of the vast complex of problems which built up tremendous pressure during the 1870's, 1880's and 1890's. There had been factories and factory workers before the Civil War, but never so many, nor from so many different countries, nor so concentrated, and concentrated not only in New England cities but in metropolises all over the nation. How would food, transportation, shelter, education, water, and sanitation be provided? Most important, how would dignity, a sense of participation, and a self-respecting identity find their way into this new sort of city population? The pressures burst forth at Haymarket in the 1880's, at Homestead in the 1890's, but they remained to be dealt with. The solution has been to enfold these groups gradually within the scope of those who "matter." And it is here that Miss Addams played a crucial role. She was perhaps the most important voice in convincing Americans that the enfolding ought to take place, and in showing them how to do it.

The result has been the kind of semi-welfare state which, for all its weaknesses, has been such a success in the United States. There are some groups who still do not "matter," and are in this sense outside the social system: migrant workers, Indians, and, most important if only because of their numbers, Negroes. Their existence, however, does not denote a basic failure of the melioristic welfare approach. There is no reason to emulate the contemporary political conservative who, when he finds someone cheating to get unemployment compensation, indignantly demands the ending of unemployment insurance. The solution is not to discard the melioristic approach but to continue its expansion.

Jane Addams was not simply melioristic; she was radical, and a part of the radical tradition in America. This is a statement out of tune with much recent American scholarship, which denies the existence of any but peripheral radicalism in the United States. The most widely influential general treatment of American political thought, Louis Hartz's *Liberal Tradition in America,* insists that Americans were all Lockean liberals, that there was neither a true conservative nor a true radical tradition in the United States. His approach, explicit in his case, implicit in the case of younger scholars, is to compare the European political spectrum with the American. He finds the latter lacks the two extremes of the former. In looking to Europe, Hartz conceived a brilliant corrective to virtually all American historical writing, but the effort carried with it its own dangers. When he compared

Europe and the United States, he stated that he found no left wing in American politics; but what he really meant was that he found no European left wing. In fact he has not so much compared the two traditions as taken European definitions and tried to apply them to the United States. To conclude that there was no left wing in this country from this logic is to make the elementary error of confusing the word with the thing.

There is another basic logical error in the conclusions of those who find only a middle-ground consensus in American history—and this quite apart from any disagreement I might have with their conclusions on specific historical issues. These scholars have confused a stance towards politics with a particular political program, and thus their discussion of the term "radicalism" has become distorted. The word has been much defined with complications as unnecessary as they are misleading. There is a perfectly adequate definition of radicalism which is also simple: Radicalism is a direction along a continuum. People who want to change a lot of important things rapidly are more radical than people who want to change less important things, or fewer of them, or less rapidly. Radicalism is thus a stance towards the political process, not any particular program. In some countries capitalism is a radical program; in others socialism may be radical. Thus recent writers have quite properly referred to a "radical right" in the United States.

Those historians who belittle the melioristic approach do so in the service of one form or another of the rejection of the capitalist system, no matter how regulated that system may be. They identify radicalism only and exclusively with a program which will reject that system. This view comes from eyes attuned to Europe, where it is true that most recent radicalism has been Marxist; but radicalism and Marxism are not synonymous. To point out that this sort of radicalism has been weak in the United States is indeed important—but it is merely a beginning, not an end to the question.

If one defines radicalism as wanting rapid change in important areas, radicalism has a long tradition in the United States, from Puritanism to the so-called New Left. By definition the Puritans were one extreme of the Elizabethan compromise and, in fact, were off the continuum. In an age when matters of faith were as important as politics are to a modern age, the Puritans insisted on a rapid and complete change of fundamentals. That they established an orthodoxy in Massachusetts, against which well-known new radicals rebelled, is simply further evidence of the necessity of seeing radicalism as stance rather than content. Whether the American Revolution was a conservative or a radical movement is very much a moot point in scholarship. Probably, it was both. Whatever the case, the constitution-makers were impressively radical in Philadelphia in 1787. If one sets to one side the historiographical controversy about which economic groups supported and which opposed the adoption of the Constitution, and looks at the document itself in its historical context, one must acknowledge its shocking political radicalism. Even historians often seem to forget that the document was written in the eighteenth century, before the French Revolution, before even the first limited franchise reforms in England. To establish a political system based on a broad popular franchise, with a head of state (not merely a head of government) elected every four years was, and was acknowledged within and without the United States to be, a form of extremism.

The older myths about Jacksonian Democracy as the age of the common man can no longer be seriously maintained, but certainly the nature of politics changed between Jefferson's time and Jackson's. John Adams and Thomas Jefferson had argued politely, near the beginning of the century, about whether the country should be run by an aristocracy of birth or an aristocracy of merit. Some few Jacksonians might say that they longed for a return to those days, but in fact both sorts of aristocracies, in the sense that Jefferson and Adams used the terms, were irrelevant in the age of King Andrew.

Not all the abolitionists were radicals in the sense that I have used the term, but some clearly were. Thoreau in gentle tones and Garrison in strident ones rejected the document that was symbolic of nationhood and—since the age was now political rather than religious—this was desecration of the temple. At least some few of the post-Civil War radicals were actually radical, proposing as they did that the social and economic system of the South be turned inside out, and that black men be considered fully human.

But the real issue for this book is what happened at the end of the nineteenth and the beginning of the twentieth century. Conglomerate reformist labor unions were succeeded by exponents of bread and butter. Explicitly socialist political parties either died natural deaths or were successfully repressed. The greatest outcry for reform came at least in part from those most eager to prevent rather than hasten inevitable economic change. At least part of the impulse behind Populism was a desire to hold on to a disappearing America where farmers were dominant; Theodore Roosevelt argued for limited reforms as a way of staving off major change. Where then was radicalism in the populist and progressive period?

"I suppose I am sort of a socialist," Jane Addams once replied to a newspaperman's question—but she did not say what sort of a socialist she was. Certainly she was not a Marxist. She did not want victory for one side in the class war; she wanted to eliminate class warfare. She did not believe that one's relation to the means of production determined one's ideology, but that changed moral ideas could alter the means of production. Norman Thomas often said that when socialism came to the United States it would be called something else. If we look at content rather than labels, Jane Addams does emerge as "sort of a socialist"—and not such an unusual sort at that. She was simply a utopian or Christian socialist, in an American version. She asked for moral change before anything else. She asked for a "social ethic" to take the place of an individualistic ethic and thus hoped to achieve something of a peaceable kingdom. She was asking for an absolute and all-embracing change in the ideology of the United States— a change which by any reckoning must be counted as radical, but radical in an American rather than a German or an English sense.

It is understandable that she has been misinterpreted. She seemed so Victorian, so old-maidish, and (worst of all!) so proper. She inherited railroad and banking money, attended the Rockford (Illinois) Female Seminary, and was a lifelong member of the Daughters of the American Revolution. It is easy to look at the old pictures and laugh at lady bountiful, billowing among the poor in her long skirts, distributing charity and moral uplift. Perhaps, after all, it was simply her way of compensating for not having a husband and bearing children.

Being good and being Victorian were, however, only the starting points for Jane Addams. For forty years she lived, not as a visitor, but as a resident, in a Chicago slum; and she let her surroundings teach her things she never learned at Rockford Female Seminary. She learned from children things she had never really known about childhood. She learned from the young working girls in factories and sweatshops. She learned from John Dewey, Harold Ickes, Richard Ely, and Florence Kelley. She learned about the impact of government on her neighbors from the ward to the federal level. She learned from garbage, from suicide, from dirt. Most of all, of course, she learned from trying things at Hull House. What services did recent immigrants need? What kinds of education did children respond to? How could a city councilman be influenced? How best could the quality of life—in Chicago, in America, in the world—be raised and refined?

From what she learned, she developed an ideology and a program that constituted a fundamental challenge to the nation as she found it. In regard to ultimate ends, the nation has not realized Jane Addams' vision. But as Walt Kelly has said, the conflict between means and ends is academic: we are all struck down in mid-means. The point of view which Jane Addams represented has produced fruitful criticisms and long-lasting reforms of American society.

PART I
Jane Addams and Hull House

1

Childhood

> Myself, wife left Kreidersville, Northhampton Co. Pa. the home of Sarah's on the morning of July 29 1844 at four o clock A. M. with Theo. A. Enen in a two horse conveyance accompanied by mother and Harrison Weber as far as Easton, 16 miles from home where we arrived at ½ past 7 all safe.[1]

THUS did John Huy Addams describe the beginning of his trip from the older, fully settled eastern portion of Pennsylvania to northern Illinois, sparsely settled and not many years beyond the pioneer stage. It was typical of the man that, before sunup, he should wake his bride of only a few days to begin what was a combination honeymoon and exploratory expedition. John Huy Addams always was up early and on his way with a firm stride. It was just as typical that Sarah Weber Addams should be ready at four in the morning, for she had the strength and resolution to match her husband stride for stride.

As they drove through the countryside towards New York City, John Addams kept close note of the type of land they passed, what crops were grown, and whether the area seemed prosperous or not. He was thinking ahead to the kind of judgments he would have to make when he got west of Chicago. Neither John nor Sarah Addams had any liking for New York. They continued their way by boat up the Hudson to Albany, took a leisurely ride to Buffalo along the wondrous Erie Canal, and then another boat from Buffalo to Chicago. Here was his base of operations. From here he planned to explore the surrounding area to find a place where an energetic young man of twenty-two, with a miller's trade and financial backing from his own and his wife's parents, might make his fortune.

He took his time deciding where the best place might be. Summer was wet that year and the roads were sometimes more like muddy swamps. The Addamses spent many days at roadside inns while pouring rain kept them off the roads entirely. They were occasionally discouraged, but John Addams pressed on energetically; and while he was solicitous of his wife's needs, he expected her to come along without dragging her feet, and she did so. When Sunday came the journey would be interrupted by a day of rest and service at whatever church happened to be handy. If none were handy, no matter, church would get skipped that week, for John Addams was more interested in land than in sermons. One day, finding himself in far western Illinois, he journeyed a few extra miles to the Mississippi River and hired a large sailing canoe to take him across. Once there he stood briefly in Iowa Territory; then, with his ambition satisfied, he returned to Sarah, who had watched his exuberance from the Illinois shore.

After many months of exploration he decided that northern Illinois, near the Wisconsin border, was fertile enough for prosperous farming and had streams which could provide the water power to drive his grist mill. Cedarville is now the place, though it was barely a town at all in 1844 when John Addams settled into what was to be his home for the rest of his life. His wife's father established a mill of his own a few miles away.

Addams is, of course, an English name, though John Addams was only half English. He had a German branch in his family tree, going back to one Abraham op den Graeff, who is supposed to have come from Crefeld in Germany, though his name sounds Hollandish. Abraham op den Graeff is also supposed to have come to America on the very ship which carried William Penn to the New World for the first time. Abraham and his wife, Trintje, made their home in Germantown, Pennsylvania, where he and two brothers who followed him to America became pillars of the community. Their daughter, Gertien, married Richard Addams, the son of an Oxfordshire squire. A grandson of Richard and Gertien Addams, Isaak Addams, was living in Reading when the Revolution broke out. He joined the American side and rose to the rank of captain; later he served as a member of the assembly of the newly independent state of Pennsylvania. Isaak had five sons, the third of whom, Samuel, married Catherine

Huy, the descendant of a family which reached America from the Palatinate in 1741. Samuel and Catherine Huy Addams had ten children, including John Huy Addams, Jane Addams' father, the man who took his bride from Kreidersville to Cedarville. At twenty-two he had been to college, knew surveying and milling, and was confident of his ability to prosper in the near-pioneer environment of northern Illinois in the 1840's.[2]

He also had a head on his shoulders, which he was not content to keep only within his mill. With broader vision, he considered the economy of the region, how his mill fit into it, and what else he might turn his hand to. He knew that the rolling hills around Cedarville could produce rich crops of corn and wheat. He could see in incipient Chicago a major entrepôt for the lake and river trade, and for the canal system then slowly working its way westward. Perhaps he could even see that railroads would soon reach Chicago. The problem was to put all these assets together. An efficient way had to be found to get Cedarville's grain to Chicago. Canals seemed the most obvious answer to many of the early inhabitants of Stephenson County, for though many canals had been built on speculation and their backers had gone bankrupt, in recent years sound financing had taken the place of the boomers and the success of canal transportation was beyond question.

John Addams, however, put his faith in railroads, an innovation still new enough to seem adventurously speculative. He had seen railroad systems work in Pennsylvania and was convinced that they would offer a better solution than canals to Cedarville's need for transportation. After living in Cedarville only six years, he embarked on organizing a railroad. For four years he traveled all over the county, and sometimes to Chicago, pleading the cause of rail transportation and raising the money to finance it. More than anyone else he was responsible for getting the Chicago and Galena—later the Chicago and North Western Railroad—extended to Freeport, only a few miles from Cedarville.

The decade between 1844 and 1854 had seen John Addams realize goal after goal in ordered succession. His mill had prospered and he built a newer, more modern one in 1853. In that year he also built a substantial brick, two-and-a-half-story house. His railway plans had been fulfilled, and he was esteemed and respected by his neighbors. In 1854 they expressed their regard for him by electing him their representative to the state legislature, and they re-elected him for the next sixteen years until he voluntarily retired. This decade had seen a change in the man, too. There had been no diminution in energy, nor in self-confidence. As he became older, however, these became not the energy and confidence of a young hopeful, but those of a man of achievement. In his prime John Addams had presence. He was not a particularly large man physically, but in any group, whether of family or associates, he tended to dominate. Photographs show him fairly glaring out of dark eyes in a face which looked nearly stern. His dark hair and full beard added to an air of probity and dignity.

Indeed, probity characterized his dealings with man and God. He was a Quaker—a Hicksite Quaker—which faith he had chosen rather than been born to. His Quakerism often seemed stern to all but his daughter, for John Addams knew his way by an inner light, and he followed that way whether others said yea or nay. He was known during the Civil War and Reconstruction as a man who had not only never accepted a bribe, but as almost the only man who had never been offered one.

Marriage to a man with a sense of direction as strong as John Addams' might have been a difficult task. For Sarah Weber Addams, however, it was perfectly suited. She had enough of love and loyalty to follow where her husband led, yet she was made of strong enough stuff herself so that she was not crushed by the weight of his personality. Sarah Weber was five years older than her husband, and in many ways had been his social superior. Indeed, her aunt (who had introduced the two) later felt that Sarah had thrown herself away on a man both young and untried when she could have had the pick of many older, well-established suitors. The full details of Sarah's years of growing up are far from clear. A shadow of a previous courtship appears, however; a relationship which was apparently discouraged by her father. Colonel George Weber had sent Sarah off to boarding school to discourage that first suit, and she acquired some French and music but no love for either. When John Addams came courting, she permitted, rather than returned, his ardor. Once she had decided to become Mrs. Addams, however, no objections from an aunt or anyone else were allowed to interfere.

Life in Cedarville must have required a substantial adjustment for a woman used to eastern Pennsylvania, but Sarah Addams made the adjustment with gusto. She thoroughly enjoyed the planning and managing of what was far more than a family home. With the aid of a hired girl she provided meals for workers in the flour and saw mills, for the hands in the fields, and for those who brought their grain for milling. She made soap, rendered lard, preserved meat, wove rugs, and produced a steady stream of mittens and socks, running what amounted to a domestic factory. She also understood thoroughly the work of the mills, and when her husband was away in Springfield or on business trips she took charge of these as well.

Like her husband, Sarah Addams had confidence and presence. The Addamses attended alternately the Methodist and Presbyterian services. Although John Addams was not a church member, he conducted classes at the "union" Sunday school for many years. This was for him perhaps as much civic duty as religious expression. He and the children would depart early Sunday morning. Later, Mrs. Addams and the help would arrive at church in time for the sermon. With her small entourage, Sarah Addams would sweep up the aisle, her skirts rustling, nodding to friends on one side or the other. When she reached her pew her husband would rise, half bow, allow her to sit down, and then sit down beside her. This ritual was enacted Sunday after Sunday.

Sarah Addams brought up her children with the same sureness with which she managed her household and greeted her neighbors. She bore eight children, five of whom lived beyond infancy: Mary in 1845; Martha in 1850; James Weber (always called by his middle name) in 1852; Alice in 1853; and finally, Laura Jane Addams on September 6, 1860. For Sarah Addams it was normal to have one child nursing, another in the cradle, and at least two romping in all directions about the house. Keeping order was no problem for her; she was a stern disciplinarian. The two eldest children, Mary and Martha, were biddable and serene, but Alice and Weber were imps, and being only a year apart in age, could egg each other on. Sarah's punishment for extreme transgression was to imprison the transgressor for precise periods of time in the closet beneath the stairs, a prison occupied by Weber more than any other child. There was no lock on the door and the prisoner had only to lift the latch to escape. This he would never do, however, though he would howl and kick the door until he had served his time and was released.

Sometimes "Weeb" and "Alie" would disobey the supreme command that they were not to play by the millrace, where the water of the creek was diverted toward the mill wheel. A child who fell into the race might be swept down and crushed. Yet the rapid current was so tempting for small boats and sticks. One day Sarah Addams saw the two children once again disobeying her stern command. Both children were so absorbed in their play they did not hear her approach. With a determined push Weber was flung into the race. Quickly Sarah ran downstream and pulled out the choking, terrified child. No more remonstrances were required. There was no further play by the millrace.

In pursuit of her neighborly duty, Sarah Addams often attended to neighbors in time of need or sickness. In January of 1863, seven months along in her own ninth pregnancy, she helped a neighbor to give birth. She overtaxed herself, however, and soon was in need of nursing herself. Her eyesight began to fail; then she had convulsions which brought on the premature birth of her child, a daughter who did not live. She then lapsed into a coma which seemed to foreshadow death. After two days of coma, the family was startled by a loud shriek from two-and-a-half-year-old Jenny: her mother had half raised herself, could see again, and was lucid. The family dared hope that Sarah might recover, but within a few hours she was back in the coma from which she did not recover. She died on January 14, 1863.

Sarah Addams was a woman of dignity to whom management and command came easily. Resourceful and self-contained, she was perfectly suited to be the wife of a young man of ability and ambition making his way in a new community. Under the pressure of post-frontier conditions and the vision and drive which they shared, other facets of John and Sarah Addams' personalities did not develop. Neither had much lightness, gaiety, or sense of humor, nor any appreciation of trivial pleasures. They lacked any serious regard for music, painting, or letters.

When her mother died, Laura Jane Addams—"Jenny," as she was called—was the baby of the family. Mary, the eldest at seventeen, managed the household in her mother's place but without her mother's firm control. Martha helped, and Alice and Weber were at least old enough to more or less look after themselves. The whole family deferred to the wishes of little Jenny. She was indulged in her whims and disliked being crossed. With no sister or brother near her own age, she learned to play much alone and became an introspective and in fact a somewhat gloomy child. Though she was a pretty little thing, with wavy brown hair and a bright bird-like look, she had a slight spinal curvature, and because of this she thought of herself as an ugly crippled child.

As the last link with Sarah, Jenny was the particular darling of her father. In the five years between her mother's death and her father's remarriage, Jenny and her father drew very close. He delighted in her; she worshipped him. With no mother to model herself on, for Mary was housekeeper rather than substitute mother, the little girl directed all her affection and admiration toward her father and longed to be like him in every way. Years later, when she had become Jane Addams of Hull House, she recalled her doglike devotion to him, and indeed in her autobiography she spoke of him almost to the exclusion of all other relatives and friends. As she grew up she tried to model herself on him in all ways that were physically possible and perhaps even in some which were not. As a miller he had developed a flat "miller's thumb" from constantly feeling the coarseness of the grain between thumb and forefinger. Jenny spent hours in the mill caressing the flour, hoping against hope that she too could develop a miller's thumb. When the stones were being dressed she stood nearby with her hands out so that the chips of stone would scar her hands as they had his. Recalling his tales of rising at three in the morning as a miller's apprentice, she too tried to waken at three to share vicariously the hardships of his youth. Later when she learned to read she tried to read straight through the village library, not through love of learning but because John Addams had read through his own village library. She could laugh at herself in later years, at least a little, for these signs of devotion; but at the time she took them and herself seriously, as indeed her father and mother had taken themselves seriously.[3]

Jane Addams later said that her father had been the one who first drew her into "the moral concerns of life." It was his forgiveness she craved when she told some childish lie, and his approval when she achieved success. She was too young to understand the turmoil of the Civil War, but she understood the admiration which her father had for his political colleagues first in the Whig, then the Republican party, Abraham Lincoln. The image of her father crying at Lincoln's death stayed with her, and the family treasured letters from Lincoln to John Addams as well as pictures and other mementoes. In the mind of the little girl, the character of her father and that of the president he admired merged a little, and she always thought that John Addams had something of Lincoln in him.

Not all the children were so satisfied with Addams family life. Martha felt sharply the lack of music in the house and begged for a piano. To John and Sarah Addams, and John alone after Sarah's death, this seemed pure extravagance, so Martha had to find her music elsewhere. The Addams knew the family of a miller in Freeport named William Haldeman.[4] They had a piano and Anna, William's wife, played. There Martha went to a house full of music to take lessons, for Anna Haldeman would as soon have been without a stove as without a piano. In her, Martha found some of the things her mother lacked. Both women were strong, both were capable and efficient managers, but their differences were greater than their similarities. One can picture Sarah Addams impressing her neighbors on a Sunday morning, but one can also picture her carrying turnips to an earth cellar, telling men where to drive their carts of grain, and serving dinner to a dozen or more people. While Anna Haldeman was an accomplished horsewoman and a poised hostess, in the daily process of running a house she never did any more physical work than arranging flowers or straightening a picture. Her help did the rest. Anna had grown up with two brothers who both became doctors, both of them had keen minds and saw the value of poetry, music, drama, and literature. For Sarah Addams the highest value was competence; for Anna Haldeman it was beauty. The difference is important, because Anna Hostetter Haldeman was to be John Addams' second wife and the mother who brought up his daughter Jenny.

For nearly six years Jenny Addams lived in the bittersweet state of being her father's, indeed the family's darling, yet with a deep loneliness and feeling of inadequacy. Suddenly, or so it must have seemed to an eight-year-old girl, a strange personage was thrust between her and her father. When Anna Haldeman was widowed in 1866, John Addams waited a decent amount of time, then began calling on her. Within a year Martha, the child who had forged the strongest link between the two families, died. Shared sorrow brought John Addams and Anna Haldeman closer together, and in mid-November of 1868 they were married. With a rush the style of living in the Addams' house changed, becoming at once more sophisticated and gayer. A new bay window, a piano, white tablecloths, and gold-rimmed china were merely symptoms of a far more important change in atmosphere. Instead of devoting his attention to his delicate little daughter, John Addams was caught up in the social whirl created by a wife who loved the role of hostess. Jenny's placid introspection, laced with self-pity, was interrupted with exhortations to go out and enjoy the sunshine. She was urged to ignore her spine rather than defer to it. Anna Haldeman Addams brought two sons with her into the family. Harry, the elder, was in Germany studying medicine. George was a few months younger than Jenny—so now she had a playmate her own age. The years of being the indulged pet of the family were over. Jenny was now subject to kind but firm control by a woman with clear ideas about what young girls should do and what should go into their minds.

After a brief period of open rebellion, Jenny seemed to adapt to the new situation. Yet outward acquiescence served merely to disguise, even from herself, the fundamental resentment against her second mother. Jane Addams' knot of bitterness did not evaporate; it merely sank deep inside, where it lay like a weight the rest of her life. One might read her autobiography, written when its author was mature and accomplished, and hardly know that Anna Haldeman Addams existed. To the best of her ability Jane Addams erased her stepmother from her life. In later years when she visited Cedarville she did not stay at the old family home but in her brother Weber's home to avoid the explosive scenes between her stepmother and herself. The second Mrs. Addams was the only one in the family who had virtually nothing to do with Hull House. Jane Addams wrote to her only on those occasions when duty demanded it, and then the letters were devoid of any real communication.[5]

Her Cedarville neighbors also showed a little resentment, perhaps mingled with awe, at the new Mrs. Addams. The move from the city of Freeport to the village of Cedarville meant something of a change for Anna Haldeman Addams. Rather than attempting to fit into the new environment, however, she brought her old one with her. Her easy familiarity with the world of art and letters led some of Cedarville to regard her as a snob—which she probably was. Also, since her life had been lived among educated, accomplished men, she had a little of the genteel coquette in her. John Addams admired her extravagantly and was obviously proud of having such a woman as his wife. Sometimes she accompanied him to Springfield for the sessions of the legislature, and there she was a great hit as a hostess.

While Jenny may have resented her new mother, she did learn from her. Aimless mealtime chatter became conversation directed by Anna. Instead of reading straight through the village library, Jenny was directed towards the classic European and American authors and taught to value some more than others. She was introduced to a world far wider than that of Sarah Addams. As the daughter of a state legislator, a railroad and bank director, and the stepdaughter of a lady, she was also introduced to the manners and attitudes of what was, for western Illinois in the 1870's, the aristocracy. Mrs. Addams accepted her beauty, accomplishment, wit, and social position with ease and grace. These things were hers as a matter of course because she was Anna Hostetter Haldeman Addams and because she was married to perhaps the most important person in that part of Illinois. Later, when Jane Addams met the very best Chicago society had to offer, she could move freely because of what she had unwittingly learned from her stepmother. When, many years later, she spent summers at Bar Harbor, she was clearly from the same social stratum as her neighbors because of what she had learned from her stepmother. Perhaps, too, her sense of social responsibility took on a faint cast of *noblesse oblige* from Anna Addams which at times in her later years verged, no matter how much she might deny it, on condescension for those whom she helped.

But all that was far in the future. Though she did not remember it that way, she lived the normal life of a village girl. She and her friends climbed up the bluffs behind the mill, half scared, half thrilled by their height. They found caves, one of which was so deep and dark that they needed a candle for its exploration. In winter there were the inevitable recreations of the cold Midwestern plains:

It is good skating and has been for a couple of weeks. George and Frank Stahl went up to the head of the dam on skates yesterday and George broke in twice but did not get wet only his feet. We will have three days vacation this week. Wenday Thursday Friday and then Saturday that will make four days whrite strait along. Polly knit George and I each a pair of new mittens mine are red and Georgie's are grey. The bell ringers are comeing to Freeport and mebey we will go to hear them. We are well and I hope this will find you the same. Mr. March preached hear to day but I did not go he preaches so long. Mrs Carey is very sick with the dropsy they do not think she will live. I have got a new water proof it is a great deal nicer than any other ever was. Budd goes visiting a good deal all alone. Mary Templeton had the chicken pox but is over it now. They had a crasy man came hear last evening and this morning he wanted to tune and play on our piano. The S.S. has a new Organ. We are agoin to have a Chrismas tree and George is in a dilogue they are agoin to have.[6]

These childhood days also disappeared from her later memories, and looking back from adulthood she saw in her own past a little girl oppressed by her infirmities and set about with dark fears. At home there was no talk of eternal damnation, and when she tried to discuss the mysteries of predestination with her father, he dismissed the subject by saying that probably neither of them had the kind of mind which could understand it. Yet she recalled that she heard about hellfire from other children and was afraid to go to sleep with any unconfessed sin on her head in case she should be "taken" in her sleep. In later years she recalled deep fears of death. She remembered the horror, lasting for weeks, of being taken by a first-grade teacher to the burial of a schoolmate's mother, and being led to look into the coffin at the dead woman. The lonely walk home that afternoon was full of terrors, ending with a breathless dash from the blacksmith shop, the last inhabited dwelling on the street, to her familiar dooryard. There she sought companionship from all the people and animals she could find to dispel her terror.

As a little girl, the death of a neighbor from dropsy was on the same level of importance as a new raincoat; but as a mature woman Jane Addams remembered herself crouching in terror on the stairs, holding on to the stability of the silent house while the rest of her family was off at a funeral, not to return until "long after you are in bed." Children have horror and happiness in their growing up, but most people remember both. Jane Addams dwelt overwhelmingly on one, and the darkness and terror thereby became the truth that mattered to her conscious mind.

Yet memories of happy childhood had their effects, too. When she wrote systematically about children she assumed their inherent gaiety and joyfulness, which she would have been unlikely to do without some of both in half-forgotten portions of her own experience.

There were tensions enough in the family, and no selective memory was required to emphasize them. In 1873 Harry Haldeman returned from Germany to begin his practice. A handsome dark-haired young man with the charm and broad education of his mother and the social position which went with his profession, he must have been an attractive person. He proved so to Alice Addams, five years his junior. When it became clear that stepsister and stepbrother had more than a sibling interest in each other, both parents became concerned. The subject of the two young people becoming engaged produced major family storms for several months. Finally Harry and Alice took matters into their own hands and married in October of 1875. They did not stay in Illinois, however, but began their married life in Girard, Kansas, some five hundred miles from home.

Alice and Harry moved away just after Jane, as she was now called, had her fifteenth birthday. She had one more year of school in Cedarville and then must think about college. There was no question but that the Addams girls would have higher education. If John Addams had not insisted upon it, Anna Hostetter Addams would have. For after all, were not women as intellectually capable as men? Alice and Mary had gone to Rockford Female Seminary, the nearest institution of higher learning. In 1876 John Addams became a trustee of the seminary, and it was assumed that the third Addams girl would go there too. But Jane Addams had been hearing about eastern women's colleges: Mount Holyoke and Smith. She mentioned that really she might like to go to the latter, and in fact took and passed the entrance examination in Northampton. At her father's insistence, however, Jane agreed to go to Rockford.

Many of the characteristics of the mature Jane Addams were clearly apparent in the sixteen-year-old who prepared to enter Rockford in the fall of 1877. Her health was delicate. She was an intensely serious and earnest young lady—though perhaps not quite so gloomy as she later remembered. She had a moral, indeed almost a moralistic, view of life, learned from her father and closely connected with him. Right was right, and it was what he would have approved of. Wrong was what he would have frowned upon. She was a Christian, though not seriously religious or pious.

Even without the help of ancient Greek playwrights, folk tradition in fairy tales, or the founder of psychoanalysis, one can perceive classic tensions in Jane Addams' childhood years. She had a glorious princely father with whom she was in love—and a wicked stepmother came between them. Most little girls grow up to find a man who can in some transformed way take the place of the beloved but unattainable father. Jane Addams, however, in a pattern far from unique, half expected and fully hoped to grow up to *be* her father. She wanted to have a thumb—that thumb flattened by rubbing—like his.[7]

On a more obvious level, marriage in her experience had brought not bliss but disruption and crisis. Her true mother, after all, had died in childbirth. Her father's remarriage had disrupted the emotional pattern and self-conception of her babyhood years. Her sister's marriage resulted in long months of recrimination, bitterness, and shrill argument.

No matter how intriguing this all may be, however, it does not "explain" Jane Addams. For a girl to be in love with and identify with her father, to hate her stepmother, and to fear marriage may lead in an infinitude of directions. The important question is what Laura Jane Addams was going to do with these tensions; whether she would let them drive her to immobility and self-destruction or whether she could deal with them both psychologically and in relation to the society she was to live in.

2

Rockford

WHEN Anna Addams sent her stepdaughter to Anna P. Sill, principal of the Rockford Female Seminary, Laura Jane Addams went from the keeping of one feminist to another, from one sort of moralistic environment to another sort. At Rockford the feminism had slightly broader horizons, perhaps, and the moralism was more social than individual, but the young Miss Addams found no essential contradiction between home and seminary.

Rockford Female Seminary had existed since 1852, a product of missionary efforts by New England Puritans anxious to bring The Word to the backsliders of northern Illinois. "The moral and religious influence of the institution shall be regarded as of prime importance, and no effort shall be spared to make this influence pure, elevated and efficient," declared the board of trustees. Yet at the same time Rockford would be no narrow Bible school, for "The standard of mental culture shall be set and maintained at the highest practicable level." Perhaps the first resolution aimed at perfection while the second settled for what was practical, but Rockford was to emphasize piety, doing good, and sound training in those early years.

Anna P. Sill also emphasized all three. The direct descendant of Puritan divines, Miss Sill lived her life in the presence of an angry immanent God. She gauged her success at the seminary by the number of confessions of faith achieved annually and by the number of missionaries or missionaries' wives produced. In truth missionaries were few and schoolteachers many, but those few were the flags which Anna Sill flew at the top of her mast. Anna Sill was also a feminist. For her this meant two things:

that women should have as good an education as men, and that women had a supreme duty to preserve morality, culture, and the heritage of western civilization. Being a good wife and mother was admirable, to be sure, but it was not adequate. One must also use one's mind and education in the service of God and man.[1]

While Jane Addams was a member of no denomination she was, in a general way, a believing Christian, and if she rejected the missionary ideal, she by no means rejected the idea of doing good. She was already a feminist of sorts, and was so serious and studious that the strict regulations of the college did not gall her. She naturally wanted to do what the rules encouraged: BE GOOD.

While being good, Jane Addams received an education broad rather than deep. Each year included some fifteen courses, though many continued from year to year. Latin, Greek, and German continued throughout the four years. Literature concentrated on the major English authors, especially Shakespeare, but included considerable attention to the romantic poets. A course in American literature emphasized its maturity and independence of England. Biblical history was prescribed in all but the sophomore year, and philosophy included only formal logic and Evidence of Christianity. Jane Addams took a surprising amount of mathematics, though none of it on a very advanced level: algebra, geometry both plane and solid, and trigonometry including spherical. She was given brief glimpses into botany, astronomy, chemistry, and geology, the latter using a text which flirted dangerously with the doctrine of evolution.

Each spring she attended graduation exercises, a ceremony well attended by townspeople and alumnae. The *Rockford Register* recorded one such:

> The most complete and interesting of the day's exercises was the examination of the Senior class in Ancient Literature, Commencing in their topics with the Hebrews, Greek, Hindoo, Roman, Arabian and Italian schools of learning. . . . The literature of each nation was divided into its various period of rise, advance and decay.

Regretfully, the *Register* noted, lack of time prevented expositions on Chinese, Japanese, and Egyptian literature. At other times during the day the young ladies demonstrated the principles of steam engines, levers, and electrical apparatus, and at another time precise knowledge of Latin grammar. With relief the report noted that the examination in botany showed that "these students rejected the Darwinian development theory."[2]

In all her courses, Jane Addams' performance was outstanding. On a ten-point scale her academic average was 9.862. At Rockford deportment was considered as of equal value with academics, and her perfect 10 in deportment brought her combined average to 9.931, at the head of her class of seventeen young ladies.[3]

She showed no signs of intellectual radicalism at college. She shared the broad unquestioned faith that the world was getting better in all ways, that oppression and tyranny would soon vanish from the earth, that faith in one's self could move mountains, and that freedom could only flourish in a well-ordered society. She was almost certainly part of the overwhelming majority endorsing the Republican candidate for presidency in 1880, and the following year she confessed herself unable to comprehend the assassination of Czar Alexander II, after he had done so much for his people. She was so dedicated to her studies that she rose early Sunday mornings to take extra Greek lessons in the privacy of the teacher's room and with greater freedom in translation than the normal classroom. She studied a little calculus on the side and took a brief practical course in taxidermy with a local practitioner of that art. Her friends and teachers regarded her with awe and admiration. While the other students sometimes referred to her as "beloved," there is some question whether they really liked her. Sometimes when the giggling and gossiping got too thick in her room, centered about her energetic roommate, Jane would withdraw to the room of one of her teachers to study or write letters home. She seemed at least as much at ease with teachers as with her contemporaries, and within two years after her graduation was a member of the board of trustees.

She excelled, too, in approved extracurricular activities. She was president of the Castallian literary society, editor of the college magazine, a member of the college debating team, and president of her class. As magazine editor she was determined to end the year in the black, and when no one else had the nerve to approach town businessmen for advertising, she did the job herself.[4]

In addition to classwork and official extracurricular activities, there were informal strolls along the Rock River or, when the current was not too swift, punting on it. Friendships developed which sometimes actually lasted for a few years after graduation. One friend, calling her Damon and signing himself Pythias, wrote about rowing on the river; another hinted slyly about a young man at Beloit. Was it he who sent her the live hawk which she killed and stuffed with outstretched wings? All these—save perhaps the hawk—were normal schoolgirl activities, evidence of neither abnormalities nor potential greatness.

With her sixteen classmates she shared a strong but vague desire for service of some sort. In their junior year these seventeen chose a class symbol of wheat and hops. "You know," Jane wrote to her sister Alice, "that 'Bread Givers' is the primitive meaning of the word lady; and there are sixteen girls in R.F.S. who mean to do all they can to restore the word to its original sense."[5] In fact the original meaning was the more prosaic "kneader of bread," and in fact the sixteen girls headed more towards the contemporary meaning of a woman to whom deference is due than to that original meaning. (Fifteen years later Jane Addams tried a brief stint of actually kneading her own bread as a way of establishing a connection with some sort of fundamental human process, but she quickly gave it up as the conceit it was.) The hops in the symbol was left unexplained. Presumably it was not meant to be mixed with malt.

The desire for some sort of service beyond motherhood and home was genuine and was seen by all the young ladies as a natural extension of the Christian spirit. Yet when Jane Addams was head of Hull House, ministers often accused her of forgetting the importance of religion. In a sense they were right, for she did not even become a church member until 1885, and then it was more *pro forma* than from deep conviction. At Rockford she stoutly resisted all attempts to persuade her to publicly profess her faith or to go and convert the heathen. In her senior year these attempts at persuasion became intense and frequent. Young Miss Addams showed a good deal of independent spirit in resisting the entreaties of her favorite teachers and in later years thought that the experience helped her resist the pleas of single-taxers, socialists, and other dogmatists to turn the settlement house into an extension of their doctrines.[6]

Still Jane Addams was glad to be at a Christian school, because she knew that the influences were on the right side—even if "slightly perverted," as she wrote Ellen Gates Starr, who provided the sounding board for Jane's theological speculation. Ellen, who became a devout Catholic and ended her years in a nunnery, attended Rockford for only one year, but the two became close friends, and they corresponded frequently after Miss Starr went to teach in western Illinois. Throughout her college years Jane tried repeatedly, never with success, to "experience," as she put it, religion. "I wish you were here," she wrote Ellen in despair, "Christ don't help me in the least. Sometimes I can work myself into great admiration for his life, and occasionally I can catch something of his philosophy, but He doesn't bring me any nearer to the Deity." While rejecting revivalism, she was sure the revivalists were after the same things she was. By the end of her college years Jane Addams concluded that for her, understanding of God had to come through reason, not faith, and that salvation meant not any flooding-in of God, but a "compliance with the good and the beautiful." In January of her senior year she made the awful experiment of not praying for three weeks and was shocked to find she felt no worse for it. In the end the girls agreed to differ. Jane acknowledged that Ellen wanted some sort of transcendent religious experience; but for herself, she wrote, "I feel that I need religion in a practical sense, that if I could fix myself with my relations to God and the universe and so be in perfect harmony with nature and deity, I could use my faculties and energy so much better."[7] Here she sounded less like an eighteenth-cenutry deist than the nineteenth-century romantic Emerson, of whom every educated young lady in the 1880's absorbed great amounts.

It would be wrong to make too much of Jane Addams' correspondence with Ellen Starr; after all, it was Ellen who was devout and who turned the conversation towards theology. It would be wrong, too, to make too much of any dramatic loss of faith or spiritual crisis in Jane Addams' college years. Faith had never been any more than a modest portion of her life. She had gone to church and Sunday school, but after all, everyone went to church and Sunday school. A replacement of childhood oversimplification—God as a bearded man on top of a mountain—with a more abstract and vague concept is simply normal growing up, not loss of faith. In fact, her religious controversy with Ellen was not over any *loss* of faith, but over the fact that Jane seemed unable to *find* the peace that passeth understanding in which

Ellen dwelt. Two years after graduation she wrote Ellen, "I wish you could tell me how to come there." In the depressing years after her father's death, she could feel "the absolute necessity of the protection and dependence on Christ." In 1890 in a Christmas letter to her brother George she wrote that "the comfort of Christ's mission to the world and the need of the Messiah to the race has been impressed upon me as never before. It seems as if the race life, at least the dark side, would be quite unendurable if it were not for that central fact." She was still hoping to find a comforting faith and pleased that there was one to comfort mankind in time of suffering, but for her it was a distant thing, not immanent.

Jane Addams explicitly adopted "Christian morality." Like most Americans, for her the word "Christian" was virtually synonymous with "virtuous." However, neither she nor anyone else in her immediate family could correctly be termed pious, and theological or other-worldly questions were not for her the important ones, either as a child, a college student, or an adult.

For four years, Rockford Female Seminary had reinforced what Jane Addams had learned at home from her father and two mothers: Christian ethics, the importance of being good and doing good, a broad role for women, a stress on accomplishing great things. What attracted and influenced her most in her readings were the English and German romantics or near-romantics: Ruskin, Carlyle who translated the German romantics into English, Schiller, and Jean Paul Frederich Richter. At almost the same time she wrote of wanting to come to God through reason rather than faith, she was absorbed in Carlyle's *Sartor Resartus,* the semi-fictionalized autobiographical essay, much influenced by Goethe, which tells the story of a German professor in *Weissnichtwo* (don't-know-where) who, relying on reason, is led first to skepticism, then through skepticism back to acceptance, and finally to an "everlasting yea." The German romantics, with their strong tension between reason and emotion and their faith in the essential rightness of natural instincts, influenced her perhaps more than she knew, for in many ways she remained a German romantic throughout her life.

Though it has been asserted that German romanticism was one of the wellsprings of Nazism, it was certainly also one of the wellsprings of German liberalism; and it was this latter tendency which Jane Addams followed. Carlyle, like the German romantics, pointed the way either towards an affirmation of human righteousness or (as he himself was led) to a scorn for popular government. What Jane Addams read of Ruskin is not clear; probably it was much of his artistic and architectural criticism, but almost certainly she read his social comment as well. As a social philosopher Ruskin is difficult to categorize. Essentially he wanted a welfare state to mitigate the harshness of the kind of capitalism he saw around him. He insisted that the "so called science" of economics must include moral judgments and that capitalism itself must become moral rather than self-seeking on the assumption, in the words of a later analyst, that "competition is an automatic substitute for morality." Did these words of Ruskin strike an echo in the mind of twenty-year-old Jane Addams?

> These—hewers of wood and drawers of water,—these bent under burdens . . . from these surely at least, we may receive some clear message of teaching; and pierce for an instant, into the mystery of life, and of its arts? Yes; from these, at least, we do receive a lesson. But . . . this message of theirs can only be received by joining them —not by thinking about them.

A romantic idealization of the poor, a belief in the superiority of nature, faith in natural human instincts, tension between reason, faith and emotion; all these were augmented by her reading and never afterward lost.[9]

Probably the most important things Jane Addams learned at Rockford were things she learned about herself. First of all she learned that she was smart, smarter indeed than nearly everyone she met. No matter how shallow Rockford's education was, it passed for advanced learning, and Jane Addams mastered it triumphantly. She also learned to lead and to enjoy leading. As class president, head of the literary society, editor of the school magazine, she took a firm grip on her fellows and they went where she thought they ought to go. Although there was a lengthy period in her life when she doubted her own competence in anything, ultimately she returned to a thorough confidence in her judgment and actions—a confidence she first learned at Rockford. In fact, at Rockford she was successful and fully happy for perhaps the first time in her life.

Little of the turmoil of America's Gilded Age seems to have affected the young ladies at the seminary. There was, to be sure, a titillating thrill in gossiping about which teachers had and which teachers had not accepted Darwinism, but "Grantism," the "stolen election," and the noise from the great barbecue generally did not penetrate the walls of Rockford. The crises visible to these girls were moral, religious, or intellectual, not political or economic. Their mission to the less fortunate was not so much to provide real wheat or bread, but spiritual solace and cultural uplift. To Jane Addams' credit, once she confronted the facts of urban poverty she could outgrow these limitations. But as she received her diploma she had not yet done so. There was no little truth, both as to prophecy and character analysis, mixed with girlish spite, in the following conversation among the gods, recorded in the *Rockford Seminary Magazine* for July of 1881:

SAGE: I will enquire as to the fate of Jane Addams, the president of the class of '81. As her brain is larger than her body, I will give the history of her brain. At three she read with fluency, and before she was six she had read the thousand and one Arabian nights. At ten she plunged into fiction, and at twleve had devoured it all from the works of Mrs. Holmes to Jean Paul Frederich Richter. Her mind was almost swamped in this case, but rebounded at the age of fifteen into Emerson's essays; here she delayed and lingered long, and after passing through a scientific infection came to Byron, De Quincey and Carlyle. From the time of her entering R.F.S., four years ago, to the present time, she has been wearied and troubled by many matters. Weary with class business, she resorts for recreation to writing editorials for the magazine, or to the laboratory, there to analyze some poisonous compound. Tell me, O Sybil, what will be the fate of this prodigious intellect?

SYBIL: What would you expect of our honored president, our valedictorian, with all her grand ideas and vast conceptions—her life work is so *broad*, the star of her destiny I see now here, now there, brightening and glimmering but never disappearing. All her thoughts and energies have finally settled on this great undertaking, this great benefit of mankind. She will make glass eyes for dolls, bushells and bushells of the most perfect blue eyes for dolls.[10]

Jane Addams' choice for making "perfect blue eyes" was neither missionary endeavors in Turkey nor yet teaching school in Illinois. Her way of serving the world, of "giving bread," would be as a medical doctor. Upon graduation she planned to enter the Woman's Medical College in Philadelphia. First, however, there would be a summer of relaxation beginning in Cedarville, then a family excursion to northern Michigan combining vacation with a chance for John Addams to look over some possible investments in copper mining.

3

Uncertainty and the Scheme

JOHN ADDAMS spent August 17 of 1881 climbing hills near Marquette, Michigan, looking over land for possible investment. He had taken Jane with him, for she would soon be leaving to begin her medical studies in Philadelphia. In the middle of the afternoon he developed a stomach pain which turned into acute appendicitis. Within thirty-six hours he was dead.[1] A vacation with her beloved father thus turned into the supreme tragic experience of Jane Addams' life. With her father's death began the crumbling of the *persona* so recently constructed at Rockford, and the period of darkness, depression, and lethargy which very nearly paralyzed her will. In fact the whole family experienced a series of crises and disasters which threatened to destroy emotionally those left whole physically. It was as if John Addams' strong personality had supported the structure of the family's existence, and when the support vanished the structure trembled and slowly collapsed.

The trembling and collapse did not come right away. Plans already made had enough momentum to carry the Addamses for a few months. Jane, a month after her father's death, began her medical studies in Philadelphia, trying to forget herself in the hard work of memorizing bones, muscles, and internal organs. She was brought with a shock to realize the difference between a genteel and well-rounded education at Rockford and the hard professionalism of medical school. Here she was no longer the hero of classmates and teachers alike. Here no generalized intelligence or cultural sensitivity sufficed. She was certainly capable of the work, though not perhaps of excelling in it, and she successfully completed her first semester. There was no joy in the studying, though. By the end of the semester the trembling—soon to be collapse—began.

The manifestation was an insistent backache. Her spinal curvature was in fact slight. Horseback riding was painful, but her normal activity was not restricted. Her back had not bothered her through the four years at Rockford. The hard, stressful work of medical school and the agony of her father's death had imposed new tensions, and it was these which exacerbated a back itself only slightly ill.

She sought treatment in S. Wier Mitchell's Hospital of Orthopedic and Nervous Diseases in Philadelphia, and no better place could have been chosen. Mitchell was a brilliant physician, both as practitioner and innovator. On the side he was a highly successful novelist, a socialite of the Philadelphia aristocracy, a poet, and a man respected for his universal genius. As a doctor in the Civil War he had become an authority on gunshot wounds and wrote a work on that subject which was considered authoritative through World War I. After the Civil War he began to develop startling ideas on the relationship between physical ills and mental condition, especially among women. His interest in what would now be called neurotic women led him to use them as chief characters in more than one of his novels. His medical practice among the wealthy of Philadelphia brought him into repeated contact with the aristocratic semi-invalid, pale of visage, weak of smile, for whom a half hour of sewing was an exhausting activity and who, from couch or bed, might be the dictator of the household. His cure for this and other "nervous" diseases was to prescribe a period of absolute rest in bed, of from six weeks to two months, followed by a return to vigorous activity. It is reported that when one of his female patients refused to get up at the end of the period of rest, Dr. Mitchell began to unbutton his waistcoat, saying, "Get out of bed by the time I count five or I'll get in there with you," a threat which proved effective.[2]

When Jane Addams, ostensibly not writing autobiography, later discussed the strain imposed upon college-educated women torn between traditional family duties and a desire for broader activity, she said with remarkably clear perception:

> When her health gives way under this strain, as it often does, her physician invariably advises a rest. But to be put to bed and fed

on milk is not what she requires. What she needs is simple, health giving activity, which, involving the use of all her faculties, shall be a response to all the claims which she so keenly feels.[3]

Since her apparent problem was a bad back, she entered the orthopedic section of the hospital where she had the resting part of Wier Mitchell's cure. After several weeks, her strength began to return and Jane went home to Cedarville for the summer.[4]

In Cedarville Jane Addams concluded that medical study was not for her. She recalled her desire, five years before, to go to Smith College instead of Rockford. Now there was no obstacle, and with a new sense of vitality she made plans to enter as a special student for one year. She wrote excitedly of her plans to a friend who had graduated from Smith and to her favorite teachers at Rockford. First she thought she could not travel until Christmas, but with her back remarkably improved, she decided to go in September of 1882.[5] As the time for departure approached, however, her back spoke loud negatives. September found her not studying in Northampton, Massachusetts, but once again bedridden in Cedarville.[6]

All through the fall she remained in pain. Finally, at the urging of Alice, supported by the admonitions of Ellen Starr, she agreed to let Harry try to help her. She visited the Haldemans, now living in Mitchelville, Iowa, and in November Harry operated on her back. It was a painful operation, but it cured her spinal curvature. There is a family legend that during this operation Harry found that she was physically unable to bear children.[7] No operation for spinal curvature, however, could possibly tell even the most skilled physician anything about his patient's reproductive capacity. There may have been a mixup between this and later operations; but more likely the whole thing was a fabrication. Perhaps, in spite of all of Jane Addams' triumphs, there lingered some embarrassment about her tendency toward masculinity, her rejection of a woman's role.

As if to emphasize that her back was symptom rather than cause of her illness, her spirits remained submerged in "lassitude and melancholy." She remained so for months, trying to comfort herself with heavy reading, this time Carlyle's *Frederick the Great.*[8] In April of 1883 a second tragedy struck the family, and, since she was needed, Jane roused herself to help deal with it.

With no warning, her brother Weber was seized with a fit of insanity and was placed in a state institution in Elgin. Jane's own invalidism was put aside, and she went to help care for Weber's wife and baby. Once again plans for going to Smith were postponed. Anna Hostetter Haldeman Addams began to feel the strain, too. With the death of a husband, the collapse of a stepdaughter, and the insanity of a stepson, she and Jane decided that for the health of all concerned Anna and her stepdaughter should go to Europe. "It seems quite essential to the establishment of my health and temper," Jane wrote Ellen Starr, "that I have a radical change."[9]

Change she did have. The daughter recovering from physical and emotional collapse, and the stepmother attempting to avoid them, sailed for Europe on August 23, 1883, to spend nearly two years on a sort of grand tour. Not sure what they were looking for, only sure of what they wanted to leave behind, they moved restlessly around the British Isles and the continent. First there was a month in Ireland and England, mostly in London but with a visit to the lakes. Berlin was big and noisy but they were impressed by Bismarck, whom they saw address the Reichstag. They were in Dresden for ten weeks in midwinter, then slowly moved south: Munich, Florence, Rome for five weeks, Athens, Sicily. In June they were in Switzerland where George met them for his summer vacation from the Johns Hopkins medical school. The winter of 1884–1885 they spent half in Berlin, half in Paris. Finally, in the spring of 1885, they returned to the United States.

There was no need to worry about money, for by the time John Addams' estate was settled, the family was well off. He left an estate of nearly a quarter of a million dollars in cash, stocks, and land. One third went to the widow, and the rest was divided equally among the children. Jane's share came to about fifty thousand dollars. Probably an income of ten per cent would not be an unreasonable expectation, so young Miss Addams could count on a comfortable income the rest of her life.[10]

Her Puritan conscience shrank from simply enjoying her life, however. While in Europe she tried to give a gloss of serious purpose to a journey which had one, but not one which seemed adequate. Museums, concerts, and cathedrals were pursued as though they were big game. In each country, Jane took language lessons, and in fact became quite fluent in German and French, but her honesty did not allow her to claim that she had been anything but idle. "I have constantly lost confidence in myself, and have gained nothing and improved in nothing," she wrote Ellen from Geneva.[11] Her health and temper had not been established by radical change.

In fact, four years after her father's death, Jane Addams seemed to have lapsed into permanent aimlessness. She busied herself for a few months with affairs of the Rockford alumnae fund and visiting with family; then she and her stepmother moved to Baltimore where George was studying. Apparently it was during this period that Anna Haldeman Addams began seriously urging that George and Jane marry, as Harry and Alice had done. George in fact proposed. Though very fond of George, as a brother with whom she had skated on streams and climbed hills, Jane had no interest in marrying him. She had no thought of career to choose over marriage, as her niece later suggested. But marriage in her experience led to conflict more often than bliss. Most important, John Addams constituted her ideal of manhood. Perhaps no man could meet her idealized picture of her father, and George—rather slight, studious, very bright but hardly a dominating personality—simply did not measure up. Soon afterward, George began a decline into an insanity which kept him in and out of institutions for the rest of his life. Even when out of institutions, he was a recluse in the Cedarville home, coming downstairs once in a while to play chess or converse briefly, then retiring again from a world he could not deal with. Near the end of his life, Jane visited him in the old house. "He is not as well now as when I saw him in Oct[ober]," she said, "and he is very much discouraged. He had hoped that getting home would free him from his aural delusions instead of which they have been worse of late than usual. He keeps control, but is under great mental stress, and is anxious to get back to the hospital. He is making a great effort to stay at home until after Xmas but I almost doubt the wisdom of it. I had a long talk with him on Sunday afternoon, although he fairly wrung my heart."[12] He died a promising young man who had been cowed by the world.

George's insanity was the third great tragedy which shook the Addams family in the 1880's. His mother, in later years, tended to blame his insanity on Jane Addams, and open hostility often flared between the two women. The dances in Springfield and parties in Baltimore were permanently behind Anna Haldeman Addams, and she clung to her bitterness like a life preserver. She became thin and subject to violent tempers, so that even Alice feared to enter the house. After George's death in 1909, Jane Addams and her stepmother restored a thin veneer of civility between them, but never any affection.[13]

George's decline was at first gradual, however, and the three Addamses continued their lives with winter in Baltimore and summer at Cedarville or Girard, Kansas, with Alice. For Anna Haldeman Addams it was the social life she loved, had enjoyed in Springfield, and missed in Cedarville. There were dinner parties and concerts, calls on people and being called upon. Her stepdaughter, not knowing what else to do, followed with neither enthusiasm nor hostility: went to parties, trimmed Christmas trees, read more Ruskin, and engaged in a little genteel philanthropy by becoming "interested" in a Negro orphanage:

> They take little colored girls and keep them until they are fifteen, training them to be *good servants,* the children themselves expecting to be that and having an ambition for a good place. I heartily approve of the scheme.[14]

How different from the Jane Addams who helped found the NAACP and fought to keep the Bull Moose party from its lily-white southern policy!

In early spring, 1887, Mary Addams Linn, now the wife of the Reverend John M. Linn, fell ill, and Jane Addams went to Illinois to care for her and assist with the children. She then went on to be with Alice for the birth of her sister's first child, Marcet. After spending the fall in Cedarville, she and Sarah P. Anderson, a teacher at Rockford, left for a second trip to Europe.[15]

It was on this second journey that Jane Addams lifted herself out of the blackness in which she had been living for seven years. This had been an extended period of agony; yet in kind, if not duration, these apparently fruitless years were not unique to Jane Addams. Young people generally go through what Erik Erikson has called an "identity crisis," which young people since the 1920's have called "finding themselves." To be sure, Jane

Addams' crisis was long-lived; wealth gave her the prerogative of long convalescence. Yet all young men and young women, when their roles are no longer defined as "child" or "student," have to find an adult self. For some people, especially where society or strong internal drives prescribe a role, few real choices exist, and the crisis is almost nonexistent. For others, choice may have been anticipated for years and the mechanism of choice institutionalized. Here too the crisis may be muted. It can be acute in any case, but where neither society nor internal drives prescribe, and where wide-ranging choice has not grown familiar over many years, the definition of one's adult self can be especially painful.

This was precisely the situation of the first generation of college-educated women in the United States in the last quarter of the nineteenth century. They had grown up seeing women almost exclusively in the role of mother and wife, yet were trained to skepticism or discontent with that traditional role. Jane Addams was particularly sensitive to the tension between generations, both in relation to herself and, later, to recent immigrants and their children. In college young ladies of Jane Addams' generation were brought into contact with a wider world than their mothers. Often they were urged toward good works of some kind. With the responsibility of their special privilege resting heavily on their shoulders, they were thrust into a world only imperfectly ready to receive them. There were no institutions to help guide them to satisfying occupations, and in fact relatively few occupations were open to them. In the 1890's, she was beginning to have the option of being emancipated *from* one sort of life, but what was she being emancipated *for*? Business was almost entirely a man's world, though after Harry's death Alice Addams Haldeman became a banker. The law was entirely masculine. A few brave souls survived the criticism of peers and parents to become doctors. Even the nursing profession was underdeveloped, though it did offer employment for some women.

In addition to the normal crisis of growing up, then, college-educated women at the end of the nineteenth century were pioneering a new role for women in general. In the older tradition, "the family logically consented to giving her up at marriage when she was enlarging the family tie by founding another family," wrote Jane Addams a decade after founding Hull House, but denounced any attempts at other sorts of life as "foolish enthusiasm." Not quite talking of herself, she said, "The grown-up son has long been considered a citizen with well defined duties. . . . In the case of the grown-up daughter, however, who is under no necessity of earning a living and who has no strong artistic bent, taking her to Paris to study painting or to Germany to study music, the years immediately following her graduation from college are too often filled with a restlessness and unhappiness."[16]

Restlessness and unhappiness in turn drove many strong-willed and capable women into social reform or social service of some sort. The temperance, settlement house, and suffrage movements all benefited from the leadership of this sort of woman. But Jane Addams seemed to have no thought of social service when she and Miss Anderson landed in Southampton three days before Christmas, 1887. Ostensibly buying paintings for Rockford, they went first to Paris, then Stuttgart, then Munich where Ellen Starr joined them, and then down to Florence and Rome. With great satisfaction Jane found herself addressed as "Madam" on this trip, rather than "Fraulein" as on the previous one. "I feel perfectly at my ease and dignified all the time," she wrote Alice.[17] Clearly she was beginning to find an adult role for herself, at least when she was away from her usual environment.

Then, in Rome, they learned of the death of Mary Linn's daughter, also named Mary, from whooping cough. The letter from her sister to Jane Addams describing little Mary's death was heart-rending; just before she died, the little girl had asked for "Aunt Dane." Within a few days, "Aunt Dane" was once again in bed with a back so painful she could hardly move.[18] Family life and the agony of sudden death, of love crumbling into tragedy, overrode any mere operation for spinal curvature, and Ellen Starr spent a month nursing her friend in a Rome hotel room. Then for a while the other ladies toured southern Italy while Jane convalesced in Rome. By spring she was well enough to travel to southern France and to Spain. She then spent the summer in Paris.

It was during that spring and summer of 1888 that Jane Addams' ideas about living among the poor began to take clear shape. She had begun to notice the poor, out of the corner of her eye as it were, on her first trip to Europe. In November of

1883 she had been taken to see one of the tourist attractions of London: a Saturday night auction of almost spoiled food which would not keep until Monday. These cabbages and turnips, cast off as unfit by the rest of society, were bid for eagerly by hoards of the "submerged tenth" in London's East End. Struck by the vision of hands reaching in supplication for garbage, she became more sensitive to poverty in Italy, France, and Greece, but her awareness took the form of a vague unease, neither a program to combat abject poverty nor even a clear desire to do so. In later years she was shocked not so much at the poverty, for she had become used to that, but by the fact that she was not expected to do anything more than look at it—as one looked at Buckingham Palace.

She recalled, years later, a parallel experience on her second European trip, but its importance seems to have been vastly increased by her highly interpretive memory. In Spain she watched a bullfight without the disgust she thought she ought to have felt—simply as another tourist attraction. She wrote in her autobiography that in the evening "the natural and inevitable reaction came." How, she asked herself, could she watch the killing of five bulls and many more horses with equanimity? Was she becoming morally indifferent, so caught up in the world of books and pictures that the real world of human beings could not touch her? To absolve herself from this charge, she resolved to speak to Ellen Starr about a vague plan which had been forming in her mind. Perhaps, Jane suggested to Ellen, if a young lady—or two young ladies—of education and leisure were to live among the very poor, some good might result. What sort of good one could not say, but at least it would be impossible for the young ladies to ignore the harsher realities of the world they lived in. At least it would be impossible for them to bury themselves in books as a way of hiding from reality. At least, and finally, it would be something to do!*

Somewhat to Miss Addams' surprise, Ellen Starr quickly agreed

* Jane Addams' letters home describe both the trip to East End London on her first trip, and the bullfight on the second trip, in a thoroughly routine fashion. The letters give no hint that either experience had any special importance. This may mean that her memory injected more importance into them than they really had. On the other hand, her letters home may not be a certain index to her mental state at the time.

to become a partner in what for the next few months they called "the scheme." "The scheme" in April of 1888 was not the founding of a settlement house with clubs, music school, theater, restaurant, and gymnasium. Their idea was much vaguer than that, and in fact was only a short step away from the inactivity in which Jane Addams had been languishing for nearly seven years. They would find a place to live in a poor neighborhood and live there just as they would anywhere else. They would call on their neighbors and, they hoped, their neighbors would call on them. Perhaps in return for being rescued from the illness of moral indifference, the college-educated women could provide some benefits to their neighbors. Beyond this impulse, which was itself clear enough, they made no detailed plans.

Jane Addams and Ellen Gates Starr knew that similar schemes had already been put into practice. Churches had "missions" in poor sections of cities, and there was Toynbee Hall in London, which they had visited on their way back to the United States. Toynbee Hall was very impressive. And yet they thought they had a slightly different idea. They arrived home in late summer and spent the fall visiting their families. In Kansas Jane spent long hours talking over her plans with Alice. As she explained things to her sister, the idea seemed to grow clearer in her own mind. Finally, in the first weeks of 1889, Jane Addams and Ellen Gates Starr went to Chicago to look for their house among the poor.[19]

4

Hull House: The Context

WHEN the young Misses Addams and Starr invaded Chicago, they carried with them the mental baggage of their upbringing. They were, after all, college-educated Christian young ladies engaging in a new kind of home mission. No matter how vaguely they might describe the details of "the scheme," they knew they were doing good. Their residence in Chicago put these attitudes into abrasive friction with the realities of nineteenth-century industrial slum life. Each reacted differently. Ellen Starr retreated into preciousness and piety. Jane Addams, more flexible, more open to learning from her environment, more energetic, grew into a person quite different from the young lady who was first in her class at Rockford Female Seminary. Her experience modified her genteel missionary approach to social reform, her lady bountiful approach to poverty. She developed a social philosophy which had a profound influence on the way America would deal with its social problems in the twentieth century.

"We discover so many similar undertakings," Jane Addams wrote Alice from Chicago, "the 'Neighborhood Guilds' in New York, the 'Denison Club' in London, etc. but we still think we have a distinct idea of our own."[1] Their first purpose, as Ellen told an early supporter, was that she and "Miss Addams intended to live there naturellement" and "get acquainted with the people & ask their friends of both classes to visit them."[2] But before they could do that, they had to find a home. For months they stalked the slums like hunters after a very special species of wild game. Jane's talks with Alice meant that in Chicago she could learn from other sorts of institutions without falling into their pattern or losing her own vision. People at the Armour mission were especially helpful. The mission workers took the two young ladies around the slum areas, and the board of directors listened to the presentation of the scheme by Jane. Some of the directors even became enthusiastic supporters. Within a few weeks Ellen's aunt, Eliza Starr, had them in the Chicago Women's Club, and by March Jane was getting tired of making speech after speech to clubs, mission boards, and church groups. Apparently money was not going to be a problem. Offers of financial support were rapid, numerous, and generous. Newspapers interviewed them, and they became celebrities even before they found their new home; but somehow the papers always gave a wrong tone. After one such interview Jane said wryly, "I positively feel my caller peering into my face to detect 'spirituality'."[3]

Jane wanted badly to make use of her now fluent French and German, and sought slums where she could. Unfortunately the people in the slums all seemed to speak Italian, Russian, Polish, Yiddish, Czech. The Irish slums were most unattractive. The Italian slums gave her glimpses of Naples, however, and she abandoned her French and German.

Allen Pond, a young architect on the board of the Armour mission, became her guide around the city. In May the two were walking south on Halsted Street and came across a large brick building which Jane had seen earlier and admired. Now, after months of failure to find anything else, the building seemed just right. After finding out about its owner, it turned out to be ideal. Charles J. Hull had lost and won several fortunes in Chicago's rough real estate business and had spent his declining years rich and philanthropic. He had built and lived in the house, but had moved out several years before Jane Addams stumbled upon it. Charles Hull had died early in 1889 and left house and fortune to his cousin and business associate, Helen Culver. Miss Culver had been heavily involved in the philanthropic portion of her cousin's life and therefore had a natural sympathy for the two young ladies who wanted to rent a portion of the old Hull mansion. The first floor was being used as storage space by a furniture factory; the second floor and entrance were rented by Jane Addams and Ellen Gates Starr. Within the year Helen Culver was to grant them free leasehold of the entire building and eventually of much of the adjoining land.

"Bien!" wrote Ellen to a college friend. " 'We' take a house, i.e. Jane takes it, and furnishes it prettily. She has a good deal of furniture and she intends to spend several hundred dollars on some more & of course we shall put all our pictures and 'stuff' into it."[4]

Jane spent not several hundred, but eventually several thousand dollars of her own money fixing up the house. She fussed over it like a young wife moving into her first real home. She told her sister the details of the color schemes and furnishings, and concluded, "Our dining room is one of the prettiest things I ever saw so many people of good taste have said so it cannot be bias."[5] Miss Starr and Miss Addams could not go so far towards being "bread kneaders" as to do their own housework, so after engaging a housekeeper they moved in on September 11, 1889.

In a literal sense they did not know what they were moving into. Both young ladies came from prosperous families. Their knowledge of economics, history, or what would now be called sociology was superficial or nonexistent, and their perception of the world was vaguely romantic. They did not realize that what they were moving into was very nearly a revolution. A very few years after Hull House opened its doors the greatest American historian of the age would look back upon the previous few years and say:

> This then is the real situation: a people composed of heterogeneous materials, with diverse and conflicting ideals and social interests, having passed from the task of filling up the vacant spots on the continent, is now thrown back upon itself, and is seeking an equilibrium. The diverse elements are fused into national unity. The forces of reorganization are turbulent and the nation seems like a witches' kettle.[6]

Frederick Jackson Turner, as much crying in lamentation and foreboding as engaging in historical analysis, expressed the idea well, for it was in the last decade or so of the nineteenth century that the nation began to undergo one of those great reorientations which come but rarely in any national history. The old dreams had run out, been bypassed, or been found to be of base alloy. The United States was confronted with phenomena which, while not unique in the world, were new to Americans. Americans had to find new concepts which would deal with the new phenomena and yet provide at least a veneer of continuity with familiar concepts. This reorientation was a great mental and emotional wrench in the American consciousness, and it was manifested in bitter labor disputes, a virulent 1896 presidential campaign, a revived racism, and eventually, perhaps, the emergence of a new consensus. Jane Addams, and the institution she founded, were important participants in this reorientation.

Essentially the reorientation involved a consideration of the proper relationship which should exist between individuals and their society. What one historian has called the "Alger myth" had produced men of notable accomplishment who had managed to strive and succeed; but it had also produced enormous problems for which no solution seemed readily at hand. Put in its simplest terms, the idea that each individual was essentially in control of his own fate, with perhaps a little neighborly assistance now and then, began to seem absurd to a growing number of Americans after about 1880. The rejection of this sort of individualism and the substitution of an alternative is still going on.

Institutions of production and distribution were at the root of the need for a new *Weltanschauung,* but in the train of economic systems came systems of ideas: social Darwinism, which raised unregulated competition to the stature of an eleventh Commandment; "stewardship," which raised businessmen nearly to the stature of givers of the Commandments; the absolute privateness of property, contract, and business operations generally.

To be sure, there were also attacks on these ideological systems and their social consequences. Late nineteenth-century antibusiness writing did not follow the basically Luddite positions of Jefferson or the transcendentalists. Henry George and Henry Demarest Lloyd, for example, asked not that the new industrial system be abandoned or destroyed, but that its fruits be more widely distributed. In 1894 Lloyd said, "mankind are crowding upon each other in the centres, and struggling to keep each other out of the feast set by the new science. . . ." The feast was there, and Lloyd did not want to return to the days of famine; he simply wanted everyone invited to the bountiful table.[7]

Yet when Hull House opened its doors in 1889, these challenges to the individualistic ethic were little more than hints of what was to come. Jane Addams, although she did not know it, was to mount an effective challenge to a view of man as a selfish individual engaged in ceaseless battle with other selfish individuals.

Both the feast which Lloyd saw and the price of the new industrialism were most obvious in the cities of America. Like the new types of industrialism, the new sorts of cities also demanded changes in ideas. Concepts of community control developed in hamlet or village became meaningless. Town-meeting democracy was becoming impossible even in the towns where it had originated; in the new cities it was unthinkable. Moreover, in a city where most inhabitants were recent arrivals whose daily round was confined to a few blocks or a round trip on a streetcar, the idea of community was either nonexistent or confined to a neighborhood. A few boosters might feel pride in "Chicago," but most of Hull House's neighbors had never even seen the lake. Neighbors were no longer fellow members of one's village, but fellow victims with whom one might band together for protection against one's town. The idea of private property in home ownership was utterly remote to a family on the fourth floor of a "three-decker" tenement. The city may have been good for producing, transporting, buying, and selling—but it was no place for living.

Like corporate individualism, the city had been under attack all through the nineteenth century; but the attack always seemed aimed at eliminating cities. It was not until the generation of Jane Addams and John Dewey that intellectuals accepted the city, albeit critically, and tried to reform rather than to eliminate it. To them the city was not, as it had been to Jefferson and Jackson, too civilized; rather it was not civilized enough.[8] The old question—How can cities be limited or eliminated?—was replaced by a new one: How can cities be made fit places for human beings to live? The older question was not eliminated, it had simply become irrelevant. Jane Addams, among others, proposed that solutions to the problems of cities lay not alone in better streetcars, or even better housing, but in re-establishing that sense of community which she remembered from her childhood, as most city dwellers remembered it from theirs, whether in Illinois or Italy. This conclusion was formulated only after she set her assumptions about human beings against her hard experience with Hull House's neighbors.

When Jane Addams and Ellen Starr moved to Polk and Halsted they were honest when they said they did not know what they were doing, but their move was not without precedent. Like so many American reforms, the settlement-house movement had its origins in England. Probably at the base of the impulses which produced social settlements was a view of Christianity which implied, nay required, a degree of social justice. This political-economic view of Christianity could appear anywhere within the British class structure, from tailors creating a producers' co-operative to peers of the realm speaking in the House of Lords. Probably it was more influential among dissenters than in the Church of England. The direct ancestors of the settlement workers were those members of England's upper classes whom this Christian imperative impelled to action. Robert Owen perceived earlier than most that healthy, contented workers produced better than exploited ones. When these speculations proved correct, Owen broadened his radicalism to include all aspects of his workers' lives and to create at New Lanark in fact not a model factory but a model community. Far higher up England's social ladder than Owen, Lord Shaftesbury worked for decades to produce the first effective factory legislation in 1833, the beginning of a series of increasingly tough laws designed to use governmental power to force employers to treat their employees as human beings. During the very decades that laissez faire seemed as immutable as gravity in international economics, the British government became increasingly interventionist within the national borders—just the reverse of the American situation.

New elements were added to these impulses after 1848. That year saw the continental revolutions, partly social, partly nationalist, come and go. The English equivalent was Chartism, technically a demand for further parliamentary reform, but in fact symbolic of a more general dissatisfaction with the state of England. Eighteen forty-eight also saw the publication of the Communist Manifesto. Christian paternalism, Chartism, and Marxian socialism were enfolded by the English genius for compromise, and emerged as Christian Socialism. More inchoate impulse than clear ideology, Christian Socialism was less paternal than previous reform movements, more interested in a general change in the economic system as against mere patching of weak points, and above all, emphasized working *with* the oppressed rather than *for* them. As a direct antecedent to settlement houses, the Christian Socialist Brotherhood established the London's Workingmen's College in 1854, staffed by teaching volunteers. Within a few years Oxford, Cambridge, and London universities established extension services, thus bringing well-educated Englishmen into contact with working-class districts.

The first university man who consciously chose to live among the lower classes as a means of educating himself, rather than them, was Edward Denison of London. Denison's move to the East End in 1867 was, in a way, the founding of the first settlement house. Denison, John Ruskin, and the vicar of Denison's parish were about to invite other university men to join them, and thus found a full-fledged settlement house, when Denison's health failed, and the project was abandoned.

The next logical step beyond Denison's work, the residence of a group of well-educated upper-class young men in a poor district, did not come until fifteen years later. Samuel A. Barnett, vicar of St. Jude's, Whitechapel, a post he chose because it was the most wretched parish in London, had for several years been speaking at Oxford on conditions in his parish. In 1883 a group of Oxford students asked his help in starting a workingman's college. He advised them that true success would only follow upon their actually residing among those they hoped to teach. The result was that on Christmas Eve, 1884, the first residents moved into Toynbee Hall, the first settlement house in England. Toynbee Hall was the example that was rapidly followed by half a dozen other houses in London, and soon in other parts of England as well.

The first American settlement was copied directly from Toynbee Hall. Stanton Coit heard about the English settlement while doing postgraduate work in Berlin. He became a resident for three months in 1886, and in the summer of that year moved to New York's lower east side to found the Neighborhood Guild, later called University Settlement. Though copied from the English prototype, the American settlement house had a somewhat different flavor. There was less of *noblesse oblige,* less confidence that the upper classes were giving to the lower. Three years after the opening of the Neighborhood Guild, two of Coit's associates founded America's second settlement, College Settlement, also in New York. A few months later Hull House became the third.[9]

The settlement thus came into existence at a moment of greater than normal stress in the American social structure and mode of thought. Every period of history is, of course, "an age of transition," but in some years the stress of change is more palpable, more apparent than others. After about 1885, Americans knew that the old society was becoming irrelevant, that something new was in the making—and they did not know exactly what to expect.

5

The Daily Round

THE story is told that one of the pioneer English settlement workers, early in the life of his settlement, was pressed by a lady to explain precisely what this new institution was. When no amount of explanation seemed to clarify the matter, he finally exploded in exasperation, "Dammit, madam, we *settle*!" And indeed that was the essence of the settlement house. Residents came to reside, and the institution developed in accordance with the personalities and perceptions of the residents confronting the situation of the neighborhood. Jane Addams had no precise ideas about what to expect when she moved into Hull House. She had, however, the kind of mind which could tolerate and even thrive on uncertainty and new experiences. She could thus help her countrymen towards an understanding of, and modes of coping with, their own stress.

Early in the life of the settlement, a delicate little child was deserted in the Hull House nursery. No trace could be found of its mother or father, and within a few days, in spite of every attention, the child died. Jane Addams recalled:

> We decided to have it buried by the county, and the wagon was to arrive by eleven o'clock. About nine in the morning, rumor of this awful deed reached the neighbors. A half-dozen of them came, in a very excited state of mind, to protest. They took up a collection out of their poverty with which to defray a funeral. We were then comparatively new in the neighborhood. We did not realize that we were really shocking a genuine moral sentiment of the community. In our crudeness, we instanced the care and tenderness which had been expended on the little creature when it was alive; that it had every attention from a skilled physician and a trained nurse; we even intimated that the excited members of the group had not taken part in this and that it now lay with us to decide that the child

should be buried, as it had been born, at the county's expense. It is doubtful whether Hull House has ever done anything which injured it so deeply in the mind of some of its neighbors. We were only forgiven by the most indulgent on the grounds that we were spinsters and could not know a mother's heart.

To this Jane Addams added the most revealing sentence of her account of the incident: "No one born and reared in the community could possibly have made a mistake like that."[1]

She was continually learning, always on the alert for ways in which day-to-day realities ought to alter her way of thinking. Thus when she sat down to write about infants, children, adults, or society, she spoke from years of experience. To be sure, she theorized and synthesized beyond any simple compilation of anecdotes, but her experience gave a certain toughness and resiliency to her theories.

While Miss Addams approached the situation of the neighborhood with an open mind, there were some things that she was sure of. The first was that she was moving into her home, not founding an institution. She insisted on calling her neighbors neighbors, not clients or cases, and she continued to insist on such things long after Hull House had become a very elaborate institution indeed. She was also sure that she was not a philanthropist. "Our temptation was to give," she wrote Alice in 1889. "I saw it plainly at the time, and that giving may be as much self indulgence as anything else." During the search for Hull House, Allen Pond had introduced her to a gentleman who was "much interested in newsboys. I did not see the connection at first until I remembered that I was playing the role of philanthropist too. . . . I insisted that I would not talk until he gave me a love of newsboys." She did develop a love for newsboys, but not for philanthropy. Nearly a quarter of a century later she still felt the necessity of denying "the usual mistake" of regarding the settlement as a charitable institution.[2] The residents simply settled, and dealt with the situation of the neighborhood.

And the situations came flooding in on them. There were a few days of hesitancy while the neighborhood wondered what in the world these two young ladies were doing—but they soon found out. Within three weeks there was more activity than the house could handle. One fashionable young lady traveled from northern Chicago to run a kindergarten every morning. She had two dozen children and a waiting list of three times that number. There were, almost immediately, girls' clubs, boys' clubs, an informal lending library, music programs, a social science club, all with waiting lists. Jane herself ran a boys' club Tuesday nights and within a few months added a club for Italian girls. "They are all so anxious to come and so very respectful," she said with mingled pride and amusement.[3]

"It is my impression," Robert A. Woods pontificated to Miss Addams after a visit in 1895, "that there is too much activity and not enough repose . . . the time has come for the more experienced residents to give up just as far as possible the notion that you are members of an emergency corps subject to call." Certainly serenity and repose were in scant supply. The problem was that there were so many emergencies, and so many calls which could not be ignored.[4]

When Hull House was only a few months old, a young woman rushed through the door saying that a girl in her tenement house was having a baby all by herself and "hollering something fierce." None of the neighbor ladies would touch "the likes of her" because she was not married, and none would call a doctor for fear of being stuck with the bill. No relatives were available, so while one of the residents called a doctor, Julia Lathrop and Jane Addams set out to help. The doctor arrived only after several hours, by which time he found the young mother lying quietly in a clean bed with a healthy young boy, to be named Julius John after his deliverers, by her side.

Walking home and musing on birth and death, Jane Addams suddenly exclaimed, "This doing things that we don't know how to do is going too far. Why did we let ourselves be rushed into midwifery?" To which Julia Lathrop replied pointedly that they were ignorant of almost everything and, "If we have to begin to hew down to the line of our ignorance, for goodness' sake don't let us begin at the humanitarian end."[5] If calls like this one came, how could anyone take Robert Woods' advice and not respond to them?

There were scores, hundreds, perhaps thousands of emergencies over the years to which Jane Addams responded. Most of them are unrecorded, and even those that are recorded are impossible to date accurately, but when anything went wrong on the west side of Chicago, when anyone had troubles too great to bear, the natural place to go was Hull House. And Hull

House, often its chief resident, *always* responded: to the "worthy," the "unworthy," the drunk, the sober, the honest man or the thief, the victim of criminal attack or the criminal. While responding, while never "hewing down to the line of our ignorance," Jane Addams was always also putting her experiences together, adding up what she saw, and deriving from her experience a theory of society.

A peasant woman from Germany, bewildered by Chicago, unable to understand the language, could earn only a meager living as a washerwoman. Her three teen-aged daughters learned English and, rather than endure the hardships of their mother, turned to prostitution. The mother, in despair, came to Jane Addams overjoyed to find a sympathetic ear, and what was more, an ear which could understand German. Miss Addams, with the help of other residents, spoke to each of the daughters, two of them pregnant. They persuaded the father of one of the expected babies to marry the woman he had made pregnant. A second man was sued for the support of his child, which the courts eventually compelled him to supply. The third daughter chose to continue the life she had begun. Miss Addams persuaded the mother to move out of the city which so overwhelmed her into a little house in the country which the settlement helped her find.

The Taboshi family was one of the few oriental families in the neighborhood. One Saturday evening Mrs. Taboshi came quietly to Jane Addams and informed her that Mr. Taboshi had just shot himself. Miss Addams offered sympathy, helped make arrangements for the funeral, and, rather than send the family back to the apartment associated only with terror and sorrow, offered the wife and two children the use of her own room where they stayed until the shock somewhat abated.[6]

One spring day after Hull House had been in existence several years, a group of enraged Italians rushed into the house looking for Miss Addams. They told her a confused story, the nub of which was that a policeman named John Baganski had got into some sort of a scuffle with a group of Italians. Scuffle had turned into battle, and Baganski had pulled his gun and shot two men. She calmed them as best she could, tried to get their story straight, and, since there was really nothing she could do herself, helped them to find a lawyer.[7]

A couple of years later, just after President McKinley had

been shot by an anarchist, another group of outraged immigrants burst into Hull House, this time Russian Jews. In a general roundup of anarchists, the police had arrested Abraham Isaak, the editor of an anarchist newspaper, and were holding him incommunicado in a cell beneath City Hall. "You see what becomes of the law you boast of," Isaak's friends said, "they will not even let him see a lawyer." By this time Jane Addams had access to any mayor of Chicago, and she and a young clergyman named Raymond Robins went to see Mayor Carter Harrison at his home. Harrison agreed with her that even an anarchist should get a fair trial, but that just now it was "too dangerous" to let Isaak see a lawyer. Miss Addams explained that his friends were much enraged and worried about his safety. He was perfectly well, the mayor insisted, and offered to let Miss Addams visit him and see for herself. She and Raymond Robins did just that. They talked to Isaak for a few minutes and found he was shaken and scared but essentially well. Did he want a lawyer? Miss Addams asked. No, Isaak thought it would not be necessary, he would answer all questions put to him. He assured her he had had absolutely nothing to do with the McKinley assassination. After a few minutes talk the two left Isaak and reported to his friends that he was all right and did not want a lawyer. After a few days he was released unharmed.[8]

On a less extreme level, Mrs. William Dennis, mother of a neighborhood family, came to Miss Addams telling a tale of alcoholism which she could not cure no matter how much she wanted to. The two women worked out the following pledge which Mrs. Dennis signed: "I hereby solemnly pledge in the presence of Jane Addams, that from this day forth, hence forevermore, that I will abstain from all intoxicating liquor. I also promise that in the case of overwhelming temptation, I will come and see said Jane Addams."[9] There is no way of telling whether or not the plan was successful.

Jane Addams would try to find work for an unemployed man or offer haven to a young wife whose drunken husband beat her. Somehow she had the ability to talk to anyone and put him at his ease: a visiting Beatrice Webb shocked by Chicago's filth, or a young newsboy shivering from the cold. He had, he said at the door, been given a dollar to bring a message to Miss Addams. She was in bed but came down and sat beside him in front of the fire while he warmed himself against the journey homeward. His shyness slipped away as he talked and joked with her, and he remembered the incident his whole life.[10]

In a more dramatic incident, Jane Addams was sleeping one night when she heard a thief climb softly in her window. Where most women would have screamed in terror, she calmly watched him as he fruitlessly searched the room for valuables. As he began to climb out the window she said, softly so as not to frighten him, that he should go down the stairs since he might fall climbing out the window. Soon thief and victim were in conversation, and she learned that he was just starting his career as a second-story man and did not much care for it. She told him to come back the next day and she would try to find a regular job for him, which she did.[11]

In dealing with individuals she was superb. She never judged or moralized as visitors from charity organization societies did. She did not investigate the character of the supplicant or calculate whether or not he was "worthy" of help. She refused to apply the standards of the middle class—hard work, sobriety, and thrift—to neighbors for whom these standards were remote, impossible, or fraudulent. She had been brought up with middle-class standards, but it was her genius that she could perceive, where others like her could not, their irrelevance to the society of the urban poor. Partly through dwelling among them, but even more because her mind was always observant and willing to learn from observation, always consciously groping toward understanding and consciously trying to avoid preconceptions, she taught the nation as a whole what kind of society it was becoming.

Jane Addams learned much from her personal contact with the neighborhood, but her perceptions would probably never have been transformed into a broad social theory without the presence of other great residents of the settlement. A remarkable collection of individuals, they not only multiplied Miss Addams' experiences but theorized, talked, wrote, discussed, generalized, and argued about everything around them. As with her direct experience, Miss Addams took all this in, modified it as it modified her original ideas, learned from it, and emerged eventually with a coherent social theory.

The first of the great residents after the original two was Julia Lathrop, a friend of both Ellen and Jane from college days. The Lathrops were among the founding families of the town of Rockford. Julia's father participated in the incorporation of the village into a city, and her mother was a member of the first class of the seminary. William Lathrop was a lawyer, businessman, and politician. Like John Addams, he had been one of the founders of the Republican party in Illinois, was a state representative, and a colleague and strong supporter of Abraham Lincoln. Julia's father was also a strong supporter of the movement for women's rights. He drew up the bill permitting women to be lawyers in Illinois, and the first woman lawyer read law in his office. Julia's mother was a strong suffragist in those long, discouraging years when the cause had no real hope of success. Julia, like Jane, grew up as a member of a prominent family in northern Illinois. She entered Rockford College with Jane Addams, but left after a year and graduated from Vassar. After graduation she became a secretary in her father's law office, all the while reading a good deal of law herself. She was also involved, in a minor way, in running two successful businesses in Rockford. When Jane Addams and Ellen Starr told her of their "scheme" she was interested in spite of her father's coolness, and within a year of the founding she came to live at Hull House.

At Hull House Julia Lathrop concentrated on trying to improve public charities in Illinois. In 1893 she was appointed a member of the State Board of Charities and investigated every charitable institution that the state ran. At the same time she worked hard to get better training for the people who ran the institutions and to keep politics out of their appointment. Failing in this last, she resigned with a sharp letter in 1901. Four years later, with a new governor, she was again made a member of the Board and served until 1909. In 1912, a vigorous campaign by her associates was successful when she was appointed first head of the United States Children's Bureau in the Department of Labor where she served until 1922.[12]

One snowy morning between Christmas and New Years of 1891, there was a knock on the Hull House door. Jane Addams was minding the baby of the cook, who was late getting breakfast. The infant was fat, heavy, and squirming to get out of her arms. At the same time a five-year-old was pulling at her skirts, demanding attention. Thus encumbered, Miss Addams opened the door and found there Henry Standing Bear of the Kickapoo tribe, and Florence Kelley. They were welcomed as cordially as though they had been invited. Henry Standing Bear remained at the house for seven months as the janitor's helper. Florence Kelley stayed for seven years as perhaps the most popular resident the settlement ever had. She had a quick and merciless wit, a sharp tongue, and was a devotee of "plain speech" from a strong Quaker heritage. Her father was "Pig Iron" Kelley, a strong free-soiler and high-tariff man who had run for Congress on the Free Soil ticket. He was one of the first Republicans in Pennsylvania, was elected fourteen times to the House of Representatives, and was part of the Republican cabal which counted in Rutherford P. Hayes and counted out Samuel J. Tilden in 1877. Florence's mother came from English Quaker stock of firm moral rectitude, and what that side of the family thought of the Hayes-Tilden deal went unrecorded. Florence remembered one of her aunts as so devotedly anti-slavery that she would neither wear cotton clothes nor eat sugar since both were products of slave labor. Florence adopted both the moral rectitude of the Quakers and the blunt determination of the self-made businessman. Where Jane Addams disarmed an opponent with charm and gentleness, turning him into a friend, Florence Kelley carried an enemy's fortifications by direct assault, demanding and usually getting unconditional surrender.

Florence Kelley was educated at Cornell and, when no graduate school in the United States would admit a woman, at Zurich where she translated Engels' *The Condition of the Working Classes in England in 1844*. Marriage to a Russian-born doctor in Switzerland ended by divorce five years later. Although they were living in New York City, the Kelleys got their divorce in Illinois because of New York's strict laws. In Illinois Florence Kelley began research into child labor, and it was natural that she should live at Hull House. Her three children were sometimes at the settlement house and sometimes in the home of Henry Demarest Lloyd in the northern suburbs of Chicago.

At Hull House she first did what would now be called vocational guidance, and then she carried out research for Carroll D. Wright, U. S. Commissioner of Labor. In 1893 Governor John P. Altgeld appointed her the first Chief Factory Inspector in Illinois after previously offering the job to Lloyd. Her job was to enforce the Altgeld administration's brand-new law prohibiting child labor and limiting women's hours, which she did with vigor until the law was declared unconstitutional in 1895. After 1899 she went to New York, where she spent most of her career as head of the National Consumer's League.[13]

Julia Lathrop and Florence Kelley were good friends at Hull House, but though they agreed on basic questions they could always find some issue on which to differ. Often it was the justice of court decisions, with Julia Lathrop defending the majesty of the law and Florence Kelley insisting on its idiocy. Anything Florence Kelley talked about became dramatic, entertaining, funny, and of the utmost importance. Alice Hamilton recalled how the other residents used to bribe her with hot chocolate in the evening to talk about what she had done, seen, and thought that day.[14]

In speaking of Julia Lathrop—but in words which might as well have applied to Florence Kelley or herself—Jane Addams wrote, "It is curious how children catch the glow of the moral enthusiasm of their elders and absorb opinions by listening even though the issue touches them remotely."[15] In these three residents there was not only an ideological, but also a direct biological inheritance from the pre-Civil War fervor of abolitionism to the "moral enthusiasms" of the progressive movement. All three had strong-willed, important fathers; all three families were strongly abolitionist; all three went through the moral trauma of Civil War, emancipation, the assassination of Lincoln, and Reconstruction. In addition, all three families had some flavor of feminism, and two of them had a measure of Quaker influence. If the abolitionists were, as has been suggested, Puritans looking for a new definition of salvation, these progressives were abolitionists looking for a new slavery to abolish.[16] Since the old slavery was already gone, they turned to attacks on the new slavery—which John Calhoun, the greatest defender of the old slavery, had been among the first to attack.

This formulation, of course, does not hold for all the great residents of Hull House. Alice Hamilton remembered her family's position on slavery as "to be sure, it must be hard on the slaves, but we did have to have cotton." Instead of moral fervor her family had an amazingly broad cultural background. Her older sister, Edith Hamilton, became an eminent classicist, and her younger sister, Norah, was the artist who illustrated both

Alice's and Jane Addams' autobiographies. Reared in Fort Wayne, Indiana, Alice Hamilton studied medicine at the University of Michigan and then, after a year in hospitals, did further study in bacteriology and pathology at Munich. Unable to find the research job she wanted, she continued her studies at Johns Hopkins. In 1897 she was appointed to the faculty of Northwestern University Woman's Medical School. Having heard Jane Addams speak in Fort Wayne, she resolved to live at Hull House. There she was inevitably drawn into the life of the neighborhood, first in an investigation of a typhoid epidemic, then in an attempt to stop druggists from selling cocaine to young boys. From this, she was asked by the governor to look into industrial poisoning in Illinois. These efforts led her into a lifelong crusade against industrial illness, a subject she eventually taught at Harvard.

Alice Hamilton did not have Florence Kelley's aggressive sharpness. She tended more toward the quiet and modest, and by temperament preferred the solitude of the research laboratory to the battles of industrial medicine; but she could not resist the claims of poisoned and injured workers. She had a first-class intellect and along with a few others did truly pioneering work in diagnosing and preventing industrial illness. At Hull House she was looked up to for her expertise. Miss Addams respected her, partly, perhaps, for achieveing what she herself had been unable to achieve. Alice Hamilton was one of the few people who could tell Jane Addams what to do with any hope of compliance. It was Alice Hamilton who worried over Miss Addams' health, told her when she overtaxed herself and when she needed a vacation. Particularly in Miss Addams' later years, Alice Hamilton became a close companion.[17]

Alice Hamilton was drawn into reform through her research in a special branch of medicine. Similarly Grace Abbott was drawn into reform through her researches into the life of recent immigrants. She was a Nebraska girl who had attended the University of Nebraska and was, in 1908, working on her doctorate in political science at the University of Chicago. When Jane Addams asked Sophonisba Breckinridge, who was to head the University of Chicago School of Social Work but was at that time on the regular faculty of the university, for a "bright young man" to undertake some research on immigrants, Miss Breckinridge recommended Grace Abbott. Grace and her sister Edith were both to have distinguished careers in social work: Edith mostly in the development of professional social work education, Grace in work with children. Eventually Grace was to become Julia Lathrop's successor as head of the United States Children's Bureau, and Edith became Sophonisba Breckinridge's assistant and colleague at the school of social work.[18]

Alice Hamilton recalled in her autobiography when "a young girl from Iowa, Jessie Binford, arrived at Hull House with a vague interest in doing something with delinquent children." That was in 1905. In looking back through more than half a century, Jessie Binford recalled the sense of bewilderment she had felt at first as she was virtually ignored in the whirl of settlement activities. Everyone but she seemed so busy. Everyone but she seemed to know just what to do. After an aimless day or two, Jessie Binford timidly plucked at Miss Addams' sleeve and asked what she should do. Somewhat surprised by the question, Jane Addams suggested quietly that perhaps she should do nothing for a while, that after being at the settlement for a few days, or weeks, she might find something which no one had ever thought of before.[19] Jessie Binford did find something, and for many years she was head of the Juvenile Protective Association. In fact, she was at Hull House off and on for the next fifty-eight years. In 1963, when all but the original Hull mansion was to be razed for the University of Illinois Chicago campus, a determined Jessie Binford stood against the bulldozers to the very end. She marched proudly out of the settlement less than twenty-four hours before the wreckers were to arrive.

There were many others, less distinguished perhaps but all contributing to the excitement of an institution which seemed directly at the center of a whirlwind of ideas: there were Russian revolutionaries escaping from the Czar's wrath after 1905, artists, writers, and young men and women of wealth and leisure. At times there were as many as fifty residents. "We had a fairly intimate life," Alice Hamilton recalled of the '90's when the group was still quite small, "if one can use such a word to describe a relation which was almost entirely devoid of personal intimacy."[20]

Strong-minded individuals like these could only flourish in a free atmosphere in which experimentation was rampant. Jane Addams knew everything that was going on in the settlement, but she was never boss, never directed. Each resident was expected as a matter of course to be alert to the needs of the neighborhood and to respond with whatever ingenuity and expertise she (occasionally he) might possess. Miss Addams might gently suggest, might offer advice or demurral, would usually offer encouragement or a sympathetic ear, might select the person to be in charge of a larger project. On the whole, however, each resident was on his own.

As a result, administrative machinery was haphazard at best. Perhaps the best term to describe the Hull House organization would be something like "autocratic anarchy." In the early years, when the number of residents was quite small, Jane Addams attempted to systematize the house through regular weekly residents' meetings. Here matters of program and personnel were subjected to collective decision, though Jane Addams' views clearly carried the most weight. These meetings made frequent attempts to bring order out of the chaos of Hull House finances—attempts which always failed. Should they start a co-operative coal yard? What hours should the playground be open? What wages should be paid in the coffee house? The residents worked out schedules for waiting on table, answering the door, "toting," or guiding visitors around the house. At these meetings Julia Lathrop frequently indulged her habit of napping after dinner, so that a constant joke was to "wake up Julia Lathrop and see what she thinks about it." By 1895, these meetings fell into disuse. Instead of dealing with the entire operation of the settlement at one meeting, Miss Addams dealt piecemeal with one branch or another as necessity demanded. This led to an even greater degree of disorganization. Usually, however, the disorder was creative.[21]

A typical day at Hull House, if there was any such thing, might begin with the newsboy placing a broad selection of Chicago newspapers outside the door.[22] If it were winter, the streets would still be dark and he might meet the first working mother bringing an infant to the nursery. The resident in charge of the nursery would have had breakfast already, but by seven-thirty the main body of residents began to gather in the coffee house for breakfast. They did not all come at once, as some had been up late the night before with clubs and reading groups, and others had to leave early for jobs outside the settlement. Those with obligations might have to leave, but soon Miss Addams would come in bearing the daily stack of mail. One morning the earliest arrivals in the coffee house decided that the settlement custom of calling everyone by his last name, or in the Quaker fashion by both names, was too formal and that first names would prevail. As each resident wandered in, he was greeted cheerily by his given name. When Miss Addams arrived with her mail, the game collapsed in an embarrassed pause; then she was greeted as she always had been, as Miss Addams. She probably did not even notice, already engrossed in the day's mail, glancing through each to see what the subject was and distributing it to the resident most concerned: "Here, Grace Abbott, this is an immigration matter."

Then the discussions would start. All the residents agreed basically on the need for social justice, but some were socialists, some were not, some moderate, some radical. On any specific issue one might find a dozen different shades of opinion. By the time the group gradually dispersed after breakfast, the discussion would be vigorous and loud. Each faction would be mustering its heaviest artillery, but breakfast discussions would be left unfinished. As the residents went to their various activities they would be mulling over plans for destroying their opponents' arguments when the combat was renewed at dinner. After one particularly vigorous argument, Marie Sukloff, one of those who had escaped after the 1905 Russian Revolution, sighed contentedly and remarked, "I haven't felt so much at home since I first joined the terrorists."[23]

By this time the nursery, called a crèche, would be filling with infants, and the kindergarten would have its complement of four- and five-year-olds, for Hull House always concentrated on children. Often there was some pressing emergency for Jane Addams to cope with, but if there were not, she would spend the morning attending to the vast pile of correspondence or, increasingly after 1900, to her writing. Many of the letters were from people in other cities who wanted to establish settlement houses, or from established houses looking for a new head resident or a specialist in some particular field.

There was no gathering for the midday meal; people took it on the fly. Frequently Miss Addams would have a luncheon and afternoon meeting of some of the scores of organizations with which she was involved. These meetings were usually held in downtown office buildings, and the elevator boys got to know Miss Addams well. As she entered an elevator one day in a building where two meetings were scheduled, the boy quite casually asked, "What are you eating with today, Miss Addams, garbage or the social evil?" "Garbage," she replied, and rode to the fourth floor with as much dignity as she could muster.[24]

In the afternoon the kindergarten training class would meet to spread the gospel of the movement, the women's club might be listening to a distinguished speaker and, as school let out, the house would be flooded with all ages of children—always the children!—swarming in and out to clubs, classes, athletic contests. This was the time when Jane Addams would meet her group of girls or boys—apparently never a mixed group. After a few months, however, she allowed these groups to drift into the hands of others since she was not at her best with groups or clubs. Her charisma inspired great loyalty and even love in individuals, but it was not of the infectious or enthusiastic sort that carried a group of young boys or girls. Ellen Starr read the great sagas to a group of boys with such effect that one day as Jane Addams came in the door of the house she was practically knocked over by a distraught young man from Ellen's club. He slammed his way out the door saying, "There is no use coming back here any more. Prince Roland is dead." This did not happen in Jane Addams' clubs, where the reading was more likely to consist of Josiah Royce's philosophy.[25]

At six the residents would gather for a rather formal dinner in the dining room, served by a cook or housekeeper. The discussions of the morning would be resumed; antagonists would sit at the same table. Arguments thought up during the day would be brought to bear. Almost always there would be a distinguished guest, for Hull House very quickly became one of Chicago's well-known "sights" as well as one of the centers of the city's intellectual life. John Dewey was a regular visitor, as was Henry Demarest Lloyd. Kier Hardy was there in 1895; John P. Altgeld on a number of occasions. Young Harold Ickes hammered out some of his political ideas at Hull House. Sometimes Clarence Darrow came to dinner. The anarchist Prince Peter Kropotkin, "Comrade Kropotkin" as the residents called him, charmed the settlement when he visited in 1901. When in the same year Vice-

President Theodore Roosevelt preached a sermon in Chicago, he spent the afternoon and evening at Hull House. Richard T. Ely was often down from the University of Wisconsin. One historian has sugested that Hull House was Jane Addams' salon, and in a sense this is so. Miss Addams did gather around herself a group of articulate and original, inquiring minds. Yet there was nothing precious, detached, or even self-conscious about them, and certainly Jane Addams was nothing of the patroness. She was as engaged and as battle scarred as they. If she preferred, as she did, to converse with a professor rather than a union organizer, still the union leaders came to the settlement too, and were welcome. Another scholar has suggested that the Hull House groups were more like the Fabian Society, and this may be closer to the truth, though there was less *noblesse oblige* as well as less pure literary skill.[26]

With Florence Kelley and Julia Lathrop telling tales of bureaucratic intransigence, Alice Hamilton detailing the results of working in unhealthy factories, Richard T. Ely filling in the large picture of national economics—from the viewpoint of a Christian humanist—and John Dewey talking about the nature of the child; with all this and the hundreds of details supplied by the residents from their experiences of the day, Jane Addams' own perceptions could be tested, refined, altered, and worked over. Certainly they could not remain static. While she continued good relations with Rockford College, she was in fact rapidly leaving far behind the missionary attitudes, the elitism, and the essential social conservatism of those young ladies who chose "bread givers" as their motto. When she came to write down her new philosophy, she could draw from the wide range of intellects that Hull House attracted.

6

Hull House: Institutional Growth

JANE ADDAMS wrote her ideas with pen and ink, but she also wrote them in brick and mortar, in programs, in clubs and activities at the large congeries of buildings known inaccurately as Hull House. Implicitly the institution became the embodiment of her ideas as well as their testing and proving grounds.

Surely the institution grew and prospered far beyond anything she could have imagined when, in October of 1889, she carefully recorded in the Hull House account book the expenditure of ten dollars for checkerboards, a stereoptican and slides, and a set of dominoes. On May 1, 1906, Hull House listed its net worth as $514,525, and this was not the end, for within a year another $50,000 building was to go up. Hull House had grown from a residence for two young ladies into a complex of buildings and programs exceeded in size in the city only by the University of Chicago.[1]

Whether by design or accident, the settlement served first and foremost the children of the neighborhood. Jane Addams, and presumably the other residents, saw children at the center of their efforts, and most of the additional buildings were added to take care of the exuberant children's activities, bursting the seams of existing structures. Within five years of its opening, the settlement added a gymnasium. Clearly more was needed, so in 1895 an entirely new children's building went up with club rooms, workshops, and dormitories. Within a decade even that was inadequate, so Miss Addams began discussing a new building with the settlement's most important financial supporter, Mrs. Louise De Koven Bowen. At first Mrs. Bowen agreed to pay for a building "provided it doesn't cost over $25,000 or $30,000." With this encouragement, Miss Addams began discussing plans with the architects. The building was finally envisioned as essentially a boys' club, with a large auditorium on the second floor for the women's club. The first floor would have a manual training department, a bowling alley, and a billiard hall. The second would have the auditorium and a gymnasium; the third a library, print shop, study rooms, and classrooms. The fourth floor would be devoted to living quarters where self-supporting boys could live for twenty-five cents a week plus a portion of their dining room expenses. The dining facilities and a few more bedrooms were to occupy the fifth floor.

With all this the cost estimate slightly exceeded Mrs. Bowen's limits and reached nearly $50,000. Mrs. Bowen was philosophical. "Things always do cost more than one expects," she reflected, then added, "But this building is going to be done right and we are not going to cut down and have things not right and then in a year or two pull them all down. So unless you can see something that might just as well be left out, tell Mr. Pond to go ahead." Then, as an afterthought, she admonished, "And please, you are not to ask anyone for any money for furnishings. I am going to do that myself and it's going to be just as you want it." With this sort of loyal support it is little wonder that the settlement grew.[2]

When Miss Addams came to think theoretically about what children were like, she concluded that recreation was more than simply a pastime. It was the essence of childhood. Yet the urban environment provided very few opportunities for play. That was why the children's building had a billiard room, a gymnasium, and a bowling alley, along with its educational facilities. That was also why Hull House found itself creating Chicago's first playground. As with so many aspects of the settlement, the formation of the playground was not planned. It started in 1892, when Miss Addams made a speech on bad housing and what would now be called "slumlords." She used the case of a nearby block of dilapidated tenements to prove her point and named the owner, William Kent. Kent happened to be in the audience. He was a young man who had just inherited the property and was indignant at being denounced for crimes he was not even aware of committing. He was, however, open to the idea of social responsibility. Miss Addams and William Kent inspected the property and finally determined that most of the buildings were beyond repair. Partly as charity, and partly in despair and disgust, he offered to give the whole block to Hull House. After some days of further thought, Jane Addams concluded that though the tenements might bring an income of two thousand dollars a year, the settlement could not become a slum landlord. The buildings should be torn down and the block made into a playground. Through some alchemy she persuaded William Kent not only to pay for tearing down his own tenements, but also to pay for equipping the playground and for taxes on the land. For ten years the settlement operated the playground with the help of a policeman furnished by the city. At the end of that time, public authority took it over as part of a broad system of small parks in the city. And William Kent went on to become an important progressive congressman from California.[3]

The case of the playground was typical of the kind of influence Hull House had on the city. A need or potential would be perceived, then met, by Hull House. Once the experimental stage was passed, the city would often take over the function. Public authority seemed, in Chicago at the turn of the century, incapable of originality and imagination. Once the case was proved, however, public authority seemed at least open to suggestion. This sequence of events occurred again and again: with day-care centers for children of working mothers, with public baths, eventually with such things as social casework and youth group leaders.[4]

A playground in the city, however, was only a reflection of what Miss Addams thought city children really needed—experience in the country. One of the few unquestioned articles of faith which Jane Addams held was that such experience would be beneficial. The city, which alienated man from man, was an unnatural environment which prevented natural human goodness from manifesting itself. Children needed rural experience to cleanse themselves. Miss Addams never wanted to send children permanently to the country, as had Charles Loring Brace of the New York Children's Aid Society; nor did she ever think that a rural society ought to be re-established. City children simply needed some rural experience as a method of attaching themselves properly to the long development of the human species. Perhaps recalling with nostalgia her early years in Cedarville, she was sure that a rural life was man's natural calling. Country work was far more normal than life in a factory. The personal ties of a small town were more natural where even courtship took place under the protective community eye. Anyone who had such pastoral simplicity in his early life had a haven of memories to which he could retreat from the horrors of a city. She wrote of a "drunken man, in a maudlin stage, babbling of his good country mother and imagining he was driving the cows home and I knew that his little son, who laughed aloud at him, would be drunk earlier in life and would have no such pastoral interlude in his ravings." If a child did not have the pastoral experience growing up in the city, Hull House might supply some measure of a substitute through a summer camp. Hull House was in existence twenty years before a summer camp was begun at Lake Bluff, north of Chicago. Two years later, in 1911, Mrs. Bowen donated seventy-two acres near Waukegan for the Joseph T. Bowen Memorial Camp. Here boys and girls were to exchange surroundings of garbage cans, as pictured on one side of the camp's letterhead, for a rushing brook, depicted on the other.[5]

The residents of the settlement realized that they could not establish a happy and productive environment for children within the settlement, while at the same time ignoring what happened outside its doors. Hence, as an outgrowth of the efforts of Miss Addams, Julia Lathrop, and others to create a Juvenile Court, these same people created the Juvenile Protective Association (J.P.A.). Louise De Koven Bowen was its head for many years, and tried to save children from certain types of urban pressures. The J.P.A. directed its efforts mostly toward trying to improve the morality of children. It persuaded grocery stores not to sell tobacco to minors, druggists not to sell indecent postcards, theaters to have plays which taught proper moral lessons. The association organized a spectacular and temporarily successful crusade to clean up public dance halls.

Much of the work of the J.P.A. was based on the premise that morality—and the word at bottom meant sexual morality—was a fragile vessel, that the city could easily break it, and that young boys and girls, especially girls, would be pulled into a life of sin. The group did valuable work. Large numbers of girls were in fact driven by low wages and terrible working conditions into prostitution, and venereal disease was a serious problem. Yet one cannot down the image of determined, righteous ladies, many of them spinsters, standing vigilant guard lest innocent children fall into a pit of vaguely defined but certainly horrible sexuality.

This kind of implicit condescension toward her neighbors was also evident in Miss Addams' efforts to bring them higher culture. In addition to creating an environment where the naturally benign instincts of children might flourish, Hull House had as one of its major purposes the break-down of barriers between groups in Chicago: to create a sense of community between immigrant and native, employer and employee, cultured and uncultured. Miss Addams and Miss Starr were explicit about their attempts to bring high culture to the neighborhood, and they were certain they knew what "high" meant.

It meant, first of all, an art gallery. The people of the neighborhood did not know that they did not have an art gallery, but for the Hull House residents, at least in a portion of their minds, art should be brought to the "humble." So the Butler Art Gallery was built, and visited and appreciated by the neighbors. While the city had had a public gallery since 1882, it was on Lake Michigan, far from working-class districts and closed on Sundays. Eventually Hull House prevailed on the trustees to keep the Art Institute open on the one day working people would be likely to visit it.

Music was not developed to the professional or near professional level it attained at the Henry Street settlement, though there was a music school from which a few professional musicians emerged. Hull House seems to have emphasized vocal music: a chorus for adults and one for children, preservation of folk songs from the immigrant communities, and intensive training of a few particularly talented singers. Miss Addams found the prospects discouraging, for over and over again a promising young music student would start factory work and the combination of overwork and bad air would lead to neglect of music and a ruined voice.

The theater was much more successful and widely popular. The range of plays was as wide as Hull House's neighbors. Youngsters provided stirring historical drama about the importance of women:

ACT I

Trenton

FIRST REVOLUTIONARY SOLDIER.

Ain't it fierce that we ain't got a flag for this yere revolution.

SECOND REVOLUTIONARY SOLDIER.
Yeah, ain't it fierce!

ACT II
Valley Forge

GEORGE WASHINGTON.
Ain't it fierce that we ain't got a flag for this yere revolution.

FRENCH SOLDIER.
Yeah, ain't it fierce!

ACT III

GEORGE WASHINGTON.
Gee it's fierce that we ain't got a flag for this yere revolution!

BETSY ROSS.
Yeah. (*Pause.*) . . . Here, George, you hold the baby while I make a flag for this yere revolution.

At the other end of the esthetic scale was a production of Sophocles' *Ajax* given in Greek by members of the local Greek community. Miss Addams was especially proud of this play, for at one and the same time it brought the higher life into the slum community, showed Americans that the immigrants had a rich and valuable culture, and provided the drama which the neighborhood needed to escape the routines of factory labor. Between the extremes of *Ajax* and the drama of Betsy Ross, all sorts of plays were devised and put on the boards. Each national community portrayed life in the old country. Often the second generation acted out traditions of the new. One Italian immigrant wrote a play about conflict between the generations, and his neighbors saw that their own family conflicts were not unique. Very early a repertory group of particularly interested and talented people put on the works of Shaw, Ibsen, Galsworthy, and others. By 1912 the Hull House players were good enough to be invited for a six-week engagement at the Abbey Theater in Dublin.[6]

For Miss Addams, the theater was far more than an art form. The rich, Miss Addams felt, might respond to lectures and reading, but drama was needed to educate the poor. Theater could do even more; it could serve as a "reconstructing and reorganizing agent of accepted moral truth." It could and should be didactic, showing Americans of all social classes what they were having difficulty understanding about the new industrial age.

On a more practical level, Hull House dramatics were to provide a more wholesome substitute for the cheap commercial stage.

The children—again, and always, the children—around Halsted Street seemed drawn to theaters like flies to jam. Jane Addams discussed the plays given at the "five cent theater" in terms virtually identical to those which mid-twentieth-century critics apply to television: the plays were immoral and in general stimulating in the wrong directions. Just as the coffee house was devised in part as a substitute for the saloon, the theater at Hull House was to be a wholesome alternative to the degenerate, cheap theater. She was convinced that given the choice, most people, especially little children, would choose the more wholesome.

Ellen Starr was the more artistic of the original residents. For Jane Addams, art was a virtue to be admired, but not participated in. Ellen Starr was a professional who taught drawing and painting not only at the settlement, but at the Art Institute as well. Fine arts at Hull House soon broadened to include commercial art, posters, signs, and then further broadened to crafts. Occasionally a professional artist was a resident at Hull House, but generally the art was amateur and, like the theater, therapeutic in intent. In the art classes the careworn mother was for a brief while in contact with creativity. The young factory girl, stifled all day by a monotonous job, was to have a chance at self-expression. An old world craftsman, finding no outlet in the new world for his skill, could restore a bit of self-respect.

Literature, especially the works of the great English writers, was also a way of bringing the higher life to humbler folk. The smallest children came in to listen to simple stories, older boys to heroic tales of medieval knights, and adults to Shakespeare, Plato, or William James. The Shakespeare Club, which read the plays, went to performances, and heard lectures by Shakespearean scholars, started when Hull House was four years old and continued for two decades. Julia Lathrop's Plato Club was attended mostly by old men who had read philosophy all their lives and had enough knowledge to impress even John Dewey, who occasionally led the club. The discussions of points suggested by Plato were often vigorous. One man insisted on disagreeing with the group leader "on principle." One Sunday he made a speech which sounded suspiciously as though he, Plato, and Julia Lathrop all agreed. When confronted with this possibility, the gentleman expostulated: "I agree with you, Miss Lathrop, not at all, not at all—it is you who agree with me!"

In addition to the Plato Club and the Shakespeare Club, other reading groups were offered as the taste and ability of the residents allowed. When Miss Addams wrote about these clubs, she did so directly after a discussion of the evils of class antagonism. Literature for her could thus "feed the mind of the worker to lift it above the monotony of his task and to connect it with the larger world outside of his immediate surroundings." There were also the slightly more formal courses of the College Extension in which college-educated men and women, occasionally a full-fledged university professor, offered evening courses for adults. These were predecessors of the University of Chicago Extension Service.[7]

These bouts with the higher culture continued at Hull House, as the residents never abandoned their aim of uniting the cultural heritage of different social classes. Yet the pressing needs of the neighbors turned the educational efforts of the settlement somewhat away from reproducing "the college type of culture" to more immediately applicable ends. Working daughters of working mothers could not learn to cook and manage a household. When they got married they were at a loss as housekeepers. The settlement started classes in what, in Jane Addams' youth, girls had learned without being aware of: home management. For the boys the beginning of instruction in a trade was more important. The settlement offered classes in wood and metal working, tin smithing, photography, printing, telegraphy, and electrical work. Classes in English gave new immigrants the rudimentary knowledge of the language they needed to get a job. Classes in American government and politics familiarized him with his new country and started him in the process of becoming a citizen.

In addition to clubs on a single subject or classes, whether on philosophy or carpentry, there were clubs of more general discussion. Mrs. Bowen first came to Hull House to lead the women's club, a group of neighborhood women gathered each week to discuss some topic of current interest, sometimes relating to the home or children, sometimes on what was called "political economy" or on any other subject. The club expanded rapidly, began to invite speakers, and soon needed the auditorium in the new building, Bowen Hall. The "Working People's Social Science Club" performed a similar function for men.

What was perhaps surprising was the degree of success achieved by these attempts to impose ideas on the neighborhood. Actually, they were not impositions of alien ideas, but were points at which the ideas of the residents and those of the community coincided. Each might modify plans and preconceptions, but whatever gulf there might be between Mrs. Bowen and a Greek immigrant, both could respect Aeschylus.

There was at least one attempt by the "other class" to impose its standards on the neighborhood which failed completely. This was the diet kitchen. The theory, logical enough in itself but oddly unperceptive, was that common preparation of inexpensive but nutritious meals would not only relieve working women of the drudgery of cooking, but would also provide better-balanced meals at lower cost. One resident journeyed to Boston to study the management of wholesale cooking, and the meals were carefully planned and prepared. There was plenty of advertising, but almost no one came to buy the cheap, delicious, nutritious stews and soups. Clearly the unmarried and bourgeois settlement residents had no understanding of a mother wanting to prepare her family's meals. Nor could these well-fed residents understand that making a meal nutritiously balanced had nothing whatever to do with whether people wanted to eat it or not. Soon the diet kitchen was replaced by the coffee house, an inexpensive restaurant which provided food and, the residents hoped, a center for the neighbors to gather as a substitute for the saloon. Even this hope proved vain. As one observer from nearby said when the coffee house opened, "You can have the shovel crowd, or the office crowd, but you cannot have both in the same room." It was the "office crowd" from nearby factories which ate at the coffee house, while the shovel crowd stayed at the saloon.[8] Here, again, was a combination of perceptiveness—at least in relationship to the "White Ribboners" of the WCTU—and blindness. Although Miss Addams belonged to the WCTU she would not merely denounce the saloon. She understood at least a portion of its social function and tried to find a substitute for that function without the faults of the saloon. To assert, however, that she understood how pleasant it is to drink beer with one's fellows would be claiming too much.

She better understood the pleasures of a vacation in the country from the heat of a Chicago summer. Just as a summer camp was important for children, so some rural interlude might be useful for adults. The men, of course, must work, but for the women there was the Rockford Summer School. Part education, part recreation, part social service, the summer school was entirely Jane Addams' personal idea and creation. For six weeks each summer during the first decade of the settlement, Miss Addams took over the Rockford College campus, to which she brought about one hundred women from the neighborhood around Halsted and Polk. The women paid three dollars a week and co-operated on the cooking and housework. For this they got lodging in a relatively rural spot, walks in the woods, boating on the Rock River, classes in literature if they wanted them, and a chance to do nothing at all. Partly the summer school was to bring some of the good life to some of the people who lacked it; partly it was to reveal to urban women the charms of country life; partly it was a cheap vacation for women who could afford nothing more. The educational intent was not of serious proportions, and clearly the summer students could not have been working women, unless theirs was a factory which laid off workers in the summer. Clearly, too, an expenditure of three dollars a week would be hard for the poorest of Hull House neighbors. In fact, the aims of the summer school were not so much complicated as contradictory. Perhaps beneath it all was Miss Addams' attachment to Rockford. The wonder was not that the summer school ceased, but that it lasted as long as it did.[9]

Hull House also, of course, simply responded to the needs of the neighbors, as they arose. The settlement provided social services such as a day nursery and kindergarten to care for children of working mothers who would otherwise have been unattended, established the first public baths in the city, opened a small library and a dispensary which sold drugs at low cost, ran an employment bureau, and, for a while, a coal yard. On a somewhat more elaborate scale the settlement organized a co-operative apartment house for working girls. Thus if one factory were on strike, the girls would not be forced to choose between abandoning the strike or being evicted. Other girls in the apartment house whose factories were not on strike could take up the slack. This was the "Jane Club" which eventually had a building designed and built specifically for it.[10]

The growth of the physical facilities of the settlement was as nothing compared to the expansion, perhaps explosion is a better word, of its activities. These activities grew helter-skelter, in all directions at once, responding not to any over-all plan but to the imperatives of the neighborhood, the ingenuity of the residents, and the stresses of a rapidly changing society. At one moment a new club might be formed for Greek women; at the next Hull House influence might touch the Illinois court system, the Chicago city council, the United States immigration service, the Greek restaurant association, the employees of the garment industry, newsboys, the University of Chicago. The Hull House yearbook for 1910 mentions as regular activities and organizations connected with the House: Jane Club, Women's Club, Men's Club, regular recreation in the gym, a basketball team, a music school, Hull House Theatre, a concert series, a day nursery, regular dances, a lecture series on Russia, the Municipal Museum, recreation in the playground and meetings of the Illinois Equal Suffrage Association, the Christian Socialists, the Chicago Peace Society, the National Consumer's League, the Legal Aid Society, the Juvenile Protective Association, and many labor unions. There were classes in the Bible, poetry, German, French, elocution, mathematics, civics, beginning English, United States history, Esperanto, Shakespeare and Browning arts and crafts.

Outside of the meetings of various organizations, one is struck by the strong educational emphasis in the list. The settlement's attempts to bring the "higher culture" to the poor was not primarily aimed at the moral improvement of the poor, but rather at closing the gap between rich and poor, ending class antagonism, and ultimately at creating a sense of community in Chicago and, by example, in the nation.

All these activities cost money. Money, while never a crucial problem at Hull House, was always a nagging worry. Jane Addams managed to find, rather quickly, a group of loyal supporters for the settlement among the wealthiest and most prominent of Chicago's citizens. She was always supremely confident that if something really needed doing, money could be found to do it—and usually she managed to find it. Hull House expanded rapidly, right from the beginning, and the expansion both in programs and physical facilities was always paid for in cash, not indebtedness. It was Jane Addams who had to find supporters and persuade them not only to give once, but to keep them loyal to the undertaking so that money would come in year after year.

This was one task which could not be delegated, for when the Armour, Marshall Field, or McCormick families dealt with Hull House, it was the Head Resident they wanted to see. A great deal of her time had to be spent with donors, and here again she employed her special gift for inspiring confidence, loyalty, and respect.

As refined young women with the right family connections, Jane Addams and Ellen Starr fit naturally into Chicago's upper crust. In its first few years, before Hull House had acquired any aura of political radicalism, it became one of the accepted causes which these families supported. Marshall Field & Company sent one hundred dollars a year, as did Lyman Gage. The source of the settlement's major support, however, was the faithfullness of three or four of Chicago's wealthiest women who gave large sums of money year after year.

The house itself, the land it stood on, and soon adjacent parcels came to the house as gifts from Helen Culver. The relationship between Jane Addams and Helen Culver was open and frank, but not always harmonious. Miss Culver was sympathetic to the settlement, and in the end she was generous. In the first five years after 1889 she gave, besides the physical facilities, something like four thousand dollars in cash. Years of being in business had made her cautious, however, and she always had to be convinced. It was typical that she only gave the house to the settlement after watching it operate for a year. No rush of enthusiasm for her! In an inverted sort of way, Miss Culver and Miss Addams had a business-like relationship, wherein Jane Addams would have to sell each idea to Miss Culver. Thus if the house needed a new furnace, no speech on the general goals of settlement work was needed. Instead there were excursions into the basement, long conversations about pipes, types of furnaces, and different manufacturers. In the end, Miss Culver bought the furnace.[11]

In 1894 Louise De Koven Bowen heard Jane Addams speak about the Pullman strike, a speech which later became a perceptive article. A few months later Mrs. Bowen went to Hull House to visit a friend who had become a resident, and there met Jane Addams for the first time. Within a week she was leading the Hull House Women's Club, a weekly meeting for lecture and discussion. Soon she became one of the two largest donors to the settlement. Louise De Koven Bowen came from one of Chicago's original families, a family which had grown enormously wealthy in real estate. She had a large personal income of her own, and her husband also had a fortune. She was a highly fashionable young lady and had, after seminary, occupied herself with various charities. Once she determined to back Hull House she was of enormous use to the settlement. In the first few years her gifts were relatively modest, between five hundred and two thousand dollars a year. By the turn of the century, however, she was giving over ten thousand dollars annually. Twice she gave over sixty thousand dollars, and in the thirty-three years between 1895 and 1928 her gifts averaged nearly sixteen thousand dollars per year.

Although Jane Addams' family had nothing like the great wealth of Mrs. Bowen's, the two were from the same class. Yet in personality they were entirely different. Where Jane Addams led by suggestion and hint, Louise De Koven Bowen was aggressive and assertive. Miss Addams disliked managing and giving orders; Mrs. Bowen loved it. Jane Addams made plans for settlement activity, blithely assuming that the money would be found; Mrs. Bowen had a hard-headed approach to finance, wanted always to know where the money was coming from, where it was going, and why. Moreover she had the ability to answer the questions, and Jane Addams made use of this ability and relied much on Mrs. Bowen's advice on money matters. When Hull House was incorporated in 1895, Mrs. Bowen was naturally one of the board of trustees and was, for a number of years, its chairman. Mrs. Bowen admired Jane Addams greatly, and the admiration and respect were returned. In Hull House, Louise Bowen found an activity where her energy, intelligence, and executive ability, all of which she possessed to a high degree, could be fully utilized. In return she gave to the settlement virtually whatever Jane Addams asked, and often more.[12]

With Anita McCormick Blaine, Jane Addams had still a different sort of relationship. Mrs. Blaine, the daughter of Cyrus McCormick, had neither the business caution of Helen Culver nor the abilities of Louise De Koven Bowen, but she did have money. Miss Addams gushed to her, cajoled her, made elaborate pretense of seeking her advice and counsel, and got as much out of her as possible. In one instance she talked Mrs. Blaine into providing a fellowship of fifty dollars a month on the basis of the excellence of the young lady who would receive it. When the girl could not come, Miss Addams persuaded the donor that someone else would be just as good, if not better. Later, when Jane Addams was a member of the Chicago Board of Education, she consulted Mrs. Blaine about an important appointment on which she had, in fact, already made up her mind. The boys who worked in the woodshop, which Mrs. Blaine paid for, were encouraged to write an effusive letter of thanks to their benefactor. Mrs. Blaine responded to these blandishments by making an annual contribution of five hundred dollars, and giving at least one fifty-dollar-per-month fellowship and numerous special contributions when Miss Addams asked for them.[13]

Mary Rozet Smith later became Jane Addams' closest friend, confidante, and companion, but she first came to Hull House as a donor in her own right and the daughter of another donor, the paper manufacturer Braedner Smith. Miss Smith was one of those gentle souls who find fulfillment in devotion to another. Her devotion went far beyond her substantial contributions to Hull House—to being, in fact, the emotional support of its founder. Jane Addams became closer to Mary Rozet Smith than to any other person. In the middle 1890's Jane Addams' letters to her bore the salutation "My Dear Miss Smith." By 1897 the salutation was "My Ever Dear" and by 1902 "Dearest" and "Darling." Nor was this simply a matter of an overblown literary style, for Jane Addams addressed no one else in these terms. Even long-time associates and close friends were never more than "Dear Lady." Whenever Jane Addams and Mary Smith were apart, a steady stream of letters connected them, often a letter a day and sometimes more than one. To others, Miss Addams often expressed gratitude and affection, but nothing to compare with what she expressed to Mary Smith. She wrote of the joy of seeing a letter in her beloved handwriting, the comfort each letter brought, and the anguish when no letter came. She wrote of longing to be together again. Each woman worried about whether the other was happy or sad, cheerful or depressed. The letters can only be described as love letters.

Mary Smith bought Jane Addams' clothes, paid for her travels, and joined her on some of her trips. They, with Mrs.

Bowen, went to Egypt in 1913, and with Alice Hamilton around the world in 1923. They went to Mexico together in 1925, to the Dublin Congress of the Women's International League in 1926, and to Tucson in 1931. Mary Smith did not go to Europe for either the Hague Conference in 1915 nor the Zurich meeting of the WIL in 1919; during both trips, however, Jane Addams kept her fully informed and tried to get Miss Smith to understand, if not to agree, with her peace work. When either woman was sick, and both had increasingly delicate health, the other would tenderly nurse her back to health. Often Jane Addams spent weeks at a time in Mary Smith's town house on West Walton Place. The two spent many summers together at a jointly purchased vacation home on Hull's Cove, Bar Harbor. Outside of Hull House, these were the only two places Miss Addams felt really at home. When Mary Rozet Smith died in 1934, Jane Addams was enveloped by a depression as deep, if not so long lasting, as when her father died.

There can be no doubt that each of the women filled some of the emotional requirements a spouse might have filled had either married. Whether emotional intimacy ever led to physical intimacy no one can say. Probably the strong sexual inhibitions of the age and of both women prevented it.[14] "We constantly think," Jane Addams wrote about the needs of children, "that there are circumstances in which human beings can be treated without affection, and there are no such circumstances." She knew that the words applied equally well to herself. Her life had, perhaps, less of affection than normal, but she managed to find ways to both give and receive that personal, intimate love which no amount of public esteem could replace.

Quite apart from the emotional closeness with Miss Smith, Jane Addams was spectacularly successful with donors. Asking for money was a task which took enormous amounts of her time, and a task which she carried out without embarrassment or reticence. Her success was such that though the word may seem inappropriate, Hull House *prospered.* If one stands back and considers the shape of the growth of the institution, considers the speed, shape, and thrust of the institution's growth, it is striking how the twin themes of serving the spirit of youth and breaking down the barriers between social groups managed always to dominate the activities at Hull House. Jane Addams' settlement house succeeded beyond all expectations, reasonable or unreasonable, but its founder never lost sight of her original goals.

Yet despite the success of Hull House as an institution, Jane Addams felt that her efforts were always hemmed in by the broader institutions of city and state, to say nothing of national politics. One thing forever led to another, she found: from dealing with a youthful petty thief she ended up lobbying in Springfield for a children's court. Always there was the need for political action, to set the seal on the settlement's progress and to give its efforts more than purely local scope and meaning.

7

Urban Politics

In a very direct way, it was the death of her sister Mary Linn which brought Jane Addams into politics for the first time. Mary's son, Stanley, seven years old and none too strong, was to stay at Hull House during the summer of 1894. For many months Hull House residents had, in a desultory way, been advising their neighbors that better sanitation would improve their health. Garbage could not simply be tossed into alleys but must be put into the large boxes the city provided, and the city should be pressed to empty them on a regular basis. When Jane Addams realized that bad garbage collection in fact made the neighborhood so unhealthy that a stay at Hull House was unwise for Stanley, she became much more vigorous in her efforts, "ashamed that other delicate children who were torn from their families, not into boarding school but into eternity, had not long before driven me into effective action."

The huge garbage boxes, Miss Addams wrote, "were the first objects that the toddling child learned to climb; their bulk afforded a barricade and their contents provided missiles in all battles of the older boys; and finally they became the seats upon which absorbed lovers held enchanted converse."[1]

In the summer of 1894, Miss Addams and twelve volunteer neighbors undertook to inspect the nearby streets and alleys to ensure that garbage was put in the boxes and then to insist that the boxes were properly emptied. Ultimately their goal was the replacement of the boxes by daily refuse collection. These investigations were successful in a limited way. Over a thousand violations of the city codes were brought to the attention of the city and three successive inspectors were transferred out of the ward; yet infant death rates were unchanged, and in essence the ward was still filthy. By 1895 the health of Stanley Linn was no longer at the forefront of Jane Addams' mind. Whatever had provided the initial impulse, she now saw better sanitation as an essential step in neighborhood reform. In desperation she herself put in a bid for garbage removal. With the help of two businessmen she spent days investigating and estimating. "We find," she wrote Mary Smith, "that the contractor bid $1000 a mo. when it would probably take $1500 a mo. then he actually spends about $500. If we bid what would clean it we can't get it, if we bid low enough to get it we probably can't keep it clean —so here we are!" The upshot was that she did not get the contract, but widespread public notice of the attempt persuaded the mayor to appoint her garbage inspector of the ward, a patronage job paying $1000 per year.

Jane Addams, the only garbage inspector in the city exempted from the requirements relating to uniforms, pursued her task with zeal. Out of bed at dawn or before, she made sure that her men were at work on time. Using what the neighborhood children called her "garbage phaeton," she followed the wagons to make sure they didn't drop too much of their load. She required the contractor to use more wagons; she deluged a local window-weight factory with more scrap tin cans than they knew what to do with; and she required another contractor to fulfill his duties by removing dead animals from the ward alleys to a glue factory in Indiana. She planned no career for herself in city sanitation. As she saw it her task was to bring filth to public notice, and then to have it removed. As garbage inspector she tried to act as a yardstick by which performance of other inspectors could be measured. After a year of conscientious work, she hired a university-trained deputy who continued the day-to-day operations. Here again, as in so many Hull House activities, Miss Addams perceived a need, perhaps initially from personal motives, met the need—and thereby brought it to the attention of those able to deal with it over the years. Once the pioneering stage was over and the functions she had inaugurated became routine, she withdrew and went on to other things.[2]

In the 1890's another type of reformer also was concerned with garbage collection, but from a somewhat different vantage point. The Civic Federation of Chicago, a group of progressive businessmen, many of them bankers, devoted some of their efforts to getting better street cleaning in the city. Their aim was essentially that of efficiency: to end unnecessary expenditure of tax dollars. They hired their own private garbage collectors and proved that the job could be done cheaper and better than it was being done. This method was also effective. Whereas Jane Addams acted from personal contact with filth, from the bottom of the problem, the Civic Federation members looked at the problem from above, with eyes used to balance sheets and efficiency analyses. Both acted as effective reformers.[3]

When Jane Addams was appointed garbage inspector for the nineteenth ward, one less patronage job was available to the regular politicians. Regular politics in the nineteenth ward meant Johnny Powers—Johnny Da Pow as his Italian constituents called him. After successfully defeating garbage, Jane Addams tackled Johnny Powers and was herself defeated. In many ways this defeat was more revealing than her successes, because it showed clearly the limitations of her understanding, as of 1898, of the social structure of the neighborhood in which she lived. To be sure, she learned from the defeat and showed better understanding thereafter, yet certain of the limits remained. In fact, she found that direct political action was not her forte. She was unwilling to play the game as it had to be played. When she found herself failing in political action she searched for some way to be effective in a wider sphere, and hit upon writing and speaking, the career of publicist, as far more suited to her talents.

Johnny Powers was a short, stocky man with a flaring gray pompadour, smooth-shaven, rather heavy-featured, with a bit of the brogue still on his tongue: in short, a typical city boss, except that he had not only the nineteenth ward in his pocket, but also controlled the city council and thereby the mayor. He kept his power in ways already routine by 1898; that is, he was a good fellow to his constituents. Tons of turkeys were distributed every Christmas in the ward, each with a personal Merry Christmas from Powers or one of his friends. On a day-to-day basis, he was willing to help a poor family pay the rent, find a job on the city payroll for a man out of work, provide free coal for a cold winter evening. At one time Powers boasted of having 2600 constituents on the city payroll. Perhaps most important among the social services he provided was a charge account he had at the undertakers. Though a man might have had nothing during his life, his family and friends were always determined that he should be buried in style. Where money was short, Powers paid for the extra carriage or the largest floral piece.

Nor did Powers' influence stop at merely the day-to-day personal kindnesses. At times he appeared stronger than law itself—as indeed he was. At one time an Italian *padrone* violated civil service regulations by selling city jobs to people who were eligible for them anyway. The *padrone* was fined, but Powers paid the fine, and the *padrone* returned to the ward as powerful as ever, though beholden to Johnny Da Pow. Everyone in the ward knew that saloons owned by Powers were open well after curfew, that the policeman on the beat would not dream of enforcing the law in that saloon, and that, in effect, Powers told the police that their jurisdiction stopped at his doorstep. Powers found no contradiction between owning saloons and endowing a temperance brigade whose young members he furnished with bright uniforms, complete with dress swords. To local businessmen he gave city contracts; peddlers knew their licenses were more sure of renewal if Powers was on their side; proprietors of small grocery stores knew that special assessments for street repairs would be repeatedly delayed so long as Powers was their alderman.

Johnny Powers wanted for himself only two things, money and influence, and he got a great deal of both. In return he gave what the poor of his district wanted most: a friend in the seats of power and the security that gave them. He would not give them the things Jane Addams thought they needed most. Of first importance was an additional public school, for there were 3000 more children in the ward than places in the school. Second was clean streets.

In a sense the battle between Hull House and Johnny Powers was for the allegiance of the neighborhood, and each fought with the weapons at hand: Powers with jobs and protection; Miss Addams with the higher culture and virtue. What was striking, of course, is that both Powers and Jane Addams perceived many of the same problems in the neighborhood and knew that the way to gain power was to deal with these problems. Their goals were incompatible, but their means were parallel. Powers, however, spoke more directly to and for the neighborhood. What difference could it possibly make to one of his constituents if Johnny Powers were bribed? "He had a big Irish heart"; he was a "good man."[4]

The good ladies at Hull House held aloof from the alderman for the first few years. Just before Christmas, 1893, Miss Addams presented the regular weekly meeting of residents with a moral dilemma. She had, she said, been honored with a visit by Alderman Powers, who offered some thousands of pounds of turkeys to be distributed by the settlement. The meeting agreed immediately that this offer should be rejected, but Miss Addams suggested that Hull House might furnish a list of the needy to Powers. There was a good deal of discussion as to whether the sending of such a list involved the settlement in acts of questionable morality, with Ellen Starr and Julia Lathrop finally moving that Hull House "have nothing to do with Mr. Powers and his charities." The motion was carried, and at Jane Addams' suggestion, the meeting agreed to ask her to write to Powers that Hull House had plenty of provender and that the alderman should distribute his turkeys another way.

Johnny Powers survived that social snub, but it was only the beginning of the battle between Powers and the settlement. In 1895 the Hull House Men's Club nominated one of their number as the second alderman from the ward. Powers was not threatened directly. He did not oppose the Hull House candidate, Frank Lawler, very vigorously. Lawler and the Men's Club campaigned as hard as they could and won. Once in office, however, Lawler was unable to resist the fruits of victory offered by his aldermanic colleague, and within a few months the reform candidate was a reformer no longer: he was Powers' man.

Jane Addams wrote Henry Demarest Lloyd that they were planning to attack Powers himself when he came up for election in the spring of 1896. The campaign would be on a broad front, Miss Addams wrote, "attacking Powers as the tool of the corporations, making a great deal of the fact that we have poor street car service in the Ward because Yerkes, through the Council, has robbed us of our rights. We will probably begin in the most sensational manner with placards: Yerkes and Powers, the Briber and the Bribed."[5] The candidate to oppose Powers was William Gleason, another member of the Men's Club, an Irish immigrant and former head of the Chicago bricklayers' union. Posters were printed showing Powers drinking champagne at a banquet, while Gleason sat on an unfinished brick wall eating from a lunch pail.

Almost everything the Hull House organization did that year

backfired. The posters showing Powers at a banquet attracted voters, for they wanted their representative to be up there with the best of them—no bricklayers for them. The attempt to tar Powers by linking him with Charles Tyson Yerkes simply associated the alderman with the generous philanthropist who had just made a large gift to the University of Chicago. Talk about cleaning and repairing streets made the local merchants fear a special assessment. The Hull House campaign must have had some effect, because Powers' majority was less than usual, but without any special effort on his part he was re-elected.

Between 1896 and 1898, the next time Powers' term was up, Jane Addams and the Hull House residents learned some more about politics. Various neighbors who had been supporting the Hull House candidate suddenly turned up in city jobs. A printer who had done the anti-Powers posters accepted a city contract. Since Miss Addams had entered ward politics, her supporters expected her to act like a ward politician, giving favors in return for support. When she would not play the game, they left less disgusted than mystified. At the beginning of the 1898 campaign, Powers declared that "Hull House will be driven from the ward and its leaders will be forced to shut up shop." He did not succeed in driving the house out of the ward, but Hull House was driven out of ward politics, for it is fair to say that the Hull House reformers were beaten before they even knew they were going to enter the 1898 campaign.

The decision to do so was actually prompted by Powers himself. In what may have been a political mistake, he forced Jane Addams' deputy, Amanda Johnson, out of her job as garbage inspector. The job was covered by a new civil service law, but by consolidating two agencies and pleading economy, Powers managed to eliminate Miss Johnson's job. Seething with indignation, Hull House once again determined to join battle. Miss Addams insisted that she had not reconciled herself to corrupt government. When Johnny Powers sponsored a measure in the city council in 1899 to allow Hull House to flood a vacant lot for skating, he said he was ready to let bygones be bygones. Jane Addams responded with an angry letter to the *Post,* saying that Hull House had flooded the lot for years, that they neither needed nor wanted favors from Powers. "It is perhaps characteristic of Mr. Powers that he should imagine that alleged favors shown to Hull House could change its attitude." She insisted that she had given up the fight to defeat Powers not because she was reconciled with him, but because "There is no hope of success, for Mr. Powers with his wealth and political methods could defeat any honest man."[6]

Jane Addams never explicitly accepted the idea that the alderman won the election because he gave his constituents what they wanted, and even what they needed, but she came very close to this recognition. She scolded businessmen's reform movements —and she was probably thinking of the Civic Federation of Chicago and the Municipal Voters' League—for being "almost wholly occupied in the correction of political machinery and with a concern for the better method of administration, rather than with the ultimate purpose of securing the welfare of the people. They fix their attention so exclusively on methods that they fail to consider the final aims of city government." On the other hand, she argued, the real leaders of the people see that in a democracy, the welfare of the people should be the goal of government, and, though they may be corrupt, they minister to this welfare, and thus are maintained in office by an admiring constituency.[7] Here is another instance where Jane Addams, through a willingness to deal with day-to-day details of city life, and a rare ability to learn from experience, came to a far greater understanding of the world than she had in, say, 1892. She learned from experience not only because she had the experience, but also because she was eminently teachable.

Although by 1900 she understood "Why the Ward Boss Rules," and scolded more mugwumpish reformers, she herself was not willing to fight the ward boss on his own terms. Her reforms took other directions: supporting an organization to get small parks in poor districts; pressing the city to establish public baths; helping in the City Homes Association's surveys of Chicago housing; pressing for more schools and better education in the city; and her writing. In fact, outside of her brief duties as a garbage inspector and a somewhat longer tenure as postmistress of the Hull House substation, the only office she ever held was that of a member of the Board of Education of Chicago in 1905–1908.

As with her venture into ward politics, her years on the Board of Education must be counted a failure. Many of the changes she wanted were not instituted, and those that were instituted lasted only a short while. The reasons for failure were somewhat different in the two instances, however. In the aldermanic campaigns she was defeated because of inadequate understanding of her neighbors and of the political system. Her ideas on education were, on the other hand, well formulated by 1905 and had grown out of many years of experience. She had spent long hours talking with her close friend and associate, John Dewey. She knew what she wanted and why, and she knew that it would work. Her failure as a member of the Board of Education was in implementation. As in the campaign against Powers, she showed herself to be a poor politician, or at least a losing one.

Probably in every community in the country, since public education began, there has been a conflict between those who emphasize efficiency and economy in the school system and those who emphasize high-quality education even if expenditures, and therefore taxes, are pushed higher. Essentially this was the nature of the conflict on the Board of Education during Jane Addams' tenure, but the conflict had many shadings and took on highly emotional coloration. There was the issue of how much influence the teachers ought to have in determining school policy, and this was closely connected with unionization of the teachers. Once the word "union" was mentioned, "socialism" and "radicalism" followed naturally, each with added emotional cargo. There was controversy about how teachers ought to be promoted and who ought to have the deciding voice on promotions; there was controversy about building more schools with smaller classrooms; there was intrigue about tax assessments and political influence; and there was, inevitably, conflict about salary scales. Unspoken beneath these disputes was the question of the professionalization of teaching. Were the teachers to be merely employees hired because they had a few more years of education than those they taught, or were teachers professional, expert, in something called "education?" As if this were not enough, many school board members appointed with, or soon after, Jane Addams, were known as reformers in other spheres, so the general issue of change versus *status quo* became an added burden on the board. No one of these issues alone would have been enough to create the furor which surrounded the board between 1905 and 1908, but as each reinforced the other, the lines became harder, the tempers shorter, the insults more pointed and vitriolic.

Before 1905 a competent but unimaginative Board of Education had run an economical, efficient, and relatively honest school system in the city, but at the cost of leaving many problems untouched, especially teacher dissatisfaction. A majority of the teachers joined the Teachers' Federation, a quasi-union, which carefully investigated the taxation of public utility corporations—street railways, electric companies, and the like. The teachers found that these companies were dodging nearly a quarter of a million dollars in taxes annually and thus were starving the school system. The Teachers' Federation sued for the taxes and won the case before Judge Edward F. Dunne, the new assessments to begin in 1902. But the Board of Education not only did not put this new income into teachers' salaries; it did not even pay certain back wages already owed the teachers. In 1905 Judge Dunne was elected mayor as a reform candidate dedicated to clean government, municipal ownership of street railways, and better education. Better education meant a different school board and Dunne appointed enough reformers to ensure reform—or at least so he thought. Among others, these new appointees included Raymond Robins, an associate of Graham Taylor at the Chicago Commons settlement and virtual boss of the seventeenth ward; Louis F. Post, editor of the *Public,* the most influential single-tax newspaper in the Midwest; John J. Sonsteby, an attorney associated with organized labor; Mrs. Emmons Blaine; Dr. Cornelia De Bey, a sociologist and reformer; and Jane Addams.[8]

The appointment of Jane Addams was widely praised, as by this time she was a symbol of rectitude and reform to all but a few die-hard enemies; but the other appointments encountered more criticism. Miss Addams herself received a flood of congratulatory letters, most of them asking her support for some project. Even Graham Taylor closed his letter by begging for a new school in his ward.[9]

Jane Addams attended her first meeting on July 12, 1905, when she and the other new members were formally welcomed to their new duties. She endeared herself, at least a little, to the holdover members by rising at the beginning of the meeting to remark, "Mr. President, I would suggest on behalf of the lady members of the board, that they have no objection to smoking on the part of the men." Otherwise she took no part in the meeting. In

August, Edward Tilden, the Board Chairman, appointed her chairman of the School Management Committee. This was the most important of three standing committees of the Board. Buildings and Grounds took care of the physical plant of the system. Finance was a committee made up of the heads of all other committees, and so Miss Addams was also a member of this committee. School Management had over-all responsibility for personnel, curriculum, educational supplies, teacher promotion, and salaries. As chairman of the School Management Committee, Miss Addams was in a strong position to bring about changes of major importance in the Chicago public schools—yet she did not do so.

Her appointment was generally received favorably by the Chicago newspapers, but the *Chronicle* objected because "She is openly at war with the existing constitution of society. Her mind is a nest of sociological vagaries. Her associations are revolutionary. We can regard [her appointment] as nothing more than a compliment to the socialism of the mayor and the insubordination of the Teachers' Federation."[10]

The School Management Committee made no reform proposals until February 28, 1906. The proposal the committee made then was relatively minor, but indicated the strong influence of John Dewey on Jane Addams' and Anita McCormick Blaine's ideas about education. A subcommittee of the School Management Committee, headed by Mrs. Blaine (to whom, incidentally, Dewey dedicated *The School and Society*), recommended that all prizes for accomplishment in school be eliminated. The report from the School Management Committee to the full Board said:

> The winning of these rewards involves struggle, competition and invidious comparison. The more successful a child may be in winning these rewards, the more detrimental may be the general result to him, not only in the qualities of selfishness evoked, but in the fact that such success puts emphasis on the outward result instead of on the inner result. . . . All who are following the educational ideas of today realize that the trend of enlightened methods is against inciting to excellence by appeals to these motives.[11]

John Dewey himself could hardly have put the matter more clearly, and it is not unlikely that he had an important role in writing the proposal. As a foreshadowing of events to come, this plan, though backed by the head of the most important of the Board's standing committees, was laid on the table and finally recommitted. It would have cost no money nor challenged the authority of the school principals or the Board of Education, but it looked like reform, and the full Board would not touch it. Nor was Miss Addams able to muster sufficient voting strength even to bring it to a vote.

By the fall of 1906 the reform group, now augmented by another batch of new appointees, felt strong enough to approach a more substantial issue. The Chicago newspapers, seeing that the reformers might have a chance to win some points, became abusive towards the reform members and tried to make the Board seem a collection of cranks and radicals. At stake, at least on the surface, was teacher promotion. The details were complex and technical, but in essence the issues were twofold: Were teachers professionals to be evaluated by other professionals, or hired hands subject to evaluation only by their boss? Were salaries high enough? Under the existing system, teachers' pay advanced from a starting salary, year by year, until the seventh year, when it stopped as automatically as it had risen. This barrier could only be passed by the teacher taking a promotional exam. The exam could only be taken by those who had been given high "efficiency marks" by their principal and these marks had been certified by the superintendent. Principalships and the superintendency were, to a degree, political jobs, and in any case they were not professional ones. Moreover the efficiency marks (in percentage terms) were kept secret from the teacher. This system, while not designed to be vicious, clearly put teachers in the position of subordinates, subject to the whims or personal feelings of the principal, and with no grounds for defense in the case of low marks.

On November 21, 1906, a subcommittee headed by Louis F. Post formally recommended a new plan, under which a teacher would first serve a three-year probationary period after which she would either be given a full certificate or released. If certified, she would automatically get salary increases for seven years. At the end of that time she was to be observed by the superintendent of her own district, the superintendent of another district, and the principal of the Chicago Normal School or a person delegated by the principal. The principal was Ella Flagg Young, a long-time supporter of Jane Addams, a close associate of John Dewey, and a person who regarded teachers as professional educators. Throughout the seven years of automatic increase, principals would write descriptive evaluations of their teachers, one copy of which would go to the teacher and one to the Board of Education. If the teacher was "reported as progressive" by a majority of the committee of three, she would be promoted and receive salary increases up to the maximum. If she were not "reported as progressive," she was to be dismissed. Any time a teacher was removed for cause, she could have a hearing before the School Management Committee.

Clearly the Post Plan, as it was known, was designed to eliminate secret markings and sycophancy in the relationship between teacher and principal; to reward good teachers and weed out bad ones; and to have the judgment between good and bad made by a relatively impartial group including at least one professional educator. Clearly it would cost more money, since teachers could not be kept on forever at lower salary levels, and clearly, too, the reform was but the first step in an attempt of the "radicals" to take over the operation of the public education system of Chicago.

Thus all the emotions of reformers versus conservatives were drawn to the Post Plan, like iron filings to a magnet. Obviously the plan would not have brought socialism to Chicago, nor would it even have ensured a good school system. Yet Louis F. Post and his supporters, including the Teachers' Federation, convinced themselves they were fighting the battle of education against boodle. The Chicago newspapers likewise convinced themselves that radicalism must be stopped at this point or disaster would ensue.

Jane Addams seemed nonplussed by the furor swirling around the Board. She was reticent about the episode in her autobiography, so her inner emotions are unknown, but she seems to have been dismayed by the depth of the emotions aroused. She attempted to play the role of conciliator, but neither side was open to conciliation. As chairman of the School Management Committee she was in a powerful position to get the Post proposals through the Board, and her prestige with the Chicago public could have been a powerful weapon to counter the newspapers. What the situation demanded was not a conciliator, but a general. Louis F. Post gave her the trumpet, but she blew it with only an uncertain sound. She remarked that the Post Plan was not aimed at the current superintendent personally, and she kept insisting that proposals ought to be evaluated on their merits, irrespective of personalities. At one point during the height of the controversy she persuaded the Board to hold an open meeting, but at the meeting only three people spoke in favor of the Post Plan including Post himself and Margaret Healy of the Teachers' Federation. This was no way to win a war!

The full Post Plan never passed the Board, though a number of teachers were promoted. Mrs. Blaine, with Jane Addams' approval, proposed a measure designed to allow teachers a greater voice in educational matters by setting up councils within each school through which teachers might address the Board directly. The reformers could not even obtain passage of this. The best they could get was a revival of a proposal made by Jane Addams before the Post Plan was offered: that every other year teachers might spend half a day per week, for ten weeks, studying at the Chicago Normal School, with full pay and substitute teachers hired for the time. Promotions were to be based partly on the taking of these courses. This was a step, albeit a small one, in the direction of professionalization. Yet even this small step did not last, as the new School Board eliminated the plan before it had any real opportunity to function.[12]

In the April, 1907, elections, Fred Busse was elected mayor, and he promised to clean things up in the School Board. At the May 22 meeting, the secretary of the Board read the following communication from the mayor: "You are hereby notified that by the authority conferred upon me, the following named persons were on Monday, May 20, removed." As the secretary began to read the names, he was interrupted by points of order and shouts from the removed members, but he continued reading: Louis F. Post, Raymond Robins, Wiley W. Mills, John J. Sonsteby, Dr. Cornelia De Bey. . ." and on through the list of reformers. Jane Addams and two other influential—and less outspoken—members of the Dunne Board survived the purge.[13]

Eventually, in December of 1907, the ousted members were sustained in the courts, but by the time the decision was rendered the terms of many of them had almost run out anyway. Those who did return to the Board were an ineffective minority.[14] They proposed a new taxation system, essentially Henry George's in inspiration, to get more money for the school system, but it never even got to a vote. The new chairman of the Board, Otto C.

Schneider, announced grimly that there would now be less talk, more action, and less money spent. "I do not think we will have a deficit in the future." In pursuit of this aim, a number of promotions were rescinded, and the old system of promotion was re-established *in toto*.[15]

Jane Addams quietly served out her term. She is recorded only as one of three voting against re-establishment of the old promotional system, and, in fitting irony, of objecting to changing the name of the Henry George School to the George M. Pullman School. On July 1, 1908, her term came to an end.[16]

Miss Addams later spoke of the "inglorious role" she played on the Board of Education, and this estimate must stand. She knew what she wanted in the way of education: she could point to Dewey's lab school, the ideas of Ella Flagg Young at the Normal School, and the educational ventures of Hull House. Moreover, on many occasions she clearly explained her ideas on education, ideas which have since become commonplace. She could be effective in persuading others that these ideas were sound. Yet she was ineffective in the hard-headed business of getting a bureaucracy to act, at overcoming the inertia of any large social organism, at the process of turning ideas into programs on a large scale. Experimenting in small scale, at Hull House, she could be highly effective; as a publicist and persuader she had few peers; as an administrator or politician she was a failure. Moreover she was discovering her success as a publicist at just that time that she was failing, and consciously failing, in politics. As a result she concentrated more and more on speaking and writing.

For ultimately Jane Addams was more important than other settlement workers not because she inaugurated the settlement idea in the United States, for in fact others preceded her. Nor was she more important because she ran a better settlement, for others were as good. She was not even more important for the ideas she originated, because most of her ideas were not her own. But she was supremely and uniquely effective in one crucial way: she was instrumental in changing modes of thought in the United States. It was in her role as publicist and persuader that Jane Addams made her greatest contribution to American life.

PART II

Rousing the New Conscience

8

The Father of the Man

As a writer and speaker Jane Addams was extremely prolific. A bibliography containing even the most widely circulated material would have to include over two hundred articles, ten books made up in large measure of articles, introductions to half a dozen other books, and speeches too numerous to count. Within a decade of the founding of the settlement, major speaking tours were regular features of her year. In 1902 she made a tour of the east in March and April, was on the west coast in May, the deep south in August, the plains states in late fall, and back to the east by Thanksgiving.

She quickly developed confidence as a speaker and an effective speaking style. She used no histrionics, dramatic gestures or inflections. Instead she employed a more modern, informal conversational tone. She leaned slightly forward, her hands often clasped in front of her, her head slightly thrown back as though eager to talk to each individual in the audience. Her voice was relatively low and carried better than some feminine voices. Her manner was direct, and her speeches were filled with her own experiences as illustrations of the points she was making.

Her articles were often simply polished renditions of her speeches, and both increased sharply in number around the turn of the century. Like most authors she was timid about submitting her first manuscript. Returning with Julia Lathrop from Boston in 1892, the two ladies passed through New York. Julia Lathrop urged her friend to publish the talks she had delivered in Massachusetts. Miss Addams was embarrassed and weak-kneed at the thought of peddling her own wares, but Julia Lathrop urged her on: "Don't cave in, J. A., this is our chance to give the public the pure milk of the word." The first editor they approached,

Walter Hines Page of the *Forum,* not only took the two articles Miss Addams left with him, but actually paid for them.[1] In fact the only piece ever rejected by an editor was one Miss Addams wrote in 1896 about the Pullman strike. Although the article was mild in tone and did not denounce anyone, no editor would touch it in the superheated atmosphere of that election year. It remained in Miss Addams' files until 1912, after Pullman himself had died and the fire had gone out of the issue.

Her books were in turn collections of articles. From *Democracy and Social Ethics* in 1902 to *My Friend, Julia Lathrop* in 1935, her ten books were widely reviewed, universally praised, and purchased in moderate numbers. Only her autobiography, *Twenty Years at Hull-House,* provided significant royalties for its author, but from the first she was noticed by the press: first in newspapers, then magazines, as scores of articles were written about her. As early as 1895 she had become a public personality, and only a decade later a writer in *Outlook* could say "Probably every reader of the *Outlook* has once at least had the opportunity to hear Miss Addams speak." She had become the symbol and spokesman for humanitarian reform in industrial America.

This was recognized by her contemporaries. In 1913 the *Independent* magazine polled its readership on "Who Was the Most Useful American?" Ten thousand replies were received, and the count revealed that Thomas A. Edison was in first place. In second place came Jane Addams, followed by Andrew Carnegie and Theodore Roosevelt. One reader chose Miss Addams because she was the "best interpreter of practical sociology." Another put the matter more dramatically by saying that she was most useful for "Rousing the New Conscience."[2]

From the vantage point of the Negro revolution or the War on Poverty, it may be difficult to recall how much rousing the new conscience needed. One must remember, however, that when Jane Addams and Ellen Starr opened the doors of Hull House, Benjamin Harrison was in the White House; the "Alger myth" was firmly established; the continent was not completely settled; and the huge industrial metropolis was a new, strange, and somewhat fearsome institution. Labor unions were inventions whose very existence was controversial and the strike was widely regarded as a form of anarchy. Governmental agencies, whether local or state, took only minimal, largely custodial responsibility for the needy or antisocial.

When Jane Addams died in May of 1935, Franklin D. Roosevelt had completed more than half of his first term as President. Not only had Congress passed the emergency legislation of the first hundred days, but the Wagner Act and the Social Security Act were well on their way to enactment. The ideology of the welfare state, though not so named, was, if not universally accepted, well ahead of its competitors.

This development embodied some changes in the political structure of the nation, considerable changes in its economic structure. Most of all, however, it involved a transformation of ideas. Jane Addams was an important component in producing this ideological transformation. At times she may have been important as an originator of ideas; more frequently her function was to sell ideas to the nation. Her obvious gentility, her expertise and experience, her gentle manner and absolute conviction, her hard work on the hustings and before committees of local, state, and national governments, and her speeches and her articles made her the most influential of those urging a transformation of ideology.

The ideological transformation was of major proportions, involving as it did a redefinition of the nature of man, of his relationship to his fellows, and of his relationship to his environment. Human beings had to be redefined as basically good—not in the Lockean sense of being rationally able to perceive their own self-interest, but in the Rousseauan sense of possessing a fundamental nature which ought to be nurtured rather than repressed. This nature was the birthright of all human beings of whatever social class. If human beings had this sort of nature, the new ideology argued that society had a responsibility to provide an environment in which human beings could flourish. This in turn meant a rejection of the individualistic ethic in which each man was expected to work for his own greatest pleasure, and the inauguration of a new ethic—Jane Addams called it a social ethic—in which each person would feel a sense of responsibility, not just towards himself and his immediate family but towards society as a whole.

Putting all three ideas together, the reformers argued that men were essentially good, that where they did not appear to be good they were influenced by an evil environment, and that it was the collective responsibility of society to see that each indivdual had the environment which would protect and nurture his best qualities.

Probably Miss Addams' writing dealt with children more than any other single subject. This was simply because she regarded children as human beings in the natural state, unshaped by society. In asking Americans to change their views about children, she was asking them to change their assumptions about human nature. Children, and therefore human beings in general, were inherently joyous and kind; the task of society was to protect and nurture this joy and kindness into adulthood. Society itself would thus be infused with joy and virtue. But society as currently structured ignored or scorned this fundamental goodness of human beings. It turned children into factory workers at a premature age, allowed them no opportunity to play, and thus produced people who were at best self-seeking, at worst criminal.

To nurture the best in human beings, a social reconstruction was necessary. Instead of assuming that men were self-seeking and that society should be constructed along competitive lines, Jane Addams proposed to substitute the assumption that men were kind and constructive, and that society should be constructed along co-operative lines. In this sort of society all barriers between man and man, whether of nationality or social class, would be buried beneath the acknowledgement of a common humanity. Her starting point in thinking about this social reconstruction was a reconsideration of the nature of the child, and to understand the new conscience she roused, one must start by understanding what she said about children.

Jane Addams' own childhood had been at best a mixture of happiness and confusion, overshadowed by tragedy. Her adult life partook only indirectly of family life. It is not surprising, then, to find that while she was very interested in children, she had relatively little to say about the day-to-day details of child-rearing in the home. She did refer to these matters occasionally. From her general ideas on human nature she might remark to a neighbor that children do better if you are not too hard on them, or in an article on quite another subject, note that children brought up by bullying and terror are almost certain to be vicious and stupid. She believed that parental harshness was often a cause of juvenile delinquency.[3] Her main focus, however, was on children in relation to institutions: school, industry, court. In her treatment of these issues, she revealed her fundamental assumptions about the nature of human beings.

Human beings were born with a cluster of "instincts"—natural drives which served a survival function under those pastoral conditions she thought of as "normal." There was an "art instinct," a "play instinct," an instinct for gathering food, one for finding a mate, and many others. Miss Addams used the term loosely and never attempted a rigorous definition, but she clearly assumed an essential human nature based on innate drives. At times she referred to them as "primitive" or "fundamental," though neither word was used pejoratively; always she was convinced that society suppressed them only at great cost. While it is true that she regarded the drives as innate, it is at least as important that she also regarded them as benign. Natural, inborn, innate drives were a part of the human animal. They must be sated in some manner, or they could turn in a destructive direction. She never considered that human beings might be combative or destructive by instinct.

Giving such a prominent place to instincts or deep drives was, in turn-of-the-century America, neither unfashionable nor very original. William James devoted a lengthy chapter of his *Principles of Psychology* to instinct, insisting that, contrary to views current then and now, one characteristic of human beings is that they have a great many *more* instincts than other animals. It was William James and his student (though only two years his junior), G. Stanley Hall, who brought modern psychology from Germany to the United States. American psychology, however, got "only its physical body from German experimentalism, but it had got its mind from Darwin."[4] In the United States people such as Albion W. Small, John Dewey, and Jane Addams, as well as Hall and James themselves, publicized the new psychology. They also tried to apply its precepts to the social problems which threatened to tear American society apart.

Both the technique of experimentalism and the content of Darwinism were important in the attempt to apply psychology to reform. A more broadly based experimentation replaced the traditional method of introspection, in which psychologists thought about their own mental processes, and from them tried to build a science of psychology. Such introspection, after all, could only deal with the psychology of psychologists, not immigrants, industrial workers, or children. Empiricism freed psychology to confront social problems. Thus when Dewey asked how children "ought" to be taught, he meant "ought" not in any moral sense but in the sense of testing to see what method produced the desired result. Since the educational method was based upon a hypothesis about human behavior and human nature, the result could show whether the hypothesis was true or untrue.

Of even greater importance for social reform was the Darwinian content of American psychology. Social analogies to natural selection were, of course, used as defense against change, but social Darwinism was not so much a conservative doctrine as a universal doctrine. The analogy found a home in America with amazing speed and ubiquity. The scientific community, save for the eminent Louis Agassiz, accepted it rapidly, and though various religious groups denounced it, they were trying to sweep back the tide with a broom. Darwinism was in the rhetoric of the trade-union movement and the management organizations; the immigrant restrictionists and those in favor of open immigration; the German historical school of economic planners and the proponents of laissez faire; the social workers and those who thought social workers a bunch of soft-hearted do-gooders. The idea of human beings and human groups as organisms which changed as they adapted to conditions around them became very nearly an unquestioned assumption.

In psychology Darwinism took the form of asserting that ontogony recapitulates phylogony—that the biological and mental-emotional life of each individual recapitulates the entire evolutionary process, from primal ooze to human primate. Nor was this process confined to the amoeba-to-fish-to-mammal evolution within the womb. After birth each child went through cultural evolution from primitive savagery to civilization. Thus, according to this view, a small child might be essentially in the stage of physical, moral, and mental evolution of a cave man. G. Stanley Hall asserted in the opening pages of his influential *Youth: Its Education, Regimen and Hygiene* that the years from eight to twelve "may represent in the individual what was once for a very protracted and relatively stationary period an age of maturity in the remote ancestors of our race." At this stage "inborn and more or less savage instincts can and should be allowed some scope."[5]

The experimental method and theories of recapitulation found their natural confluence and their natural application in what came to be called the Child Study Movement. Starting roughly with Hall's studies of children, the Child Study Movement flourished in the 1890's and first decade of the twentieth century, after which it was absorbed by a more broadly conceived psychology or medicine. The movement had a number of facets, including a desire to socialize the child and make him a co-operative member of society, but the root assumption beneath child study was that a careful study of children could reveal what "man" was. "The most important truths are more plainly manifested in the simple immature mind, of which the purpose is single, than in the complex mature mind," wrote one child study enthusiast; or, "The knowledge of the child is the fundamental knowledge of human nature."[6] In application, the Child Study impulse meant an education geared around the natural stages of growth of children. As Hall said, "What the child soul needs is the light touch of the hand to guide the fancy which the children are so ready to take up. The child must be left to freedom. Interest is the main thing."[7]

Miss Addams, in adopting both the recapitulation theory and James's view on instincts, was thus simply absorbing currents of thought around her, not originating anything. She did alter or misinterpret the ideas a bit to fit them to her own purposes. To Hall, for example, pre-adolescence was a state of "savagery"; to Miss Addams it was "primitive" impulses. The first meant uncivilized, the second uncorrupted.

Indeed, the basic unquestioned assumption beneath Miss Addams' views on children was the inherent rightness of children's impulses. Problems arose not when these impulses were allowed outlets but when they were repressed. The instincts themselves came from individual recapitulation of human history. "Each boy comes from our ancestral past not 'in entire forgetfulness'," she wrote, and many misdeeds of children "may be traced to the unrecognized and primitive spirit of adventure corresponding to the old activity of the hunt."[8] In her view of the mechanism of instincts she followed James very closely. James dismissed as "the psychologist's fallacy" the idea that instincts were perceived in relation to nature's goals. A fly does not lay her eggs on a leaf, James insisted, because she knows that the leaf will provide food for the maggots; to a fly it is simply obvious that eggs should be laid just there. Similarly young men are not attracted to young women by any desire to perpetuate the race but because young women are obviously so excruciatingly attractive.

Miss Addams also recognized the indirection by which nature's needs were met. "We know that nature herself has sharpened the senses for her own purposes and is deliberately establishing a connection between them and the newly awakened susceptibility of sex; for it is only through the outward senses that the selection of an individual mate is made and the instincts utilized for nature's purposes. It would seem, however," Miss Addams added ruefully, "that nature was determined that the force and constancy of the instinct must make up for its lack of precision."[9]

If all instincts were for nature's purposes—that is, if human instincts were basically constructive—it followed that they should be exploited, not repressed. Most especially did this apply to education. Curiosity was one of the human instincts which James asserted could be found very early in the evolutionary process. "It was formerly assumed," wrote Jane Addams in 1905, "that a child went to school unwillingly, and that he there entered into an unending struggle with his teacher, who was often justified in the use of coercion. The new pedagogy, which is so ably represented in New York, holds that it is the child's instinct and pleasure to exercise all his faculties and to make discoveries in the world around him, that it is the chief business of the teacher merely to direct his activity and to feed his insatiable curiosity. In order to accomplish this he is forced to relate the child to the surroundings in which he lives, and the most advanced schools are using modern industry for this purpose."[10]

Here in a few short sentences is the essence of the progressive movement in education: the assumption of inherent motivation; the teacher as guide, necessarily on a rather individual basis; the urban-industrial environment as the starting point for education.

Seen from one point of view, practically everything at Hull House had to do with education. The Labor Museum could just as easily have been called a school and was not because Jane Addams thought the word might frighten people off. The boys' and girls' clubs, the Shakespeare and Plato clubs, the athletic teams, the little theater, language classes for immigrants—indeed the very existence of the settlement—all were education, though only a small portion grew out of any desire to teach something.

A kindergarten was one of the first Hull House activities, not because Jane Addams and Ellen Starr were enthusiasts of kindergartens but because their neighbors needed one. Neighborhood families who desperately needed the wages of the mother could not be told that the sacred duties of motherhood were more important than a paltry four dollars a week; the families needed the four dollars. Instead of simply opposing this judgment from a middle-class, and therefore an irrelevant standpoint, Hull House tried to do something about the neglected child left locked in the house in winter or out of it in summer. A nursery was established for infants and a kindergarten for the four-and-five-year-olds. The children received a balanced meal, elementary training in hygiene, and a start on their school experience. All of a sudden Jane Addams found herself part of the kindergarten movement.

The kindergarten movement, as the name indicates, originated in Germany and was an outgrowth of German theories of the human being as a developing organism, to be cultivated in a garden like a plant. Frederich Froebel came into contact with these theories while a student at the University of Jena and applied them to the education first of traditional school-age children, then in 1837 in Blankenburg to pre-school children. The kindergarten was to be based on instinct for play which was inherent and to be organized in accordance with natural development. But the natural development and instincts were to be organized in a systematic way. The purpose of this was to create "a society of children engaged in play and various forms of self-expression, through which the child comes to learn something of the values and methods of social life without as yet being burdened by its technique." In this second definition self-expression appears, but, more important, the goal of kindergarten is taken to be a child learning to get along with other human beings.

Froebel himself emphasized the systematic organization of children's play by developing a standardized set of toys and activities, given to the children in a stated sequence. As with many educational theories, this one in practice often developed into rigid orthodoxy, but the idea of gently cultivating children's natural instincts towards social and artistic fulfillment survived.

The first kindergartens in the United States were German-speaking and modeled on that of Mrs. Carl Schurz, a pupil of Froebel, which opened in 1855 in Watertown, Wisconsin. The first English-speaking kindergarten opened five years later under Elizabeth Peabody of the formidable Boston family. By 1880 there were four hundred kindergartens in the country; a decade later all major cities had not only kindergartens but kindergarten associations, which were pressing city authorities to incorporate the idea into the public school system.[11]

The basis of the kindergarten movement was a confidence that the instinctive desire to learn existed in every child, that the first few years of life were crucial in deciding the direction in which the child would grow, and that the purpose of the school was to cultivate, encourage, and guide the learning instinct. But what of the later years when mere playing with balls and blocks was not enough, when children saw fathers and older siblings going off to work, when children became aware of their surroundings? How then could natural curiosity be exploited?

The answer was obvious to Jane Addams. The stuff of childhood experience around Hull House was industry and the city. Children were going to live in the city and work in industry. Hence education should focus on what was inevitably important to children: themselves and their environment. She rejected the "assumption that the ordinary experience of life is worth little, and that all knowledge and interest must be brought to the children through the medium of books. Such an assumption fails to give the child any clew to the life about him, or any power to usefully or intelligently connect himself with it." "The democratic ideal," she insisted, "demands of the school that it shall give the child's own experience a social value."[12]

A rapid glance at Miss Addams' writings might easily lead one to the conclusion that she found the means to give to the neighborhood children's lives a social value in industrial education. Indeed, industrial education was a significant component of the progressive movement in education, endorsed by manufacturers glad to receive trained or semi-trained workers. After some initial resistance, industrial education was also endorsed by organized labor. Miss Addams favored the idea as far as it went. Training could enable a man to be a foreman or an engineer instead of a machine tender. But Miss Addams was acutely aware that this sort of industrial education had nothing to say to those who were not engineers. "They graduate machine builders, but not educated machine tenders." In fact, this sort of industrial education was simply "the old paths of education with 'manual training' thrown in." Why, she asked, should the public spend money to supply industry with trained workers?[13]

Miss Addams proposed to turn the theory of industrial education upside down. Men were not to be trained to run machines; machines were to be the instrument through which men might be educated broadly. John Ruskin had written: "The great cry that rises from all our manufacturing cities, louder than their furnace blast, is all in very deed for this—that we manufacture everything there except men; we blanch cotton, and strengthen steel, and refine sugar, and shape pottery; but to brighten, to strengthen, to refine or to form a single living spirit, never enters into our estimate of advantages."[14]

Miss Addams, echoing these words, argued that the current industrial system "works automatically, as it were, towards an unintelligent producer and towards an uninteresting product. This was first said only by such artists and social reformers as Morris and Ruskin, but it is being gradually admitted by men of affairs." Like many reformers of the progressive age, Miss Addams thought that country life was more natural than city life; but she had "ceased to mourn the changed industrial conditions in which children were taught agricultural and industrial arts by natural co-operation with their parents." Since no return was possible, the inevitable environment had to be utilized. No child should ever be put into school simply to memorize what a professor thinks is important, then put into a factory to tend a machine which the factory manager thinks is important, and even worse to have no relationship between school and factory.[15] Starting from the machine which the child may eventually tend, or from the factory where his father and perhaps his mother work, the school can teach him the whole history of industry and economic development:

> A child from an "advanced school" will have reproduced and in a measure reinvented the process of spinning and weaving from the savage apparatus of a few sticks of wood to a colonial wheel and loom of his own manufacture. Such a child will never see a piece of cloth without a certain recognition of the historic continuity of effort, of the human will and ingenuity which lie back of it; but

better still perhaps such a child having learned something of the lives of textile workers for thousands of years and the part which daily habit and occupation has played in human development will be interested perforce in the textile workers of the present moment.[16]

Thus economics, history, physics, civics, and even social reform could grow out of the child's interest in, essentially, himself.

For Miss Addams this type of education was not to be confined to working-class children. A bookish classical education as she herself had received was, if not wrong, certainly inadequate. It placed literary blinders over the eyes, by which the contemporary world was obscured and distorted. Indeed, a very powerful component in her own move to Hull House was that she found with shock that she was observing everything through eyes given to her by literature, rather than observing life at first hand. She wanted to shuck off this barrier and allow life to touch her without intermediaries. Thus for future clerks and managers, education which built the curriculum out of a study of modern industrialism would give them knowledge of workmen "to know the lives of workmen, their habits, needs and hopes, not in a philanthropic spirit . . . but in the much more democratic desire to test the usefulness and validity of his own knowledge that it may run on all fours and be fitted to contemporary needs."[17]

As with all of her proposals, the purpose was to break down barriers between groups so that the essential unity of the human family might be nurtured and preserved. Yet she herself moved in a rather bookish world. Her speeches and writings abounded with literary references, she was friends with numerous professors and even taught a college course. Did she really mean to reject bookish learning? This conclusion might be read into her theories, as a certain anti-intellectualism has been read into Dewey's educational thought.[18] The conclusion would be wrong in both cases.

In the first place, the environment was not to be the end of study, but the entrée to it. Actual conditions were to be made "the basis for a large and generous method of education, to perform a difficult idealization, doubtless, but not an impossible one." In an eloquent phrase she wrote, "the man in the factory as well as the man with the hoe, has a grievance beyond being overworked and disinherited, in that he does not know what it is all about." Education should meet this grievance and supply the factory worker "with general information and to insist that he shall be a cultivated member of society."[19]

The second route by which the new education could lead to more traditional cultural values was through self-expression. Miss Addams was pleased when she saw schools encouraging "the sense of art which little children were never supposed to possess, because they were always taught to copy things and were never before encouraged to compose." She hoped that self-expression was being so rapidly developed "that in ten, fifteen, twenty years from now it must register itself in a new art awakening." The same thing was happening in music, so that there might be, in the midst of a dull factory environment "that joyousness which has been the basis for all art."[20]

In fact, said Miss Addams, "we have found at Hull-House that our educational efforts tend constantly toward a training for artistic expression; in a music school, a school of dramatics, classes in rhythm and dancing, and the school of the graphic and plastic arts. In the last, which we call the Hull-House Art School, the children are given great freedom in the use of color and clay and other media through which they may express those images which are perpetually welling up from some inner fountain, and which suggest not only their secret aspirations, but curiously enough, something of their historic background."[21] The chief aim of the art school was to remove inhibitions and allow these images to find their way to the surface. From these efforts at self-expression, valuable enough in themselves, children heard talks on art history, went to museums, and in general were introduced to the world of painting, sculpture, dramatic literature, and music. Like the more famous music school at the Henry Street settlement in New York, some graduates of Hull House went on to professional careers in the arts, but these few were merely adornments. More important were the day-to-day effects on children and their parents whose lot was bound to factory labor.

Jane Addams went so far as to believe that children educated in the way she desired could provide a moral and esthetic revival for society; could act as a saving remnant "if we only release that wonderful power which children possess and which we have so long repressed."[22] Thus it is a grievous misinterpretation of both Jane Addams and John Dewey—though certainly a misinterpretation to which both lay themselves open—to conclude that in favoring education for life they favored merely an education of life-adjustment courses. To both, an education for life meant an education which would make people aware of the broad stream of development of which they were a part, of the insights to be gained from literature, of the development of science. The starting point, however, was to be their own situation.

For adults who had passed through school and were already at work amid the monotony of factory labor, the problem was more difficult. One could hardly ask these people to add still another task requiring a certain amount of drudgery on top of their overlong work day. In fact, Miss Addams recorded as one of her keenest disappointments that by 1902 the settlement had been unable to find educational methods appropriate to the adults among her neighbors—save for those who were bookishly inclined. For all other ages, however, she was proposing an education based on the assumption that children like to learn, and that through the right kind of education, society as a whole could be redeemed.

When John Dewey reached his seventieth birthday in 1929—with still nearly a quarter of a century of activity ahead of him—he was given a birthday party in New York. Jane Addams was invited to give one of the toasts. She talked briefly of his pragmatism, reminisced about his early association with Hull House, recalled an amusing incident or two. She put the most emphasis, however, on his educational philosophy. Her trip to New York and her toast sum up the personal and ideological closeness between the two.[23]

Significantly, the article on "Play" in Paul Monroe's *Cyclopedia of Education,* published in 1912–1913, was written by John Dewey. Dewey started by rejecting the long-held theory of Herbert Spencer that play was the overflow of surplus energy. Dewey scorned this theory as based on a belief that "individuals are naturally averse to any kind of activity; that complete quiescence is the natural state of organic beings; and that some fear of pain or hope of pleasure is required in order to stir individuals to effort which in itself is painful." Dewey insisted that, on the contrary, activity was "the very essence of life." Again assuming that natural instincts were benign, needing merely guidance and direction, rather than destructive, needing repression, he argued that play was an inherent part of the life process. The task of education was to direct this activity so that it would lead by insensible process into increasingly mature stages: "In other words, the natural transition of play into work is the means and the only means of reconciling the development of social efficiency with that of individual fullness of life."[24]

Froebel had rediscovered the importance of play in the educative process, and the idea entered American thought via the kindergarten. Soon, however, the Play Movement or Playground Movement joined scores of other movements as a full-fledged reform organization. This was quite in keeping with the American practice of developing a voluntary private organization to deal with whatever ills afflicted society. By the 1880's a few private organizations like the Boston Children's Mission and the Children's Kindergarten Association of Providence, Rhode Island, were operating playgrounds. In 1897 the Associated Charities of Chicago began founding playgrounds, and a year later the Board of Education of New York took over similar work from the Association for Improving the Condition of the Poor and established twenty playgrounds with trained supervisors. From then on the idea spread rapidly, and by 1911 over three hundred cities had established more than 1600 playgrounds.[25]

In June of 1907 the Playground Association of America met in national convention in Chicago. According to Graham Taylor, "Everybody Played." Surely the high point of the occasion was when Luther H. Gulick, the dignified and mustachioed president of the association, along with half a dozen other officers, was pushed into a municipal swimming pool. "Through personal experience [wrote Taylor] they can now bear witness that Chicago's municipal swimming pools have water as clear and clean as her streets are dirty." Immigrant groups performed dances of their homelands; children demonstrated various games; enthusiasts of the playground movement gave learned, or at least intense speeches; and one hundred playground girls demonstrated how they "could wear bloomers without self consciousness."[26]

In Luther Gulick's formal address to the association—given before he was pushed into the pool—he indicated the theme that ran through the convention: play, under conditions of considerable freedom, was an absolute necessity for the maintenance of democracy in an industrial society. He went through the standard list of great advances made by technology and the standard assertions about increased interdependence. This interdependence "rendered many things socially significant which in former days were largely individualistic." This expanding area of social significance required a new growth of conscience, a new ethic—in essence what Jane Addams called the social ethic. Gulick argued that this social ethic could only be learned by experience, and experience under conditions of considerable freedom. We hear much about learning by doing, he said, but "ethics alone seems to be the exception." Social ethics cannot be learned by talking about it, nor by merely enforcing certain rules: prisoners in jail, forbidden to do harm to anyone, do not thereby learn ethics; sailors living for months under rigid routine are not known for their decorum in port. Ethics could only be learned by developing self-control and awareness of the group. On the sand pile, small children learn lessons in mutual rights, and older children learn that "the most perfect self-realization is won by the most perfect sinking of one's self in the welfare of the large unit—the team."[27]

Graham Taylor summed up his view of the convention by enthusing over the way both the spirit of commercialism and the spirit of individualism, by which he meant selfishness, had been banished. Indeed the members of the association were confident that play could protect democracy, train citizens, revive morals, and prevent tuberculosis. If these hopes were naively sanguine, the fundamental ideas that children have a natural developmental process which must be respected, and that changing conditions could in fact alleviate misery, were of the broadest social import. "To see Mary McDowell and Jane Addams . . . so completely enjoy that day," said one delegate, "you would think that the seventh heaven had suddenly set down in Chicago."[28]

Jane Addams had reason to be happy, for it was through play that she hoped to retain and preserve the natural joy of childhood and, indirectly, the conviction that life itself was worth living. In her own paper to the playground association she implicitly referred to theories of instinct and recapitulation, and argued that play was both anticipatory and reminiscent. Boys and girls learn to be older children and then adults by first playing at being older. A boy may play at being a ship captain or a cowboy, and though he may grow up to be neither, he has pictured himself as an adult and can thus more easily become one. Play could also be reminiscent. Miss Addams found the root need for recreation in the unnatural urban environment which allowed no outlet for human instincts. In the country a man gave his energy to subduing nature and saw the effect of his success in the food he grew or the game he shot for his family. In the city, however, "it is his chief business not to conquer his environment but to subordinate himself to it. . . . His business is no longer to subdue nature but to subordinate himself to man." His instincts are cut off, and the relation between his daily work and providing for his family is remote and indirect. Games of all sorts could allow outlets for his natural and subconsciously remembered needs for the hunt, chase, combat, and primitive religious festivals. When young people in the city looked about them for opportunities to play, when they tried to follow the promptings of their instincts, they found only the streets, the gang, and the cheap theater.[29]

All around Hull House, children's instincts were misdirected. Jane Addams knew that thousands upon thousands of children around Hull House were literally addicted to the five-cent theater. Children would turn to stealing in order to buy tickets, and parents often supplied the money rather than drive their children to petty theft. Miss Addams recognized the motives that drove children to these theaters: a need for seeing life in larger terms, for finding order and morality, for denying that their daily round was all there was to life. Properly done, drama could be a healthy, edifying experience for young people, as the "little theater" movement in New York and the Hull House Players proved. Yet she found the five-cent theater teaching a false and destructive morality and burying all the fine motives under blatant vulgarity. The songs in the *entr'actes* were suggestive, emphasizing the glamorous flirt, the flashy young blade. The music was valueless. Most of the plays glorified violence, crime, and revenge. Although there might be a pious ending denouncing crime, it was often the dashing criminal who was the real hero. One milkman near Hull House barely escaped with his life the morning after a gang of boys had seen a play about robbing a stagecoach. Although the milk got through that morning, the boys were serious enough about their admiration of the holdup men to fire a real shot at the hapless milkman.

Even worse than the theater were the public dance halls of

Chicago, institutions which Miss Addams saw as the source of the most horrendous sins. In the countryside, from which most Chicagoans had come, there was no dance hall. To be sure, there were dances at which young people enjoyed themselves, but they were part of a courtship procedure overseen by the benevolent, protective eye of the community, subtly enforcing rules which were readily understood and accepted. In the city, "huge dance halls are opened up to which young people are attracted . . . to procure the sense of allurement and intoxication which is sold in lieu of innocent pleasure. . . . Since the soldiers of Cromwell shut up the people's playhouses and destroyed their pleasure fields, the Anglo-Saxon city has turned over the provision of recreation to the most evil minded and the most unscrupulous members of the community." In these halls not only was there no supervision, but the entire management was bent on debauching young men and young women—and all this not for pleasure, but for profit.[30]

In the city, even the desire for adventure, beating a rhythm to which every young boy must dance, turned out wrong. In the country a boy could hunt rabbits, explore the woods and fields, and imagine himself a soldier or a pioneer. When he followed his primitive instincts in the city, where was he to go? The most exciting place in Chicago was the railroad yards. Here gangs of boys would sometimes camp, stealing a little coal for warmth and apples for food. They watched the trains and dreamed of faraway places. Miss Addams knew that some boys who thus danced to the beat of adventure were caught, tried, and convicted of stealing, trespassing, or truancy. Sometimes the love of excitement led to the passing of mysterious packets, via an elaborate underground complete with code phrases and secret meeting-places. The secretiveness and danger, Miss Addams thought, were much more attractive to boys than the fact that the packages contained cocaine.

"May we not assume," she asked, "that this love for excitement, this desire for adventure, is basic, and will be evinced by each generation of city boys?" Yet in thousands of cases, she argued, the love for adventure had led to the police court, to prison, and to the start of a life of crime. "It is as though we were deaf to the appeals of these young creatures, claiming their share of the joy of life, flinging out into the dingy city their desires and aspirations."[31]

Miss Addams, who was able to empathize to a startling degree with young people living a life which she, in a sense, never had, understood the basic striving for identity in young men and women. When she saw girls with "the self-conscious walk, the giggling speech, the preposterous clothing," she knew that, "through the huge hat with its wilderness of bedraggled feathers, the girl announces to the world that she is here. She demands attention to the fact of her existence."[32]

Understanding young people in this way, Miss Addams saw the solution to the problems of youth in the city in youth itself. The solution lay all about, the only task was to provide the social mechanism for grasping it. She was thoroughly convinced that wholesome pleasures were really the most attractive, and that petty crimes and immoral dance halls were popular only through the lack of alternatives. She noticed that the employees of numerous factories spent their noontimes cheering the practice of the factory baseball team. On Saturday the team would play that of a nearby factory. "The enormous crowd of cheering men and boys are talkative, good natured, full of the holiday spirit, and absolutely released from the grind of life. They are lifted out of their individual affairs and are so fused together that a man cannot tell whether it is his own shout or another's that fills his ears."[33] Precisely this spirit of exuberant fun, release from monotony, and feeling of fellowship must be encouraged. Boston was on the right track, she felt, with its municipal gymnasiums, cricket fields, and golf grounds. Chicago had parks with playing fields, and in many of them were halls which were provided, rent free, to groups of young people for dances. Food, electricity, plants for decoration, and supervision were provided by the city at cost, and these halls were less expensive and more attractive than the disreputable private halls.

The very conglomerate nature of poor sections of cities gave them a richness in recreational opportunities. The city schools of New York were organizing folk dancing based on the national traditions of immigrant groups. Various national holidays could also be celebrated in and out of school. "From the Chinese dragon cleverly trailing its way through the streets, to the Greek banners flung out in honor of immortal heroes, there is an infinite variety of suggestions and possibilities for public recreation and for the corporate expression of stirring emotions."[34] There was the tarantella danced at Italian weddings, the Greek pipe played through the long summer nights, the Bohemian theaters, the Hungarian street musicians.

Hull House itself, of course, tried to do as much of this as possible: a gymnasium used both for vigorous athletics during the afternoon and dances in the evenings; various national clubs keeping alive the old world dances and festivals; the Hull House Theater; a marching band with uniforms to play stirring music; the playground. But as always, Miss Addams felt that Hull House could only be a small beginning. To be truly effective the efforts would have to come from the whole community and be expressed through public bodies. Chicago was a leader in the municipal parks movement. Its first playground was the one run by Hull House on the William Kent property, but by 1898 the city had appropriated public funds for the purchase of land and equipment for playgrounds. By 1910 the Small Parks Commission of Chicago had spent over ten million dollars for playgrounds and had an annual budget of half a million dollars for their maintenance and supervision. Starting at about the turn of the century, cities all across the country, with perhaps a greater share in the northeast, adopted some plan to provide parks. By 1920, nine out of ten cities over 100,000 population had them, and by 1930 nearer 100 per cent had them. The standard journal of city planning included a section on playgrounds and recreation as routinely as a section on street repairs. Jane Addams' argument that urban recreation was a public function had been accepted.[35] No one would claim that playgrounds in slums have eliminated crime; indeed, a number of contemporary murders have been committed on urban playgrounds. But that all children need recreation and that the provision of recreation facilities is a public responsibility is now virtually unquestioned.

The value of play itself has received even more important acceptance, not so much in any explicit program of providing playgrounds, but rather as one of the assumptions beneath the progressive movement in education. These assumptions have received such widespread acceptance that they have developed an inflexibility and a devotion to their own orthodoxies—quite out of character with the spirit in which they were born—which have produced new reactions. Indeed, in those vast reaches of the nation which social historians no longer notice and on which educational theorists have little effect, the counterrevolution has arrived before the revolution. Teachers now go from pre-progressive to post-progressive without ever passing through Dewey. Like a lady who saved her short skirt from the 1920's to the 1960's, these teachers, with methods left over from the 1880's, are, in a superficial way, once more in style. It is as if all the successful experiments, all the pilot projects, all the knowledge gained during the last seventy-five years did not exist. A new generation of educational innovators is having to discover progressive education all over again.[36]

Yet there have been some gains, particularly in the well-to-do sections of cities and in the suburbs. The great days of progressive education were between the wars. The City and Country School was founded in 1914 and the Walden School in 1915 as private institutions to put the ideas of Dewey (and Freud) into practice. They were followed in the 1920's by at least a small host of others, the center of activity being New York. The leading communities in the adoption of the progressive impulse by the public education system were the wealthy suburbs of Winnetka, Illinois; Bronxville, New York; and Shaker Heights, Ohio. Denver was the first major urban system explicitly to adopt progressivism, and many of its programs and materials became models for other cities.[37]

Perhaps more typical than explicit adoption of progressivism as a system was an unacknowledged seepage of progressive education into school systems and teachers' colleges in all parts of the country. There was no wholesale repudiation of old methods and attitudes, no worship of the demigods of the Chicago lab school. Yet instead of an entire day made up of rote learning of standardized texts, children began to find themselves spending some time on projects growing out of their surroundings. Curricula, bit by bit, were revised to include manual training and artistic expression. More flexibility was introduced into the grouping of children, and students by one method or another were more frequently permitted to work at a pace concomitant with their needs. Movable furniture and movable partitions were architectural expressions of greater freedom in the schools. Teaching became increasingly professional and increasingly based on the results of the child-study movement and its offspring.

In the process some of the ideas of Dewey and Jane Addams became unrecognizable. Changing social conditions made some of them irrelevant, and the unacknowledged revolution by no means affected all parts of the country equally. Yet in one form or another, the fundamental ideas have survived: children are innately curious; schools ought to be relevant to the needs of all social classes; education ought to follow natural maturational patterns; the opportunity for self-expression, including artistic expression, ought to exist in the schools. The adoption of these ideas and points of view, though continuing to develop in unpredictable ways, is probably irreversible. Finally, and perhaps most importantly, the general assumptions which Jane Addams and other progressives made about the nature of the child have had wide impact on American society generally. On that day when Dr. Benjamin Spock's *Baby and Child Care* sold more copies than the Holy Bible, one might have said that the new era had arrived.

9

Environmentalism: Child Labor, Child Crime

"ONE generation after another," wrote Jane Addams in 1907, "has depended on its young to equip it with gaiety and enthusiasm, to persuade it that living is a pleasure." Much of the effort of Hull House and its founder was devoted to preserving and utilizing this fundamental joyousness of young people. All around them, the residents felt that this natural joy was being repressed and denied. The city, industrial society, even the school and the family prevented the basically kind and joyous child from becoming a kind and joyous adult. The institution which most supressed the natural child, which most distorted personality, at least in the Hull House neighborhood, was the factory. A child laborer, drilled in monotony from his twelfth year or even earlier, could not possibly develop his potential. Either he would become a dull person, as monotonous as his daily task, or he would turn to some form of rebellion.[1] One could cheat personality, Jane Addams argued, and what could cheat it more than to require a thirteen-year-old boy to work ten hours a day, six days a week, at a task which offered no intrinsic satisfaction, so that he might buy a pair of boots so that he could go to work properly shod?[2]

Here Miss Addams was asserting a new version of an environmentalist argument almost as old as European settlement in North America. From Crèvecoeur through the Jacksonians to Frederick Jackson Turner, American intellectuals had insisted that environment shaped the individual. The traditional version of environmentalism, however, usually took the environment as given, and as natural. Miss Addams and others argued that the environment was also the social environment.[3] In fact, in the city the natural environment almost disappeared. The entire environment was man-made, whether one considered society itself or its artifacts. Many Americans missed the difference and transferred their environmentalism from nature to the city, assumed that both were immutable and that individuals must simply adapt, whether they lived in wilderness Kentucky or south Chicago. However, those who noticed the difference between the two argued that since the new environment was man-made, men could make whatever they chose. If they *could* choose, it was morally irresponsible *not* to choose, because that refusal was itself a choice. And yet the environment which men were making for their children did the reverse of cultivating and nourishing their natural instincts. Putting a child into the factory for long hours of labor not only crushed his spirit but also diminished by just that much the amount of spirit upon which society might draw.

"By premature factory work, for which youth is unprepared," said Jane Addams, "society perpetually extinguishes that variety and promise, that bloom of life which is the unique possession of the young." The source of art lay in this spirit, the source of human sympathy, of good workmanship and pride in accomplishment lay therein. "The discovery of the labor power of youth was to our age like the discovery of a new natural resource, although it was merely incidental to the invention of modern machinery and the consequent subdivision of labor. In utilizing it thus ruthlessly we are not only in danger of quenching the divine fire of youth, but we are imperiling industry itself when we venture to ignore those very sources of beauty, of variety and of suggestion."[4]

Miss Addams also paraded the standard economic arguments; but one feels that here she was simply trying to find an appeal for those to whom "the divine fire of youth" was a chimera. The hard-headed realistic argument was simply that child labor wasted a resource. Children could do simple industrial tasks at a very early age, but if they worked at these simple tasks year after year, they became useless for the more complex tasks they otherwise could perform later in life. She told of one such case in which a man, just at the age he should have been at the peak of his earning capacity, was ruined. "The physician has made a diagnoses of general physical debility. The man is not fit for steady work. He has been whipped in the battle of life, and is spent prematurely because he began prematurely."[5] Put all such individual waste together and the total was a staggering long-term loss in return for a small, short-term gain—and this in strictly economic terms.

The assumptions beneath all these arguments was that something could and therefore must be done about it. Child labor was a state responsibility. Miss Addams rejected the idea that meliorative remedial charity, such as a school for newsboys, could make up for the destructiveness of child labor. The only solution was to prohibit child labor so that youngsters who might be newsboys could go to school instead. How ridiculous it was, she argued, for the state to go to great expense to train teachers, build school buildings, provide education for children, and then completely lose interest in them. Children are trained to be obedient, prompt, and hard working, then turned over to businessmen who used them for their own profit, confident that the state would provide a new crop when these were exhausted. It was as though the state provided new machinery for businessmen and replaced it every time it got out of order, taking the old machinery back. For after a worker was "laid on the shelf" as early as his thirtieth year he might require state support for the rest of his life.[6]

Illinois was among the early states to enact effective child labor legislation, and in Illinois enforcement was particularly good. The law was gradually extended from the prohibition of children in mines to their work in factories, then in mercantile establishments. At the same time compulsory school-attendance laws were made more effective. While she was a resident at Hull House, Florence Kelley was the first supervisor of factory inspectors and, strictly in character, was a tough, hard-hitting law-enforcement agent. Jane Addams led the battle against any weakening of the law. In 1910 there was an attempt to exempt child actors from the prohibition against night work. Miss Addams argued that every manufacturing interest in the state had some reason for wanting an exemption. If actors were exempted, why not children in glassworks, or messenger boys? Soon the law would be a nullity. She became surprisingly well informed on child actors: their hours, their pay, whether they went to school, how they were treated. She testified in Springfield before the committee of the state senate considering the bill—and found herself disagreeing with the daughter of her friend, the Senator from Wisconsin—and became an effective lobbyist. The exemption was defeated.[7]

State child-labor legislation, if enforced and combined with compulsory school-attendance laws, sometimes had a remarkable effect. In one school alone, the fifth grade increased from fifty to one hundred and fifty students, all trying to learn to read so they could qualify for work permits. But state legislation was of limited effectiveness. In Illinois, perhaps, children were forbidden to work in glassworks; but when one took a glass of water in Illinois, he could not be sure the glass had not been made in Kentucky with the help of an eight-year-old boy. There was something wrong, Miss Addams argued, when the national government could legislate on the condition of a dead cow inside a can—through the meat-inspection bill—but could not legislate on a living child inside a factory. She vigorously supported Senator Albert J. Beveridge's bill to prohibit goods made by child labor from interstate commerce, and she testified in Washington on its behalf. She wished, however, that the legislation could have been more direct. Instead of stretching and torturing the commerce clause, she wished that federal legislation could prohibit child labor simply because it was wrong.[8]

Jane Addams was one of those who urged the establishment of a Federal Children's Bureau to collect the data needed for the proper national protection of young people. Florence Kelley pointed out caustically to the House committee holding hearings on the proposal that the city of Portland, Oregon, had to rely on a passing traveler who knew something of New York's legislation when Portland wanted to draw up a pure milk bill. Besides, she asked, if the government can collect statistics on reseeding clam flats, why can't it do the same on matters affecting children? Eventually the bill was passed and, at the urging of Jane Addams and others, Julia Lathrop became first head of the Children's Bureau.[9]

All this was necessary, Jane Addams argued in summary, because new industry had created a new environment with a new set of pressures on young people. There were no institutions from the earlier rural age to protect children against these pressures; new institutions had to be created. The churches could not do it. The informal nexus of community opinion was nonexistent in a multifarious city. Private voluntary organizations simply did not have the power. State power could be of some use, but in the final analysis society as a whole, acting through the national government, had to act to provide protection for those who could not protect themselves.

Looking back on the history of child-labor legislation, Grace Abbott in 1938 remembered particularly the leadership provided by Florence Kelley and Jane Addams. "Miss Addams persuaded and Mrs. Kelley spurred the public to a sense of responsibility."[10] Of course there were a great many other people persuading and spurring the public. Theodore Roosevelt and Senator Beveridge argued that child labor would produce a weakened race, unable to fight successfully in future wars. Alexander J. McKelway and Edgar Gardner Murphy put harrowing tales of childhood suffering before the public. The National Federation of Women's Clubs urged action upon individual states while the National Child Labor Committee acted as a publicity and lobbying agent in the states and in Washington. Miss Addams was a member of these two organizations and lent a powerful voice to the crusade.

Her ideas were accepted only very slowly by the nation. Between the depression of 1893, which first gave the question of child labor a pressing urgency, and the First World War, most states with sizable industry passed some sort of legislation to protect children. Not surprisingly, these laws varied widely in their provisions and enforceability. In general, northern states adopted a fourteen-year minimum age, and enforced the law sporadically. Southern states had similar laws, but such was the desire of the New South to attract industry, especially textile plants, they were seldom enforceable or enforced.

Since opponents of state regulation argued that child labor laws would drive industry to neighboring states, national legislation seemed the obvious solution. Senator Beveridge introduced the first such bill in 1906, based on the commerce clause of the Constitution. The bill lost, and during the next decade repeated attempts to pass similar legislation failed. Finally the Keating-Owens Act was adopted in 1916, only to be declared unconstitutional by a sharply divided Supreme Court in 1918. The following year another regulatory law was passed, based on the taxing power rather than the commerce clause. This, too, was disallowed by the high court. During the 1920's vigorous efforts on the part of the National Child Labor Committee, the U.S. Children's Bureau, the National Consumers' League—all, incidentally, with former Hull House residents in positions of leadership—failed to produce ratification of a constitutional amendment allowing national regulation. It took another depression to obtain the goal, not through amendment, but through legislation remarkably like the original Beveridge proposal. Actually it was not until 1940 that a more liberal Supreme Court explicitly overruled the 1918 decision and sustained the use of the commerce clause to regulate child labor. Finally the idea that society, acting through whatever organ of government was most effective for the task, had the responsibility to protect its young, was accepted on a nationwide basis.

But it was not merely working in factories that snuffed out the divine fire of youth. The entire urban setting, of which factory labor was a part, repressed the natural benignity of the human spirit. Instincts which found no constructive outlet would find their way into antisocial behavior. Thus without ever formulating a theory of criminal behavior, Miss Addams implicitly assumed that crime, like poverty, was a symptom of a misconstructed environment, not of indivdual character weakness. Statistically, most crime was relatively petty, and was committed by young people between thirteen and twenty-five. Most crimes she felt, had no rational aim, even in terms of criminal rationality, and most young criminals partook not at all of even elementary prudence. "Only a utilization of that sudden burst of energy belonging partly to the future could have achieved them, only a capture of the imagination and of the deepest emotions of youth could have prevented them."[11]

Miss Addams saw that among families of the neighborhood, where homes were tiny and overcrowded, children were not expected to invite their friends to visit. Out of doors there was no playground but the street, and in the street children formed their own, unsupervised social structure: the gang. Much gang activity could be harmless fun, though in the close quarters of the city almost any boyish activity might run afoul of the law.

Moreover gangs provided a little center of warmth and loyalty against the mass impersonalization of the city. "Nothing is more forlorn," she perceived, "than the boy who has no gang at whose fire of friendship he may warm himself." But often, with virtually no approved outlet for loyalty and exuberance, gang life became predatory, either against other gangs or against society. It was not difficult for loyalty to the gang to become more powerful than any sense of morality, law, or loyalty to another group such as the family. Miss Addams recognized that gangs had a morality, but that the morality was not society's. Youthful gang members became, without shock or division, adult racketeers or corrupt politicians, loyal to friends rather than the public.[12]

Nor was only pretty crime produced by inhuman living conditions. In 1911 six young men, without any apparent motive, murdered a gardener driving to work. They were quickly arrested, tried, and convicted; and four of them were hanged with the approval of most of Chicago. A resident from the Northwestern University settlement visited the homes of each of the young men, and found conditions "which stirred a careless city to compassion." The fathers were absorbed in ceaseless toil to provide food for an ever-growing family. Mothers were absorbed in the care of babies. There was no affection for children who were more burden than joy, and often the parents had no idea what the older children were doing. The parents only had one question of these youngsters: "How much money on Saturday?" One father indicated that he didn't care whether his sons were hanged or not: "Neither of those boys ever brought home a penny." With such a home life, young men could easily wander into gangs where the highest virtue was bravery or bravado, and into neighborhood saloons where contacts with criminals began. "Again, the desire for play, for sports fitted to the age of such boys I believe will be the only agency powerful enough to break into this intensified and unwholesome life. In fact I have seen it thus broken when gangs of boys were finally induced to patronize the public playgrounds of Chicago."[13]

Repression of natural instincts also led to the institution which Miss Addams regarded with utmost horror: professional prostitution. Sometimes a girl would become a prostitute through much the same spirit that drove boys' gangs to crime. Girls were perhaps not actual members of the gangs, but were attached to them by bonds of loyalty as strong as membership. This loyalty, this desire to be a "good Indian," often led to what Miss Addams referred to as the girl's "downfall." Apparently one such slip was a permanent stain, for Miss Addams assumed that from an initial loss of chastity, a life of prostitution was almost bound to follow.[14]

Simple desire for pleasure also led to downfalls. What could be nicer than an excursion boat ride on Lake Michigan, an evening at an amusement park, or a pretty ribbon to brighten up a drab, inexpensive dress? What could be more "hideous" than the payment men expected in return for their purchase of such delights? Worst of all were the dance halls and the liquor traffic which accompanied them. Here young girls were lured into prostitution, and young men into careers as procurers.[15]

For the Social Evil, the cure was more complex than merely providing adequate recreation, though that would help. The most important reason that young women went "on the street" was that they simply did not earn enough to support themselves in factory or domestic work. The most effective way to protect the virtue of factory girls would be to pay them a wage which would allow a modicum of comfort and even of fun. As it was, the wages of virtue were so low as to almost force girls to seek the wages of sin. This was one reason Miss Addams supported the unionization of women. In addition, reformers would have to end collusion between brothels and politics, legislate woman suffrage, and revolutionize education. The basic idea, however, was that the urban environment, by the repression of normal needs for dignity, pleasure and affection, would lead to antisocial behavior. "We constantly think," she quoted Tolstoy, "that there are circumstances in which human beings can be treated without affection, and there are no such circumstances."[16]

Affection was also needed by those who were unquestionably guilty of crimes, and were punished. The current system, Jane Addams pointed out, was simply not working. A recent study had shown that two out of three inmates in prisons were repeaters. "If our legal system cannot do better than that in dealing with criminals, we certainly have a right to challenge the whole process for there is rank failure somewhere."[17] Miss Addams was opposed to capital punishment. She was convinced that harsh punishment was no deterrent to crime. "The English records of crime were never so full as when the penalties were most severe," she wrote in the first year of the twentieth century. A quarter of a century later she was still insisting that brutality of punishment left a legacy, not of law-abiding citizens but of brutality added to the brutality of the crime. In fact the brave criminal who goes to the gallows without flinching may be a hero to the adolescent who would not admire a life of prison monotony.[18]

Capital punishment, however, was only the extreme case, and it was relatively rare. Jane Addams was much more interested in the fate of the more mundane criminal, especially the young criminal who might still be flexible enough for redirecting into constructive patterns. The first task would be to separate those who broke the law virtually by accident, as incidental to normal play, from those who broke it by intent or profession. As necessary was a separation between young offenders and older, presumably more hardened offenders. Criminal trials were constructed to deal with adult offenders and were, Miss Addams argued, basically irrelevant to the vast majority of criminals, who were young people. It was at the instigation of Hull House that Chicago established its Juvenile Court, the first in the nation. The first probation officer was a Hull House resident, paid privately by a committee led by Hull House residents and trustees. For many years the court was across the street from the settlement, and the judge was appointed, by custom rather than law, only with the approval of the committee of the settlement. The difference between the Juvenile Court and other courts was that in the latter the punishment was made to fit the crime, while in the former the punishment was made to fit the criminal. The judge had wide discretion to find a punishment which would not so much deter others, or even produce fear in the wrongdoer, but would serve as an educational experience on the road to a constructive life.[19]

This approach to young criminals was new to the nation, and indeed to the world. Jane Addams' views on education were influential, but one must ultimately credit others with the mental pathbreaking. On the issue of juvenile offenders, however, Miss Addams was in the very forefront of the pioneers. The Juvenile Court movement—for it became a full-fledged movement—had its origins in Hull House, and involved a basic innovation in society's definition of what a juvenile offender was. This, in turn, had an influence on society's view of criminality in general.

The late-nineteenth-century picture of the criminal was established in Italy by Cesare Lombroso, who did his most influential work in the decade after 1865. Lombroso concluded that criminals were biological types, physiologically different from honest men. Partly they were atavistic throwbacks to an earlier evolutionary stage, perhaps Mongolians or even as far back in the sequence as rodents. Partly the physiological differences were pathological, involving diseases like epilepsy. Lombroso first based his theories on studying only three men, but he validated his conclusions by careful examination of nearly six thousand convicts. Like so many careful investigations, this one produced the conclusions desired by the investigator. Lombrosian criminology did not totally omit environmental factors, because the biological tendencies could be hidden or brought out by stimuli in the environment, but inherent criminality was heavily emphasized.

Lombroso's conclusions were given their first thoroughgoing test by someone other than their originator in the same year that Chicago established its Juvenile Court. In 1899, an English prison official, Dr. Charles Goring, compared three thousand recidivist convicts with one thousand Cambridge undergraduates —presumed, for reasons unexplained, to be honest men. Further studies were done on Oxford students and noncommissioned naval officers. In all cases the results indicated no significant variation between the criminals and noncriminals. If there was any difference, it was that criminals tended to be smaller and weaker than other men. Perhaps, Goring hazarded, this was simply because small men tended to get caught. This study did not rule out mental differences, however, and seemed to imply that feeblemindedness was related to criminal behavior. It was this theory, developed more or less independently of Goring, which gained great popularity in the United States, especially as it related to juvenile delinquency.[20]

In 1911, two years before the final results of Goring's tests were published, Henry H. Goddard had used the new Binet intelligence tests to test delinquent children in New Jersey. Goddard found that feeblemindedness was far more frequent among convicts than among normal children. Rather than assuming that only less intelligent offenders got caught or that the test was biased, Goddard concluded that feeblemindedness caused criminal behavior. Goddard's immense confidence in the Binet tests and their later modification led him to the theory virtually as physiological as Lombroso's, for to him feeblemindedness was as real, as measurable, and as inheritable as cranial capacity or the slant of the forehead. Goddard's views became extremely popular in the United States.

Thus, in the 1890's, when the Chicago Woman's Club began talking about a Children's Court to consider juvenile offenders as something different from criminals, they were whispering an environmentalist argument in the midst of a great crowd of hereditarian shouts. The Chicago Woman's Club, through its jail committee, had been involved for many years in prison reform and had become uncomfortably aware of the large number of children confined in city and county prisons. The jail committee recommended a Juvenile Court Bill in 1895, but the project was dropped because the ladies became convinced that the law was in conflict with the state constitution. The idea gained considerable support, however, among lawyers, women's organizations, settlements, and the ministry.

At the annual meeting of the Illinois State Conference of Charities in 1898, members of the club pressed for a policy in favor of a court. The result was a Juvenile Court Committee having members of the Chicago Bar Association and of the Chicago Woman's Club, including Louise De Koven Bowen, Julia Lathrop, and Jane Addams. The committee drew up a law which was submitted to the legislature in Springfield. Mrs. Bowen was instrumental in the passage of the law and later recalled with amusement the way her opposition to political bosses clashed with her desire for the bill. Mrs. Bowen invited an important Republican leader to her house for a social call. While he was there, she told him she wanted very much to have a juvenile court. At once he went to the telephone in her library, called one man in the state house of representatives, and one in the state senate. To each he said that he wanted bill number such-and-such passed. One of the men evidently asked what was in the bill, for Mrs. Bowen heard her friend say, "There is nothing in it, but a woman I know wants it passed."

It passed.

The state bar association, in a report backing the bill, explained that the fundamental idea was that "the State must step in and exercise guardianship over a child under such adverse social or individual conditions as to develop crime." The law assumed that the child should not be treated as a criminal or one charged with a crime, "but as a ward of the State, to receive practically the care, custody and discipline that are accorded the neglected and dependent child, and which, as the Act states, 'shall approximate as nearly as may be, that which should be given by its parents.'" The obvious assumption was that it was environmental conditions which develop crime, not unalterable, inherited characteristics. The very title of the law indicated the same view: "An Act to Regulate the Treatment and Control of Dependent, Neglected and Delinquent Children." By contrast, another Chicago organization had recently referred to the same group as "the unfortunate, the vicious and the defective." For the Juvenile Court Committee, delinquent children were victims, not victimizers.

The law itself was carefully designed to avoid police stations, grand juries, the city house of detention, and the other paraphernalia of criminal procedure. Indeed the legal argument for the court was based not on criminal law at all, but on British chancery law, which in the United States became the law of equity. Theoretically the state, through the court, became not the prosecutor of a criminal but the parent of a child. The duty of the state was thus not to uphold order or the majesty of the law but to do what was best for the child.

While the law of 1899 established the court and authorized probation officers, it made no provision to pay the staff, house the children awaiting trial, or finance any ancillary social services. The Juvenile Court Committee raised the money for these things privately, eventually spending about $100,000, and at the same time pressed public bodies to assume the responsibility.[21] Gradually the functions were taken over by public authority, and the Juvenile Court Committee re-organized itself as the Juvenile Protective Association.

A clear gap in the facilities of the court was the lack of a highly trained psychologist. Probation officers and settlement residents could make common-sense judgments about some children on the basis of interviews and visits to the home, but other children needed more expert diagnosis. The first psychiatric clinic in connection with a Juvenile Court was established in Chicago in 1909, with William Healy as psychiatrist. Healy became one of the pioneers in the study of the psychology of delinquents, and his book, *The Individual Delinquent,* was for many years the standard text. The clinic did not accomplish the cures its founder hoped for, but it became, more than anything else, a laboratory for the study of delinquents. Healy, in his text, was far more careful and complex in his theories on causes of criminal behavior than was Jane Addams. In fact, he repeatedly warned his readers against drawing general conclusions, and might have echoed Marg Richmond's remark in *Social Diagnosis* that different things should be treated in different ways. He explicitly rejected the heredity-versus-environment argument by maintaining that in some cases one might be the cause of delinquency, in other cases the other, and in most cases a combination. If one were looking for cures, one might manipulate the environment simply because "in many cases it is the environment that can be more easily altered than anything in the individual's personality." Yet he insisted that merely altering the environment would be inadequate. Thus Healy's years of contact with thousands of cases modified the over-simple explanations of Miss Addams. Without her over-simple first approximations, however, neither the court nor the clinic would have come into existence.[22]

Jane Addams' views on a juvenile court received much more rapid acceptance than her views on child labor. During the first years of the twentieth century, state after state passed legislation similar to the Illinois statute of 1899. By 1914 thirty-seven states had done so, and by 1920 all but three states had juvenile courts. In roughly the same period, most of the nations of western Europe established similar systems. In the United States, the most famous juvenile court was in Denver, presided over by Judge Benjamin B. Lindsey. Lindsey was involved in virtually the entire spectrum of progressive reforms, but his fame was as a juvenile court judge. It was Ben Lindsey who, twenty-five years after the Juvenile Court of Cook County began, said that the most important contribution of such courts was in "pointing out those social and economic injustices that are responsible for juvenile delinquency and crime."

By the mid-twentieth century, however, juvenile courts drifted far from their original purpose. The concept of the court as a nurturing parent declined and the court as an agent of punishment grew. In abandoning the procedures of a criminal trial, the juvenile courts also abandoned the protections which the accused automatically receives. Most juvenile trials take place without the accused having a lawyer, and no rules of evidence or cross-examination are enforced. In most states there is no need even to convince a grand jury that an offense has been committed, and judges in juvenile courts have, and have exercised, virtually dictatorial powers. Clearly, some new reform is needed, perhaps even a new institution, to restore the impulse which animated the founders of the original juvenile courts.

The new institutions may well grow out of research into the causes and nature of juvenile crime which have, in the last half century, gone well beyond Jane Addams' intuitive judgments. The situation is now seen in much more complex terms than she stated it, and one no longer talks so easily either about the "cause" or the "cure" for delinquency. Starting with efforts like the psychiatric clinic connected with the Cook County Juvenile Court, a vast amount of data has been accumulated. The most important investigation was the Harvard Crime Study, the first volume of which appeared in 1934. Sheldon and Eleanor T. Glueck have brilliantly analyzed the data in that study, and tested and retested their conclusions.[23] While talking the language of caution, using such phrases as "pressure toward anti-social behavior" rather than "cause of crime," the Gluecks have arrived at a clear enough theory of delinquent behavior to be able to predict it with a high degree of accuracy. In essence, the most important factor seems to be whether the parents care for and about their offspring. If they do not care—or if they ask only the equivalent of "How much money on Saturday?"—the child is likely to end up in a juvenile court.

It is not surprising that a quarter of a century of research should add depth and subtlety to Jane Addams' understanding of crime in young people. Widespread crime among middle-class and wealthy families has brought into question any simple relationship between crime and poverty. Nor is it surprising that mid-twentieth-century theorists put more emphasis on relationships within the family than on the family's social and economic situation, though the two are related.

Nevertheless, the essential attitude of compassion for the delinquent or potential delinquent has replaced the thoroughly rejected idea of the criminal as a physical type or the child as inherently antisocial. Contemporary investigators now look to the environment, whether it be the physical, the psychological, or the sociological environment, as the cause for delinquency. Moreover society as a whole has clearly accepted a large portion of the responsibility to try to prevent deviant behavior. The very testing of the Glueck prediction scale was carried out by an agency of the New York City government, and every major city in the nation has a similar agency. Juvenile crime has hardly been eliminated, but the attitudes Jane Addams proposed in 1899 are now virtually national assumptions.

Within children, Jane Addams believed, was an irresistible pressure for righteousness, if only adults would let it burst forth. If children were taken out of factories, put into schools which were relevant to their social situation, provided with supervised healthy recreation, protected from demoralizing temptations, and treated with compassion when, in their innocence, they strayed from approved paths—if all this would happen, society would be flooded with a light of joy, justice, idealism, and beauty which would banish slums, strikes, corruption, crime, and misery.

Somewhere between their middle teens and early twenties, Miss Addams thought, young people in all lands and all cultures became aware of the ways in which their surroundings did not come up to their ideals. These young people burned with an ardor to put the world right, to banish hypocrisy. Most of the answers to Lincoln's call for volunteers came from men under twenty. The French and German revolutionaries of 1848 and the Russian revolutionaries of 1905 were mostly young people. Adults in their superior wisdom treat this ardor for reform as naive. Instead, Jane Addams urged adult society to utilize it, to direct it in constructive directions, to discipline it, "to make it operative upon the life of the city." "Democracy," she wrote, "like any other of the living faiths of men, is so essentially mystical that it continually demands new formulation." Where better to look for this new formulation than in the divine fire of youth?

> We may either smother the divine fire of youth or we may feed it. We may either stand stupidly staring as it sinks into a murky fire of crime and flares into the intermittent blaze of folly, or we may tend it into lambent flame with power to make clean and bright our dingy city streets.[24]

10

Environmentalism: The Culture of Poverty

"THERE can hardly be anything more opposed to conventional charity than the social settlement," Francis G. Peabody told the National Conference of Charities and Correction, meeting in Toronto in 1897. "Its representatives have an almost morbid terror of being involved in charity." A few minutes later, Jane Addams rose to address the conference, and began by apologizing for her very presence: "The settlements are accused of doing their charity work very badly. They pretend not to do it at all." She then went on to insist that there was, after all, some connection between social settlements and charity.[1]

What was striking about this exchange was not that anyone connected charity and settlements, but that anyone at all should feel the necessity of explicating the connection. Both settlement workers and the more conventional charity workers realized that each approached the problem of poverty with different attitudes. The more traditional workers tried, with a good deal of success, to learn what the settlement had to teach. The result was that the settlement workers became the leading formulators of new attitudes and methods of dealing with poverty.

Yet, in an important sense, Jane Addams was right in denying her connection with charity. Nothing could be more wrong than to consider Jane Addams a reformer of methods for dealing with the poor. She had to fight against this conception of her role from the first days of Hull House to the day of her death. The most important things she had to say, both in her own estimation and from the point of view of the influence of her words, had to do not with poor people but with people in general. Her view of education was as relevant to the wealthy as to the poor, and was in fact put into practice more at the upper than the lower end of the economic scale. What she had to say about class conflict applied to the society as a whole, not merely the "lower" class. When one examines her ideas on the poor, one finds that on that subject in its simplest form she had relatively little to say. She could talk about children who were poor, or immigrants who were poor; but "the poor" as a class were less prominent in her thinking than one might expect. In fact, Jane Addams did not like to talk about "the poor" as a group, for that tended to diminish just the humanness she wanted to emphasize. For her they were the girl out of work because she had injured her hand; the man whose low wages would not support his young family; the child wasted with overwork before he was grown. For Jane Addams each had a name, a face, and a personal history. Unlike the charity visitors, settlement residents knew their neighbors through the years, could watch them from infancy to adulthood, and could understand something of the pressures on their lives. To give her readers and auditors some taste of what this residence among the poor meant, Miss Addams filled her speeches and writings with examples. One after the other, individual people were brought before her audience and given human shape.

"I never had a chance to go into the country when I was a kid," she quoted a young neighbor as saying to her, "but I remember one day when I had to deliver a package way out on the west side, that I saw a flock of sheep in Douglas Park. I had never thought a sheep could be anywhere but in a picture, and when I saw those big white spots on the green grass begin to move and to turn into sheep, I felt exactly as if Saint Cecilia had come out of her frame over the organ and was walking in the park." For her readers, who spent their summers on a lake at Waukegan, a door had thus been opened onto the mind of one city child.[2]

At Hull House, Jane Addams wrote, a kindergarten training teacher lectured on the advantages of some permissiveness rather than tyranny in the bringing up of children. Some members of her audience were puzzled. One said, "If you did not keep control over them from the time they were little, you would never get their wages when they are grown up."

"Ah," answered another, "Of course she doesn't have to depend on her children's wages."[3]

And something of the family life of the very poor was revealed to the reader of her account.

Early in the history of Hull House a group of residents, with the influence of romantic ruralism still strong upon them, took a group of children to Lincoln Park only to be disappointed at the boredom with which the children reacted to trees and flowers. On the way home a paddy wagon rattled by, and all the tired children burst forth with excited questions about who was arrested, how many, man or woman?[4]

And readers realized that the standards of a rural age did not necessarily apply at Halsted and Polk streets.

Perhaps the most vivid rendering of the poor as people was in Miss Addams' treatment of the "daintily clad charitable visitor," who, upon entering the home of her "case," finds herself confronted not with someone who has not come up to the standards of the visitor, but who has different standards, and logical ones for the circumstances. Miss Addams is understanding of both the visitor and visited, but she shows clearly how the middle-class outlook of the one makes her standards irrelevant to the working-class problems of the other. The family being visited emerges from her pages as more sensible and more comprehending than their charitable visitor.[5]

If the poor were sensible and comprehending, why then were they poor? Jane Addams never explicitly answered the question, but her answer was implicit in virtually everything she wrote: circumstances. The poor were poor because at every turn they were prevented from being anything else. They were not only as good as the well-to-do; in some respects they were morally superior. Many were working to the point of exhaustion. Yet even if all adults in the family worked hard, spent money only for the necessities, including a little necessary recreation, income only barely met expenses. When sickness, accident, or old age disrupted earnings or created sudden expenses, the family had to go into debt or seek charitable help. Millions of people were trapped in poverty which neither they nor most of their children could escape.

Jane Addams was not alone in making these points. She was perhaps the best known of the settlement workers, journalists, and publicists of all varieties who insisted, at the end of the nineteenth century, that the poor were poor because of a misconstructed social environment, not because of a defect in themselves. But Americans in general proved highly resistant to the idea. In fact, before the closing years of the nineteenth century, the question of "the poor" had not been central in American consciousness. In the very year that Hull House was founded a writer in the *New Englander* (later the *Yale Review*) suggested in all seriousness that the cause and cure of poverty lay in the poor themselves and that the cure could be completely effected if all trade in liquor and tobacco were forbidden. Two years later Andrew Carnegie told a combined British and American readership that poverty in early life was actually an advantage to the businessman.[6]

To be sure, everyone had always known about the poor. The poor but warmhearted old widow was very nearly a stock character: half pathos, half comedy. The kindhearted criminal was another stock character, and rather more completely comedy. All of Horatio Alger's heroes started honest, manly, and poor; all had been the better for it. Before the Civil War most Americans assumed that degeneracy and criminal tendencies caused slums, and even that slum dwellers lived in filth by choice. "They love to clan together in some out-of-the-way place," said the founder of the New York Association for Improving the Condition of the Poor. Anyway "they" were not really Americans at all, but the self-selected paupers of Europe, dumped into the great eastern port cities and left there to spread their disease among the better classes. In addition to restrictions on immigration, there were two obvious cures for poverty: paternalism and self-help. Employers should be generous with their workers, help them towards temperance, cleanliness, and thrift; and the poor for their part should work hard, be obedient, and lift themselves out of their misery. Some few Americans, like Herman Melville, insisted that poverty was neither educational nor morally beneficent but debasing and debilitating—but then Melville was merely a spinner of romantic South Sea tales.

One radical approach to the individual cure of poverty was inaugurated in 1843 by Robert M. Hartley, founder of the New York Association for Improving the Condition of the Poor. Starting as a worker for total abstinence from alcohol, Hartley concluded that he was working at the problem from the wrong end. The environment in which the poor lived would have to be improved before their moral health could be restored. His association therefore called upon the needy, did casework of a sort, and investigated housing, sanitation, and health. This was an important shift in emphasis, but Hartley's purpose was to lift the impoverished to the point where certain moral preachments would be effective. The essential point of these preachments was self-help, and for Hartley this usually meant leaving the city. Tirelessly he urged the urban poor to have enough initiative to go somewhere else. For him the poor were still moral degenerates. His contribution was to suggest that some environmental reform might hasten moral regeneration.[7]

Charles Loring Brace was another mid-century innovator. In reporting his work with the poor, he entitled it "The Dangerous Classes of New York and Twenty Years' Work Among Them." His special interest was in the children of the poor, particularly those with no apparent home. He was less interested in the children themselves than with their effect on the rest of society, for he considered them parasites and incipient criminals. He detested the idea of institutional care for children since the problem was always individual. His solution was to round up waifs like wild dogs and ship them to the morally regenerating atmosphere of "The best of all Asylums for the outcast child," the farmer's home. Thousands of farmers were eager to take Brace's emigrants, for cheap agricultural labor was scarce; and in fact, later studies indicated that the program was remarkably successful in resettling children. Brace, like Hartley, did not challenge the fundamental American creed about the causes and cures of poverty. He did advance the environmentalist approach, however, and almost without knowing it he implied that some of the poor or criminal were in no position to help themselves.[8]

By Appomattox two contradictory phrases—"the poor ye shall always have with you" and "in America, no man need be poor"—had been melded into one standard ideology:

> Poverty is unnecessary [for Americans], but the varying ability and virtue of men make its presence inevitable; this is a desirable state of affairs, since without the fear of want the masses would not work and there would be no incentive for the able to demonstrate their

superiority; where it exists, poverty is usually a temporary problem, and, both in its cause and cure, is always an individual matter.[9]

The doctrine of self-help, which neither Hartley nor Brace had challenged, led to the neglect of institutions for the poor such as almshouses and orphanages. Partly in response to this neglect, and partly in the hope of making charitable work more efficient and "scientific," the charity organization movement spread from London, where it had begun in 1869, to the United States. The charity organization societies acted as co-ordinating bodies and clearinghouses for charitable work. The idea was that cases possibly suitable for charity would come to the C.O.S., which would investigate their situation. If deemed worthy of charity, the case would be referred to the appropriate charitable organization. The aim was to weed out the unworthy and then to avoid the expense of overlapping organizations. By the end of the century some of the C.O.S. were involved in charity themselves: keeping woodlots where the deserving might find work; administering low-interest loan societies; and, most importantly, employing "friendly visitors" who visited the poor, advised thrift and sobriety, and incidentally acquired a good deal of information about urban poverty. The aim throughout was to keep "watch over the poor people to guide them and help them to self help"—and to make charity cheap and uncomfortable. The poor should be driven to work by the repulsiveness of charity.[10]

The organization of all workers in the vineyards had been national since 1873 when the National Conference of Charities and Correction held its first annual meeting. The name of the organization was fitting, for until the settlement workers drew the distinction with clarity, charity was assumed to be in the same general field as the treatment of the insane and criminals already in prison. There was nothing strange in the fact that in 1885 a standing committee of the NCCC delivered a "Report on the Statistics of Pauperism and Insanity."[11]

One can see indications of these attitudes in general circulation magazines as well. In the year prior to the onset of the great depression of the 1890's, *Scribner's Magazine* ran a series on "The Poor in Great Cities." Written by different authors, the series contained a variety of points of view, but came down heavily on the side of blaming the poor for their poverty. The final article in the series summed up the general tone. In "The Prevention of Pauperism," Oscar Craig of Purdue University assumed that pauperism was the "vice or disease" of unwillingness to work; that the poor must be prevented from declining into pauperism for their own good and that of the well-to-do; that the cure was elimination of outdoor relief (that is, relief outside of institutions), emigration from cities, and immigration restriction. Craig did not mention drink as a cause of poverty, but other writers did, some maintaining that there were really no poor at all, just honest workingmen and drunken bums, usually called "tramps."[12]

One of the articles in the *Scribner's* series indicated the beginning of some change in attitudes. Robert A. Wood, who was soon to establish South End House in Boston, showed in "The Social Awakening in London" how a newer view of poverty was evolving in that city. Stronger hints of evolving attitudes appeared in Jacob Riis' *How the Other Half Lives,* published a year after Hull House was opened. The book was a harrowing collection of Riis' experiences with the life of the very poor, as police reporter and informal investigator of poverty. He picked up the lid on the life of the very poor and demanded that the wealthy see what was under it: restaurants where, for two cents, a man could sit all night with at least a roof over his head; the dingy street full of those who "don't live nowhere." Riis adopted some aspects of the new view of poverty, but in 1890 Jane Addams would still have been able to teach him much—the two did not meet until later. Basically his argument was based on the older view that poor people came in two kinds, the honest workingman or "worthy poor," and the "tramp" or "pauper," a lazy, worthless person who would never amount to anything. Both of these classes lived in the spreading slums of New York, presenting a threat to the more respectable classes. The poor of both types produced disease, crime, and a load on charitable organizations. For the "pauper" Riis had no sympathy and no cure. For the honest or worthy poor, he thought that a decent environment must be provided. At the time the book was written Riis found hundreds of thousands of people paying high enough rents to support decent housing, but living in incredible filth and overcrowding. An indifferent public and greedy landlords, requiring a return of between 15 and 100 per cent on capital, had created the slums. Riis's solution was to propose a combination of private enterprise and public control to produce new model tenements which for the rent would provide ventilation, sanitation, adequate space, and an outdoor area for a touch of the rural life. With cheap, decent housing, families would not be impoverished, diseased, or prone to crime; children would be brought up correctly and not be driven to premature work or hoboism.

Clearly Riis, as a visitor to rather than a resident amidst poverty, found his cure in the most visible aspects of slum life. Obviously better sewage and clean running water could eliminate some disease and filth; but neither then nor now has cleanliness or better housing cured poverty. Riis asked explicitly for justice rather than charity, but he seemed to think justice could be a product of the architect's drawing board. And yet Riis's book was important, for it rejected the idea that slumdwellers liked their quarters, that all of them were mere idlers, and that the rest of society could ignore them. He pointed out that conditions in the slums were horrible, and he laid the blame squarely on the shoulders of the wealthy.[13]

The depression of 1893 provided the shock which changed some American attitudes towards poverty. The question of whether outdoor relief was beneficial or harmful evaporated as city after city found outdoor relief to be absolutely necessary.[14] Some workers discovered with surprise that "tramps" were not a special breed of degenerate, but were in fact honest workingmen unable to find honest work. The attempt to uplift the poor morally became secondary to the task of finding work for the unemployed and keeping people from starving. By 1896 the president of the National Conference of Charities and Correction felt justified in titling his address "The New Philanthropy." The new philanthropy, claimed Albert O. Wright, was at the base of the new social settlement movement, the trend toward scientific sociology and, in fact, was winning its way all over the nation. And yet as Wright talked he revealed the close ties the new philanthropy had with the old, and how right Jane Addams would be when a year later she said she felt out of place at the National Conference. Wright described the characteristics of the new philanthropy:

> On the philosophical side it studies causes as well as symptoms, and it considers classes as well as individuals. On the practical side it tries to improve conditions, thus changing the environment of the defective. It tries to build up character as well as to relieve or punish,

believing that the essential cause of Pauperism or crime is usually some defect inside the pauper or criminal as well as bad conditions around him; and it seeks for prevention as well as cure.

The criminal, the pauper, the tramp, the neglected child, even many of the insane and the idiotic, are all interrelated with one another, and are mutually exchangeable.[15]

Clearly there were some new features in Wright's new philanthropy—most notably the emphasis on environment—which could easily lead the philanthropist into general social reform. The emphasis on prevention focused attention on people living at the borderline of outright dependence, who were so liable to be thrown into complete poverty by even a minor misfortune. His rejection of punishment could lead to more humane treatment of the poor, criminal, and insane. And yet Wright would not abandon the idea of a pauper as a class of defectives whose greatest need was a stronger character. The settlement house movement taught not the new philanthropy, but a still newer philanthropy. As economic circumstances forced the poor on the attention of the nation, a flood of personal accounts, sociology, fiction, and journalism shaped the reaction with which the circumstances would be met. Out of the gentility of William Howells and the statistics of W. E. B. DuBois and the brutal cry for justice of Upton Sinclair, national attitudes evolved. Through a flood of speeches and articles, Miss Addams helped evolve this newer view of poverty.

Miss Addams did not come to the poor completely free from Victorian prejudices. There were contradictory impulses in her thought and action which mirrored the struggle between older and newer ideas in the nation as a whole. Perhaps these very contradictions made her more effective. Not being too far ahead of her countrymen, she could communicate better with them. In any event, the sum total of her words and actions helped to destroy older ideas and to shape the ideology behind the welfare state. Her very move to Hull House involved some of these conflicting impulses. She divided her motives into three parts: "The desire to make the entire social organism democratic; . . . the second is the impulse to share the race life and to bring as much as possible of social energy and the accumulation of civilization to those portions of the race which have little; the third springs from a certain renaissance of Christianity, a movement toward its early humanitarian aspects."[16] Though her use of "democracy" in this passage is vague, she probably meant changing the economic system so that everyone had some measure of control over his own destiny, and was assured of enough participation in the economy to support himself and family in decent circumstances. In short, the first motive was a desire for social justice. The second motive was somewhat more condescending, in that she wanted to share the "higher things"—art, music, literature, natural beauty—with those who had no opportunity for their cultivation. The third motive was extremely vague, involving remnants of Tolstoyan renunciation of luxury and a Christian ministry of good works, as well as a basic expression of the unity of the human family across class lines.

More than she perhaps realized or stated explicitly, it was this conviction of human unity which lay at the basis of her move to Hull House and what she did once settled there. The poor were not "vicious and dependent classes" as some other Chicago residents thought; rather they were the people who had not triumphed in "the unequal battle of modern industry." Indeed, at times she seemed to think that the poor, by the very fact of their poverty, were closer to a true understanding of the world than their economic superiors. The wealthy, cut off by their materialism from these simple truths, could become wiser by knowing the poor better. Of course, to regard a poor man as wiser and more virtuous because of his poverty betrays a certain lack of understanding and implies condescension. It assumes a relationship between wisdom and income, and puts the poor into a single group quite as much as an attitude which regards them as stupid because of their poverty. To treat the poor as simple people uncorrupted by material well-being smacks of Marie Antoinette entering the dairy with her milk pail. At times Jane Addams did confess to doubts that the poor had enough social energy to change their lot.[17]

Yet the overwhelming brute fact, more important than any remnants of nineteenth-century attitudes, was that Jane Addams lived at 335 South Halsted Street. She did not visit for a few weeks or a few months; she lived there as her regular home. And living there gave her knowledge that no government survey or novel could. She saw the deserted wife who had no choice but to leave her children alone as she went off to work, and knew that the mother was neither vicious nor defective. She saw whole generations stunted by overwork early in life and knew that the tales of Horatio Alger were cruel frauds. She saw hard work for inadequate salaries and knew that workers were the reverse of lazy. The deserted mother, the overworked child, and the toiling laborer were more than mere cases for her, though they were not quite her friends. "Neighbor" was the word she used, though the equality implied in the word never quite existed.

The basic assumption behind Hull House was that the poor, like all mankind, were basically good if only they had the opportunity to express their natural impulses. Many of Jane Addams' neighbors were educated, though not in the American way; many had skills, but skills which were not saleable in Chicago; and most had kindly impulses which prompted them to give from a scanty supply to help others still more desperately in need. American society ignored or rejected these people to its own cost. From this assumption Miss Addams was able to overcome her own middle-class standards and understand the poor in their own terms. To some extent she was able to bring others with a middle-class standard along with her. She understood, for example, how a poor working girl might spend a disproportionate amount of her $4.50 weekly salary on clothes, because in an impersonal city one's appearance provided personal identity. Another type of charity worker might have merely condemned the concentration on appearances as extravagant.[18] Miss Addams understood that the middle-class virtue of thrift might be a crime when each penny was needed for daily survival. She understood how the poor might resent a charity visitor who thought that "organized" and "charity" should be part of the same phrase, or who thought some poor were "worthy" and others were not.

From this understanding, Jane Addams evolved a new view of poverty. The first part of this view was that "poor" meant not only those who were absolutely dependent. For these, public care was already available. "But for the great mass of people just beyond the line, from whom the dependent are constantly recruited," she wrote, echoing Hunter, "we do practically nothing." She pointed out that a workman with tuberculosis in New York could receive free hospital and post-hospital care, but if he had a lesser illness, one which merely made him unfit for work, he got no help unless he was ready to declare himself helpless and without resources.[19]

The second part of the new view of poverty was the belief that people were poor because society gave them less than they had a right to. Partly this was a matter of inadequate wages, partly of inadequate public services, but it was not a matter of inherent defect in the poor man himself. Her friend, Graham Taylor, put the matter succinctly. "The sting of modern poverty in prosperous communities," he wrote, "is precisely that it is not necessary, that it is the result of social neglect, of industrial exploitation, of maladministration in government, or an obsolete system of education, of our failure to adopt plans which already, at least in fragmentary and local ways, have shown their usefulness to correct particular evils."[20]

Miss Addams not only agreed with this view, she took it so for granted that she hardly was aware of it. Oh, of course, she might say, distress is due to a misorganized society; but then she would quickly move on to the question of what could be done to organize society better and eliminate distress.

Elimination of distress was not always the same as social reform. The former could be an individual matter; the latter could only deal with groups. Miss Addams' work was originally with individuals, and while she quickly was brought to social reform, her work with individuals continued. Though she did not use the term, this was social casework. "Social case work," Mary Richmonds said, "does different things for and with different people—it specializes and differentiates; social reform generalizes and simplifies."[21] Jane Addams would not have entirely accepted the second half of this definition, but the first half is a perfectly good *post hoc* description of what she did without formulating a theory. The first step in social casework was what Miss Richmond called *Social Diagnosis* in the title of her book: "the attempt to make as exact a definition as possible of the situation and personality of a human being in some social need—of his situation and personality, that is, in relation to the other human beings upon whom he in any way depends or who depend upon him, and in relation also to the social institutions of his community."[22] *Social Diagnosis* was a textbook for training caseworkers. As such it attempted to systematize what various sorts of charity workers had, at their very best, been doing. Jane Addams learned about the social institutions of the community, both formal and informal, from being in and of the community. She learned about the individual from talks with him, for somehow she could make anyone feel comfortable enough to talk. As her experience at Hull House lengthened, she often knew individuals through long years of acquaintance. Thus her proposed remedies were usually developed on the basis of knowledge as complete, or more complete, than that available to the most highly trained outside professional observer.

Yet she made mistakes. In a misguided effort to help a family without adult wage-earners she found a job for a twelve-year-old boy, and when he lost that, she found him another, and then a third. By the age of sixteen he was disgusted with boring work, weakened by a bout with typhoid fever, and, at just the age he should have been earning, had become useless.[23] On another occasion, an unemployed man who had always worked indoors was found an outdoor, wintertime job on a street project. After trying manfully to do work for which he was unfit, he contracted pneumonia and eventually died. Most often, however, she understood the individual with whom she was dealing well enough to make the right decision. An adventurous boy, working at a monotonous factory job, was brought into court repeatedly for taking joy rides in doctors' carriages while the doctors were making house calls. Miss Addams found him a job in a livery stable, and he turned into a good employee and model citizen. By sometimes bitter experience, she learned the necessity for "specializing and differentiating" and for complete "social diagnosis."

Working with individuals, Miss Addams found, often led to the second half of Mary Richmond's statement: working with groups, which was social reform. One thing led to another, so that if striking girls were evicted because they could not pay the rent, Miss Addams did not simply supply the rent, she helped found the Jane Club. Factory workers found no joy in their work, so Hull House founded the Chicago Arts and Crafts Society which gave skilled craftsmen a chance once again to employ their skill. Wives in the Hull House neighborhood never seemed to have any leisure, so the Rockford summer school was begun. As Jane Addams explained: "We at Hull House have undertaken to pave the streets in our ward, only to find that we must agitate for an ordinance that the repaving shall be done from a general fund. We have attempted to compel by law, that the manufacturer provide proper work rooms for his sweaters' victims, and were surprised to find ourselves holding a mass meeting in order to urge a federal measure upon Congress."[24] In other words, people did not need to be *made* decent; the circumstances had to be created in which people could *be* decent. In some cases the initiative came from Miss Addams, in others from her neighbors, but whichever way the ideas ran, she insisted that reform must be *with* the poor, not *for* them.

Jane Addams scorned the idea that "it is not possible for the mass of mankind to have any experiences which are of themselves worth anything, and that accordingly if a neighborhood is to receive a valuable idea at all it must come from outside." This confidence in the potentiality of her neighbors, remarkably current in tone, led her beyond the new view of poverty to a still newer view, one which is not yet fully accepted by the nation. By 1910, Jane Addams explicitly criticized the "new view" of poverty as narrow and limiting. She endorsed it as far as it went, for after all both relief and prevention were necessary; but they were not sufficient. She agreed with John Galsworthy that "while society has made up its mind that it cannot see anybody die, it is a little bewildered as to the disposition of the survivors. . . . [This] is well so far as it goes, but it is not after all sufficient, and we look about to see the next step, the one beyond the mere negative salvation of human life." In urging both relief and prevention, Jane Addams was one of a swelling chorus of reformers. In arguing that society as a whole had further obligations, in arguing that relieving all destitution was "*mere* salvation of human life," Jane Addams placed herself among a smaller, far more radical group of reformers.

She recognized this herself in her presidential address to the National Conference of Charities and Correction in 1910. "Charity and Social Justice" proposed that the goal beyond relief and prevention should be "raising life to its highest." In tracing the history of this idea she spoke of the "gradual coming together of two groups of people, who have too often been given to a suspicion of each other and sometimes to actual vituperation. One group who have traditionally been moved to action by 'pity for the poor' we call Charitable; the other, larger or smaller in each generation, but always fired by 'hatred of injustice,' we designate as the Radicals." Speaking to an audience of Charitables, she acknowledged that the Radicals had indeed perhaps moved toward the Charitables, but she spent most of her time arguing that the Charitables had become more and more Radical, and ought to continue that direction of movement.

> It would be easy from the records of this Conference to trace the gradual steps by which charitable folk were irresistibly led from Cure to Prevention, as it would also be possible to demonstrate from contemporaneous records that we are now being led in the same gradual but unresting manner from Prevention to a consideration of Vital Welfare. The negative policy of relieving destitution, or even the more generous one of preventing it, is giving way to the positive idea of raising life to its highest value.
>
> If at times the moral fire seems to be dying out of the good old words Relief and Charity, it has undoubtedly filled with a new warmth certain words which belong distinctively to our own times; such words as Prevention, Amelioration, and Social Justice.

She went on to show how charity had gradually come to proposed changes in ways of treating children, of treating widows, the role of the school, public health and industrial safety and most important of all, of a new view of the state, with full responsibility for not *mere* salvation of human lfie, but for social justice.[25]

For Jane Addams it was not enough to give a crippled child crutches, or to fence a machine so he could not be crippled, or even to keep him out of the factory entirely. It was also necessary to ensure that the child, now saved from accident, could live a happy, satisfying, and productive life. If she was vague in specifying the nature of that life, vague in delineating what "raising life to its highest value" might mean, it should be no source of surprise. She was still trying to arrive at a society of abundance, not dealing with its problems. She knew that if all the changes she wanted were instituted, new sets of problems would emerge. The point was that she envisioned that a society of abundance might exist in America, not as some faraway dream but within the grasp of her contemporary reformers, if only they would pursue it with enough vigor.

Over half a century after she formulated this ideal, and some thirty years after her death, the idea of a society which not only feeds the hungry or prevents a man from becoming hungry but also ensures him a decent, productive life has become at least rhetorically possible in American national life. In 1964, at the behest of President Lyndon Johnson, Congress established the

Office of Economic Opportunity, designed not only to eliminate poverty, but also the culture of poverty. Its lineage to social reformers of the progressive era is easy to trace.

The torch was kept burning through the discouraging decade of the twenties in large part by the social workers, a term not yet invented when Hull House was established. In 1917 the National Conference of Charities and Correction changed its name to the National Conference of Social Work. This was a somewhat belated recognition of what was indicated when, in 1909, the journal *Charities* changed into the *Survey*. Dealing with the poor was both symbolically and actually detached from dealing with the criminal. Even more important, no longer were the poor dealt with through charity, but through surveys and social work. The great trend of social work in the later pre-war years, and more clearly in the 1920's, was a self-conscious drive toward professionalization. This meant the development of special training for social work, as contrasted with the amateurs who founded settlements; it meant the development of specialties within the field; it meant dividing the accredited and acceptable sheep from the untrained goats, even if the goats had spent long years in their jobs, but lacked the proper training in the proper schools. Probably professionalization was not only inevitable but good, for more people could more competently perform the tasks that social workers set for themselves. Yet there were costs in professionalization too, not the least of which was a concern with technique and treatment and a declining interest in broad social reforms. Yet social workers, especially caseworkers following the guidelines laid down by Mary Richmond, accumulated the vast amount of experience without which the reforms of the New Deal would not have been possible. While many succumbed to bureaucratization, some social workers kept alive the broader idea. In her presidential address at the National Conference in 1926, Gertrude Vaile set forth the aim of social work as the positive one of securing a "more abundant life" for all.[26]

"These social workers are frauds—they talk big but really at heart don't want any legislation passed and endorsed which will in time abolish the necessity for their kind of work."[27] This condemnation by a socialist leader in Buffalo was patently too sweeping, yet the broad drive for ensuring "a more abundant life" went on outside the ranks of professional social work. The

American Association for Labor Legislation carried on the unsuccessful battle for national health insurance, the American Association for Old Age Security fought for old-age pensions. Settlement workers too continued the fight, especially in relation to child welfare and housing improvement. Through publicity, speeches, and research these people strove during the twenties to convince Americans that all was not the best in this best of all possible worlds.

In fact, the lesson was not learned until the boom was replaced by bust and depression. In 1933, the AAOAS changed its name to the American Association for Social Security, thus indicating that not only old-age but also unemployment insurance was part of their program. The announcement was made by Nicholas Kelley, the son of Florence Kelley who, during and after her years at Hull House, was involved in virtually every aspect of social reform. Slowly a few states, notably Wisconsin and New York, and a few firms, including Hart, Schaffner and Marx, tried to work out schemes for some sort of unemployment insurance, but these efforts were scattered and ineffectual.

Under the prod of worsening depression, however, social workers moved back into the fight for social security, led by private Jewish social-work agencies in New York. These groups had followed Al Smith into the Democratic party and were in a position to become important participants in the Roosevelt coalition. They had a friend in court in the person of Frances Perkins, long-time associate of Florence Kelley in the National Consumers' League.

On the advice of Miss Perkins, Governor Franklin D. Roosevelt of New York had proposed in 1930 that the several states establish a system of unemployment insurance. As President, Roosevelt felt the pressure of his associates, of Congress, and of the Townsend movement to put together unemployment and old-age insurance. The result was the Social Security Act of 1935, signed into law about three months after Jane Addams died. Had the Depression and F.D.R. not combined, social security would not have passed. Yet when F.D.R. needed social-security legislation, the concept was virtually at hand, and needed only to be polished and pushed through Congress. He gave it effect, but the program was the product of long years of discouraging work by the old-time progressives and their heirs. Yet even the Social Security

Act was hardly the deathblow to poverty for which Jane Addams had called in 1910. It contained no health insurance, and its benefits were sharply limited. It did nothing save give small incomes to its beneficiaries—hardly "raising life to its highest."

Thirty years later, a protégé of Franklin Roosevelt declared war on poverty. The war was far more than economic; it was devoted to bringing the poor—many of them second- or third-generation recipients of welfare checks—out of the wilderness of poverty and into the fabulous prosperity that the nation enjoyed.[28] The war on poverty proved to be more difficult than Lyndon Johnson had imagined, as did the war in Vietnam, and the war in Asia ultimately defeated the war in America. Yet the terms on which the war on poverty was waged were much more in the direction of Jane Addams' ideas than was the New Deal.

11

Community: Immigrant and Native American

If man's nature was in fact good, and if the goodness of that nature was distorted by a misconstructed social environment, what sort of environment did Jane Addams believe would be more in keeping with human nature? In part the answer was already implied in the criticisms she made of specific flaws in the society around her: there should be better schools, no child labor, a decent wage paid to all workers. and so on. However, this was not enough to fulfill man's nature, not enough to allow each life to be lived to its fullest potential. There also had to be room for man's naturally co-operative nature, his desire for common effort and common identity with other men, to assert itself. In short there had to be a society constructed on the basis of what Miss Addams called the "social ethic" and might also be called "community." Barriers between groups of men had to be broken down, not so that all groups might be the same, but so that a sense of the community of all mankind might be maintained. There was no barrier between man and man, she believed, which was not overwhelmed by their common humanity.

Yet probably no place in the United States seemed to have less sense of common humanity than Chicago. Recent immigrants were resented and in turn resented older inhabitants, and various immigrant groups resented each other. Class conflict made Chicago one of the most strike-prone cities in the nation. Jane Addams made it her task to try to lower these barriers and make at least a start toward a sense of community: "Whatever other services the settlement may have endeavored to perform for its community, there is no doubt that it has come to regard that of interpreting the foreign colonies to the rest of the city in the light of a professional obligation."[1]

Perhaps the best known, and certainly the most characteristic, of Miss Addams' attempts to interpret foreign colonies to the rest of the city was the Hull House Labor Museum. It was Miss Addams' personal creation, and it was based on a complex of emotions. One fall day in 1900 she was walking down Polk Street, bothered by her inability to communicate as fully as she wished with her Italian neighbors, and bothered more generally by the lack of understanding between European immigrants and native Americans, and between the immigrants and their own children. Looking up, she noticed an old Italian woman spinning thread with a distaff, a method more ancient even than the spinning wheel. The children and grandchildren of the old woman were probably working in nearby factories, some perhaps in textile establishments. Could there not be, she wondered, some way by which the children might see the grandmother demonstrate "the inherited resources of their daily occupation"? Was there not some way that native Americans could understand the long traditions and ancient practices behind their own industries?[2]

For Jane Addams, the next step was obvious: talk things over with John Dewey. Of the essence in Dewey's ideas about education was that education should start (though not end, as some later practitioners seemed to believe) with what was already important to the students, and gradually to reveal to them the connection between these familiar activities and the wider world. Thus "experience," to use one of Dewey's central words, would be reconstructed. The result would not only be education, in the sense of learning new knowledge, but also a heightened awareness of the place of one's familiar activities in the contemporary structure and in the historical development of society. Dewey and Jane Addams decided that these ideas could easily be translated from the laboratory school to a more informal educational institution. In order not to sound too bookish, Miss Addams called the institution the Hull House Labor Museum.

A month after her talk with Dewey, a room in the settlement had been fitted out for the Museum. Within a few blocks Miss Addams found four varieties of spinning with distaffs or other very simple devices, and three based on a spinning wheel. Women skilled in the use of these devices were invited to come to the settlement and demonstrate skills learned long ago in another country. So eager were the neighbors to participate that one Syrian woman had a particular kind of spinning wheel sent to Chicago from her homeland. The various types of spinning were arranged in order of their increasing complexity, more or less as they had developed historically. Soon the spinners were joined by weavers on five looms, the last run by electricity. The weavers were supplied with most of their thread by the spinners. Thus, each Saturday night, when the whole process was in operation, one could see the development of the entire process of textile production, from the raw wool through various methods of carding, spinning, and weaving. Pottery, bookbinding, and metalwork were added to the Labor Museum, but never were so elaborately developed or so popular as the textiles.

The Labor Museum was not simply for show once a week. Classes in the various crafts were held every afternoon and some mornings, and spinners and weavers came to work whenever they had the time or inclination. Immigrant women who had been out of place in their new industrialized surroundings now found their highly developed skills valued, and their products sold for good prices. Jane Addams conceived of the Museum as having a variety of important results, though the actuality was not quite so influential as she thought. Immigrant children were brought into a different relation with their parents. One Italian girl came every Saturday to cooking class at the same time as her mother went to the Labor Museum, but the young girl always entered the settlement by a different door. She was ashamed to be closely associated with a woman who wore a kerchief over her head and still carried with her the atmosphere of the Old Country. One evening the daughter saw her mother surrounded by admiring students from the School of Education at the University of Chicago, and concluded that her mother was the "best stick-spindle spinner in America," to which Miss Addams agreed that she probably was. From then on mother and daughter entered the settlement together through the front door.

The Museum, Jane Addams said, "often put the immigrants into the position of teachers, and we imagine that it affords them a pleasant change from the tutelage in which all Americans, including their own children, are so apt to hold them." Thus, she thought, the immigrants were brought closer not only to their children, but to native Americans.[3] Immigrants were once again given the opportunity to use long neglected skills, and their children and native Americans were shown the virtues of a way of life they had scorned—and yet all was preserved in the Museum like an Egyptian sarcophagus or an Indian tepee: honored but not incorporated into the present.

Even if the Labor Museum was but an imperfect realization of Jane Addams' overt objectives, the very statement of these objectives constituted an argument. Immigrant customs *could* make a contribution to the United States. Differing value systems *should* be acknowledged. The social structures of the immigrant communities *ought to be* understood. Americanization *ought not* to blot out all knowledge of or respect for the old traditions, heroes, and customs.

Hull House, though not Miss Addams so directly, also concerned itself with the more practical problems of the day-to-day life of recent immigrants, through the Immigrants Protective League. Grace Abbott was the inspiration for the League, which was founded in 1908. After she became head of the Children's Bureau, the leadership passed largely to Jessie Binnford. Growing directly out of the problems that flowed to the doors of Hull House every day, the I.P.L. was formed with six major objectives: to secure a Federal Bureau of Immigration; to visit new arrivals, especially girls; to prevent exploitation of new arrivals by private employment agencies; to learn of and deal with exploitation by steamship agents, cabmen, expressmen, and banks; to co-operate with those engaged in prevention of the "white slave" traffic; and to interpret foreigners' problems to the community.

To carry out these aims, the League arranged to regularly receive lists of unattached girls arriving at Ellis Island and destined for Chicago. During the early years the League tried to meet each of these girls on arrival, guide her to a respectable boardinghouse, and secure her a job. The I.P.L. was successful in securing regulatory legislation relating to employment agencies, though unscrupulous agencies continued to function. Relatively little was done by the I.P.L. itself to interpret foreign communities to the city or nation, and by far the greatest amount of time of the workers in the I.P.L. was spent in dealing with hundreds of individual problems. The League would search for the father of a family in Europe now destitute because of his departure; recent arrivals would be helped to fill out forms or affidavits necessary for applications for a job or for citizenship; a deserted wife would be directed to welfare organizations, not always Hull House. Eventually the League did what can only be described as casework.[4]

These activities were mostly what Miss Addams would have called "negative," in the sense that they merely patched up a tattered situation. Some were "preventive," such as the laws against exploitation by employment agencies, but none were truly "positive" in the sense of "increasing the positive value of life." Miss Addams suported the I.P.L. and Grace Abbott, for negative and preventive measures were important, but these activities never engaged her attention as much as the Labor Museum.

Interpreting foreign communities to native Americans did engage her attention, particularly in times of crisis. The "Averbuch case" in 1908 was such a crisis. On the evening of March 1, 1908, police commissioner George Shippy heard his maid admit a caller. Going downstairs to see whom it might be, he saw approaching him a young man, obviously poor and unkempt, who said something to him. Convinced that the young man was an anarchist there to assassinate him, the chief drew his gun, shot his caller twice, and then, as he turned to flee, shot him twice again. Young Averbuch fell dead in the hallway. Immediately the police put out a dragnet for all anarchists; the young man's sister Olga was taken into custody together with printed material of "anarchist tendency" and some of the religious objects of the orthodox Jew.

At once the battle lines were drawn. At first the dead man's identity was uncertain. The Italians feared he might be of their nationality, the Russian Jews that he might be of theirs. When his identity with the latter was established the Russian Jews rushed to Hull House. Memories of Old World pogroms were fresh in their minds, and the police dragnet and sensational newspaper reports did nothing to quiet their fears. DRIVE ANARCHY FROM CHICAGO—POLICE SLOGAN read one newspaper headline. The subhead added: *Investigation of Hull House Settlement Institution where Meetings of Revolutionaries are Held and Sedi-*

tionary Theories are Taught to be Examined. While some newspapers counseled against panic, the atmosphere in the city reminded older citizens of Haymarket. Jane Addams, of course, counseled calmness, but she went much further. She acted as a central collection point for relief funds for Olga Averbuch and as a communications link between the Russian Jews and the Chicago government; she pressed for a full investigation of the shooting itself; she persuaded Harold Ickes to act as legal advisor to the Russians.

The more radical members of the Russian colony planned a parade of protest against the police to take place as Averbuch was being reburied in accordance with the requirements of his religion. Miss Addams and Graham Taylor feared that such a parade might set off further violence, and was certain to inflame rather than calm public feeling. The only way to avoid the parade was to keep the time of the reburial secret. This was difficut, however, because a reburial required certificates and permissions from various offices of the city government, the actions of which were public knowledge. The newspapers and the radicals stationed agents to watch the city bureaus and inform their fellows whenever the certificates should be issued. The settlement people knew they had to obtain the certificates quickly and quietly, and rebury Averbuch before the noon editions of the newspapers could let the city know the reburial was taking place and before the young radicals could assemble their fellows. The three necessary papers were, with difficulty, obtained secretly through the co-operation of city officials. The body was disinterred, a noted pathologist performed an autopsy, and the body was quietly reburied with appropriate Jewish rites. The deed was completed before the city was aware anything was happening, and a demonstration was avoided. Nothing could be done to bring the young man back to life, and there was no investigation of Chief Shippy's action in killing Averbuch. The best Jane Addams and Harold Ickes could do for his distraught sister was to help her do what she wanted to do, which was to return to Russia.[5]

In later years, Miss Addams sometimes bent to public opinion, sometimes choosing the road of caution as against risk. In this case, however, she stood against the tide of opinion and endured, with seeming calm, the consequent insults.

Two months after the shooting, with the case still under investigation and feeling still high, Miss Addams explained her position in a vigorously written article in *Charities.*

It is deeply to be regretted that instead of using this opportunity to present to the Russian Jewish colony the sharp contrast between the two forms of government, the republican government right on its own ground and in the hands of its friends should have fallen into the Russian method of dealing with a similar incident, and that because the community was in apparently a state of panic it should have connived at and apparently approved of these very drastic methods on the part of the police.

Since the event of the membership in all the radical societies in the Russian Jewish colony, irrespective of names and creeds, has increased with incredible rapidity.

She insisted that there was no evidence that Averbuch had any intention of killing Shippy, that there was no evidence to connect Averbuch with the anarchists, and further, no evidence that anarchists as a group advocated killing public officials or anyone else. She interlarded her points with condemnations of murder, treason, and revolution; but she insisted that the best, indeed the only way to deal with crime was through due process and fair trial, protection of freedom and an open society. Throughout the article she tried to make clear to the people of Chicago how the police action and public panic appeared to the Russian Jewish colony, just as, in her actions, she tried to calm the Russian Jews and control their more violent reactions.[6]

As a result many of the Russian Jewish community thought she had become a tool of the bourgeoisie, while the Chicago newspapers denounced her as a dangerous radical. She was bombarded with letters of condemnation. "When any one says a word to comfort, aid, abet, encourage or anything similar for anarchy, I admit prejudice and all other radical and one sided things," wrote one correspondent. "There is no room in this country for this sort of truck."[7]

Though her success may have been only partial, her aim was to convince the immigrants that the American system could produce justice, and to convince the wider city that immigrants should not be considered a dangerous alien group. In fact, she insisted, immigrants were *people.*

Polk and Halsted was certainly the place this argument had

to be made, for if there was a melting pot in America Hull House was in the middle of it. *Hull House Maps and Papers* showed that within a few blocks of the settlement lived Italians, Russians (many of them Jews), Poles, Bohemians, Swiss, French, French Canadians, Irish, Chinese, Dutch, Germans, Scandinavians, and a few Greeks and Arabs, not to mention Englishmen, some of whom were also recent arrivals.

Jane Addams had chosen the neighborhood precisely because it contained a wide variety of immigrants. Just as her conception of the unity of human society impelled her to establish communication across class lines, she was impelled to break down barriers between people of different national backgrounds. The poor were people, children were people, women were people, even Negroes were people—and so were recent arrivals. Breaking down barriers for her did not mean homogenizing the various national cultures; it meant teaching native Americans to respect the immigrants.

Jane Addams' general views on children have gradually come to be widely accepted. With respect to immigration she did not represent what came to be the dominant view. Her broadly tolerant attitude toward differing origins and mores contrasted sharply with a rising nativism in the United States resulting, in 1921, in immigration laws based not only on a desire to restrict the number of people entering the country, but on racist prejudices as well. In clinging to the idea of unrestricted immigration, she was holding on to an older American ideal which most of her countrymen were ready, nay eager to abandon. She still saw America as the haven for the politically repressed and economically exploited of the world. Yet in a strange way this holding to older ideals also put Jane Addams ahead of her time. Now, over thirty years after her death, the element of racism has finally been eliminated from American immigration laws.

Hull House was, in fact, founded at just that time when anti-foreign sentiments were growing rapidly in several directions, having attained violent expression in the Haymarket affair in May of 1886. New anti-foreign societies were formed and old ones revived; Americans of old stock, led by Henry Cabot Lodge, mourned the passing of "the great Anglo-Saxon race"; economists announced that the immigrant stream was an economic and social liability while eugenicists trembled at its biological implications; organized labor feared that the newcomers would, as in fact they did, have a depressing effect on wages.[8]

In the 1890's, organized charity was concerned with immigration only in a very narrow sphere: how the newcomers affected charitable institutions. The National Conference on Charities and Correction was worried by too many poor new citizens, but there was no trace of racism in this worry—there was no greater worry about Italian paupers than German or English ones. On the other hand, the National Conference paid no attention at all to what happened to the immigrant as he confronted American life. Americanization was simply not an issue. Presumably the assumption was that all newcomers were quickly and easily absorbed into American culture.[9]

In the decade between 1899 and 1909, organized charity paid no official attention to immigrants, and when the subject reappeared it was in an entirely new guise. In the ten years since the Conference had considered the issue, over eight and a half million immigrants had entered the country; and increasingly the immigrant stream was dominated by the "new" immigrant. No longer was there a "Committee on Immigration and Internal Migration," but rather a "Committee on Immigrants." Of thirteen papers, only one was concerned with the process of immigration; all the others were devoted to the immigrant in confrontation with American society. Titles included "The Immigrant and the Public Health," "The Foreigner Before Our Courts," "Night Schools," and "Child Life on the Streets." The articles emphasized the problems met by immigrants and the discrimination recent arrivals experienced. Only one was racist. In general, the attitude was that immigration was an asset to the nation, and that the Americanization of the immigrant should be made as painless and rapid as possible. There seemed to be no doubt in anyone's mind that immigrants should adapt to American ways, and no suggestion that immigrant mores, precisely because they were not American, might enrich American society. Over-all, however, was an undeniable sympathy with the lot of the recent arrival and a desire to mitigate its harsher aspects.[10] The chairman of the Committee, in a few introductory remarks, pointed out that in these decades of enormous immigration the nation had paid virtually no attention to the immigrant. The chairman was Jane Addams of Hull House.

Almost another decade was to pass before this sort of concern again stirred the charity establishment. In 1912 the Committee again became the Committee on Immigration, and was sharply split as to whether a literacy test should be required for entrance into the United States. In 1918 the Committee concerned itself with "Americanization." The chairman, Charles C. Cooper of Kingsley House, Pittsburgh, again and again asserted his own loyalty to the war effort and stated that he had not one drop of Austrian or German blood; but he insisted that immigrants were being unfairly discriminated against, and that Americanization often ruined people. Again, it was a settlement resident who argued for the immigrant.

After the war the forces of racism and restriction gathered strength in the United States to rush toward the national origins quota system of the 1921 law. "One-hundred-percent Americanism," which had reached unprecedented heights of foolishness during the war, could not be cut off merely by signing an armistice. If immigrants did not melt in the pot, most Americans seemed to think, then they should be shipped back where they came from. Yet official charity sounded a protesting countercurrent to nativism and xenophobia. Now the Committee on Immigration had become the Committee on the Uniting of Native and Foreign Born in America, and its chairman in 1919 explicitly rejected the simile of the melting pot as too fraught with the idea of homogenization. Instead he proposed the image of the loom, in which different strands of warp and woof could create a rich complexity of design.[11]

At the 1922 Conference of Social Work, it was Edith Abbott who protested vehemently against the national origins system, castigating the Immigration Service for becoming a prosecuting service and pleading that if immigrant numbers must be decreased, a more just standard be discovered than national origin. But by 1925 charity workers had lost the battle against the quota system and, though continuing their objections, concentrated once again on making the lot of those who did immigrate somewhat easier.

Thus it was the charity workers, particularly those who had

some connection with settlement houses, who fought the long, discouraging, and ultimately losing battle against racist nonsense in American immigration laws, and who tried to deal with new arrivals with a respect for them as individuals and for their culture. It was this group for which Jane Addams provided much of the ideology and for which she was a continuing spokesman.

In making her argument, Miss Addams had the advantage of springing from the genteel, Anglo-Saxon civilization which provided the basis for the national origins ideology. Her experience at Hull House and her openness to learning from that experience caused her to diverge from the tradition. Had her own views grown from sources thought at the time to be radical she could have been dismissed as a crank. As it was, she spoke the language of those she hoped to convince. Her failure to convince them is one testimony to the strength of xenophobia during the war and postwar years.

The striking fact about Miss Addams' position is not that she seemed at times to retain vestiges of the genteel tradition, but that she was able to move as far as she did toward recognition of the values of immigrant culture. In a sense this too was prejudice of a sort, at least to begin with. An occasional course at Rockford might emphasize the Americanness of American literature, but the truly great books were written by Englishmen and Germans. This respect for the venerable cultures of the Old World was reinforced by her European trips. Later, when she entered an Italian section of Chicago, her first reaction was that it was almost like Italy. Throughout her life she had a strong respect for things German, a respect continually revived by that nation's advanced social legislation. Thus, behind each Italian she saw the shadow of Mazzini, the Medici, or the dome of St. Peter's; behind each German, the University of Berlin or a social-insurance law.

This undercurrent of respect for Europeans simply because they were European ran parallel to a contradictory pride in things American. Her chauvinism was a back-eddy in her thought, not its main tendency—yet it was there. She spoke of Southern Italians as "primitive," and while this was sometimes a term of approbation, in the sense that they were close to natural truths, it frequently meant simply that they were uneducated and dirty. American workmen in the stockyards of 1904 "represented a distinctly superior standard of life and thought" in relation to the Slovaks, Poles and Lithuanians.[12] She complimented these superior creatures for their solidarity with the recent immigrants, but she was certain who was superior and who was inferior. Her strongest links with a genteel past were expressed in a romanticism about immigrants which ran parallel to her romanticism about the poor. One cannot say that this tendency declined over the years to be replaced by a more empirical, or realistic, or complex view, for her idea of immigrants as more virtuous, wiser, closer to truth recurs throughout her life. This current was soon joined by others which eventually became stronger than romanticism; but the romanticism never disappeared.

In fact what Jane Addams expected from immigrants, like what she expected from children, was nothing other than salvation. "Our final help and healing," she said in a phrase reminiscent of the gentle tones of an Easter sermon, would come "from those who have been driven by economic pressure or governmental oppression out of a score of nations." These people "worship goodness for its own sake," they "serve God for nought."[13] No doubt by 1906 the Christian terminology had social rather than spiritual denotation. Salvation would be expressed "in public baths and gymnasiums, parks and libraries," and yet more important than these buildings was the spiritual reawakening of which they would be the expression. In any case, the demand and the models for these expressions of salvation would spring from immigrant communities.

Not only domestic reform but also international comity could grow out of immigrant communities. The newer ideals of peace could grow where, in these communities, the "synthesis of the varying nations should be made first at points of the greatest congestion." "It is not," Miss Addams admitted, "that they are shouting for peace—on the contrary, if they shout at all, they will continue to shout for war—but that they are really attaining cosmopolitan relations through daily experience."[14] On a more practical level, Miss Addams saw much in immigrant customs which might be of value to their new homeland, except for America's blindness to "the possibility of using these great reservoirs of human ability and motive power." For instance, she argued that the American system of farming isolated quarter sections might not be as good as the Italian system of having villages of several families, surrounded by fields. Italian mutual benefit societies provided a model of collective responsibility which the nation as a whole might emulate. Or perhaps the experiment in communal ownership of the Doukhobors could be useful to other groups.[15]

Obviously a view of immigrants as saviors of a materialistic America shows understanding of neither the immigrants nor their new nation, but it does reveal the ideals of Jane Addams, who imputed her values to the "simple" people around her—much as a certain type of white American in the mid-twentieth century imputes superior virtue to black Americans simply because they have been oppressed. Yet, just as the latter view can open a white man's circle of experience to include contact with black people and thereby teach him to overcome his stereotypes, so Miss Addams' romanticized perception enabled her to learn about immigrant communities.

Jane Addams made Hull House a place where groups of people from the same country could gather together to celebrate the old holidays, put on traditional costumes, sing the traditional songs, and reminisce about days gone by. Thus, she fought against the tendency of immigrants to "lose the amenities of European life without sharing those of America."[16] It was right that new arrivals should develop a patriotism toward their new land, but not to the point that it blotted out fond memories of Garibaldi, or the battle for Greek independence from Turkey. Always alert to generational conflict, she was distressed at the frequency with which second-generation immigrants scorned the ways of their parents, and she praised those young people who honored Old World customs.

She explicitly and implicitly favored a pluralistic society in which assimilation did not mean an elimination of differences. Indeed, her plea for the Doukhobors and the Italian landholding system implied a vision of America far less uniform than has ever occurred. Property could be held in common in one community, individually in another, and by some intermediate arrangement in a third. While the restrictionists argued that certain groups should be excluded from the nation because they were unassimilable, Miss Addams thought that a degree of nonassimilation was good.

This recognition of the value of pluralism was the first step toward an understanding of the intellectual and social structure in immigrant communities. From the death of the foundling and the Italian women's objection to having it buried at public expense, she learned something of Italian views on childhood and death. She understood the traditional relationship between an Italian worker and his *padrone*. She understood and tolerated the position of the saloon in the world of her immigrant neighbors, where a more narrow-minded reformer might simply have condemned both the institution and its customers. In speech after speech, all over the country, she argued that immigrant traditions and values could enrich American culture, and should neither be scorned nor assimilated out of existence.

To what extent she succeeded in interpreting the immigrant community to the wider public it is difficult to say. Certainly in times of xenophobic excitement Hull House was condemned as a hotbed of foreign radicalism, and Jane Addams was considered to be far too friendly with anarchists. And yet by about 1910, many of her basic ideas began to gain greater general acceptance. In that year popular magazines printed articles explicitly rejecting the simile of the melting pot and proposing instead a mixing bowl, in which the characteristics of each nation might be preserved. "Our problem," said one author, "is to make our immigrants co-operating members of our civilization, and we cannot do this by repressing the peculiar social impulses each group brings with it."[17] Had war not intervened to give the superpatriots and exclusionists of all varieties both fervor and popularity, the history of American immigration legislation would probably have been very different.

But the war came. The drive for one-hundred-percent Americanism, the racism of Madison Grant, and the fear of labor surplus by the A. F. L. had the opportunity to combine and pass the national origins quota act of 1921, and its further racist modification in 1924. By 1921 Jane Addams was heavily involved with her efforts to bring about a modification of the terms of the Versailles Settlement, to gain American participation in the League of Nations and to make the Women's International League for Peace and Freedom an influential force. Along with many other Americans, she did not become as excited about the 1921 law as she would have in less hectic times. She had always opposed immigration restriction of any sort, including a literacy test. Restriction betrayed the mission of the United

States to act as a haven for the politically and economically oppressed and showed an inadequate appreciation of the resources of both the immigrants and their new country. At the height of postwar xenophobia, she urged social workers to redouble their efforts at persuading native Americans that immigrants "are surprisingly like the rest of us" and that unrest in immigrant communities stemmed from injustices done them, not from any radical desire to overthrow society.[18] She made this plea almost exactly three months after A. Mitchell Palmer and J. Edgar Hoover organized the mass arrests of the citizens and aliens, communists and noncommunists known as the Palmer Raids, and in her gentle way she clearly criticized the Department of Justice. As she spoke, however, congratulatory editorials and letters were pouring in to Palmer and Hoover, and there was no stopping arrests, deportations, and increasingly harsh antiforeign legislation.[19]

Not until five years after the 1924 act did Jane Addams sum up her views on national attitudes toward immigrants. When she did so, she put her criticism in the broadest possible terms, attacking not simply the details of the law but also the attitudes implied by it. Anti-immigrant feeling was part "of our exaggerated acceptance of standardization. Every one wants to be like his neighbors, which is doubtless an amiable quality, but leading to one of the chief dangers of democracy—the tyranny of the herd mind." This, she supposed, was a result "of the intolerance for differing opinion during the war and after."[20]

Jane Addams insisted that immigrants were not a source of radicalism or crimes of violence, but that "the immigrant is continually blamed for conditions for which the community is responsible." She denied that one could blame immigration for unemployment, for "we have no national system of labor exchange which might show how much of the apparent unemployment is maladjustment of the supply to the demand and how much is oversupply." In fact she pointed out, immigrants were not only job-seekers; they were also consumers and therefore job-creators. More specifically, she objected to the prejudices in the law against Japanese, Latins, and Slavs, and to the wave of illegal and questionable arrests and deportations which antiforeign feeling inspired. Families were broken up; broken families could not be re-united; men and women were deported from the United

States to European ports and there unceremoniously stranded; whole national and linguistic groups were treated as undesirables.

She would have been willing to approve of a temporary cessation of all immigration for a few years to give "immigrant groups already here a breathing space," but the new law was an "iron bound quarantine against newcomers" indicating we were "so afraid of them that we applaud the immigration officers and the naturalization agents for every device which makes more difficult the entry of immigrants and their procurement of citizenship papers."

While swimming against the stream of popular opinion and criticizing the attitudes of her contemporaries, Jane Addams clung to the hope that further research would bring understanding. She noted studies of "The Polish Peasant in Europe and America" and "The Race Relations Study of the Pacific Coast" and thought she might "venture to hope for wisdom at last in our national immigration policy."[21] These words were written about a half-dozen years before Miss Addams' death, when she was nearly seventy years old. Thus in 1929 she was holding fast to a vision of America formed in the 1880's and the 1890's and violently rejected by most Americans in the postwar years.

And yet by the time the Second World War had run its course, and after a Red Scare longer if not quite so virulent as the first, Americans seemed to have recaptured at least a portion of her vision. Almost exactly thirty years after her death the discriminatory aspects of the quota law were eliminated in the Immigration Act of 1965, signed with much ceremony on Bedloes Island. Then again, perhaps the new law does not indicate a new tolerance for diversity in the nation. Perhaps it was simply the result of a political accident, and passed in a fit of absence of mind.

12

Community: Labor and Management

IN most instances when Jane Addams had anything to do with class conflict—specifically disputes between labor and management—she sided with labor. Thus it might appear that she was engaged in the war between labor and capital, and that she favored the victory of labor. This, however, would be a misreading of her position. She favored labor organizing only as a temporary tactic in long-range strategy the aim of which was a society in which there would be no class struggle, nor even any consciousness of economic classes. In the misarranged society around her it might be necessary to support labor in particular conflicts, but a far more important activity was the re-ordering of the society so as to eliminate the conflicts. This re-ordering, she believed, would have to be accomplished through a broad and rapid expansion of the role of the federal government, which she believed represented American society acting as a unit.

Yet to begin with she did favor labor unions. "At Hull House," Alice Hamilton said, "one got into the labor movement as a matter of course, without realizing how or when."[1] It was obvious to anyone living in a working-class neighborhood of Chicago that one way to diminish misery was to raise wages, decrease hours, and improve conditions. As a matter of course, then, one supported the aims of organized labor. On a day-to-day basis Miss Addams nearly always was on the side of the strikers in an industrial dispute and was often of major practical help to the Chicago unions. In her public statements she usually supported the details of union positions. Neither those in the labor movement nor those in opposition to it noticed that essentially her views on the nature of the relationship between social classes were incompatible with that of organized labor.

Miss Addams spoke frequently in favor of unionization and was held in high regard by union leaders. Samuel Gompers trusted her, and she was often a speaker or participant at union meetings, picnics, and parades. Many years before she was on the school board, she favored unionization of teachers and hoped the union would join the American Federation of Labor. The thought of a teachers' strike did not alarm her—as a matter of fact, she thought it might be useful. When John Mitchell of the United Mine Workers was in town and had lunch with Chicago's labor leaders, it was natural that Jane Addams be invited. When an occasional dispute went to arbitration, both sides trusted a board of arbitration more if Jane Addams were a member. Hull House was always available for union meetings or speeches for union causes.[2]

At least as important as repeated speeches in behalf of unions in general was the support which Jane Addams and Hull House provided for unions and their leaders in times of stress and discouragement. Mary Kenny, one of the key figures in the formation of the Women's Trade Union League, after a brief period of suspicion of Jane Addams' upper-class origins, lived at Hull House, and it was in the settlement that the sewing trades were organized for the first time in the city. "The needle has ever been the refuge of the unskilled worker," Jane Addams noted, and as a result the sewing trades were overcrowded with poverty-stricken women, and some men, each trying to undercut the others. The result was a wage on which no one could support a family and barely enough to support a single penurious life. After a disastrous failure of a strike in 1891, the Women Dressmakers were organized at Hull House, and a year later the Cloakmakers. When Mary Kenny moved away from Chicago she left behind four viable unions, and Miss Addams as a member of the executive committee of the Women's Trade Union League.[3]

Jane Addams was helpful in many strikes: the terrible stockyards strike of 1904; strikes among the building trades; a strike of waitresses in downtown restaurants. In this last, Ellen Starr was arrested for inciting disorderly picketing, though with Harold Ickes' help she was acquitted.[4] Jane Addams' most important intervention, however, was in the strike of garment workers against Hart, Schaffner and Marx in 1910.

Although the strike of clothing workers, involving more workers than any dispute in Chicago since the Pullman strike, began in the Hart, Schaffner and Marx factory, the three partners were by no means antilabor. In fact all three were philanthropists of sorts, all three had contributed generously to Hull House, and Schaffner was, at the very moment the strike began, in the process of organizing evening education for workers. The strike itself was more a disorganized walkout than a planned work stoppage, for the only union among male clothing workers was the United Garment Workers of America with its chief strength in New York and only about two thousand members in Chicago, all skilled. In September, 1910, when a few workers walked off the job in protest against a reduction in piecework rates, most of the other workers treated the matter as an isolated incident. Soon, however, some cutters walked out in sympathy—and by October most of the eight thousand workers at the Hart, Schaffner and Marx plant, plus perhaps ten thousand from other Chicago factories, were on strike. The secretary of the U.G.W.A. in New York was clearly afraid to get involved in such an uncontrollable situation, but eventually, after a trip to Chicago, called for a strike of all clothing workers in the city. Within a few days the strikers' numbers grew to forty thousand. The strikers, typically more militant than the U.G.W.A. leadership, soon threw up new leaders who were more representative of rank-and-file views—most importantly, Sidney Hillman.[5]

Jane Addams first entered the picture purely on the basis of organizing relief for needy workers. With Ellen Starr she organized a strike fund, then a milk fund to keep babies alive. Relief work brought her into contact with Hillman, and the two found that their ideas had much in common. Although more militant than U.G.W.A. leaders, Hillman was a moderate among the Chicago strikers. Ultimately, it was he who persuaded the workers to accept an agreement which did not include the closed shop. Like Miss Addams, Hillman believed that industrial warfare involved great waste, and that better ways to solve labor-management disputes could be worked out. Thus Miss Addams found herself in a uniquely privileged position of being trusted and liked by both the factory owners who had contributed to Hull

House and by one of the new young leaders among the workers. By December of 1910 she had become something of a channel of communication between the two sides.

Joseph Schaffner was the founder of the firm, but had dealt almost entirely with the financial side, leaving labor problems to his partners. At first he held to his principle of not interfering with labor, but in December of 1910, as Chicago newspapers, the city council, and finally even the state legislature began investigations, he decided to step in himself. He asked Earl Dean Howard, a professor of economics at Northwestern University, to investigate conditions, and almost the first thing Howard did was speak to Jane Addams. She shocked him by saying that what was happening in Chicago was no ordinary strike, but a spontaneous, leaderless revolution based on long-standing hatreds and injustices. Hearing this report, Schaffner offered terms of settlement slightly more generous than previous offers, and after a stormy meeting Hillman persuaded the Hart, Schaffner and Marx workers to accept it. Unfortunately the other firms were not so generous, and the workers had to accept lesser settlements.

The Hart, Schaffner and Marx settlement meant neither victory nor defeat for either side. The most important part of the agreement was an arbitration board to settle grievances before they reached the point of boiling resentment. The purpose, largely successful, was to avoid both strikes and the bitterness which created them.[6]

This type of settlement was precisely in line with Jane Addams' views on the proper relationships between economic classes. She was often accused of being prolabor, too radical, or too socialistic, particularly by the Chicago *Chronicle*. In one of her rare moments of public pique, Miss Addams snapped at one *Chronicle* reporter after such an attack, "We have no apologies to make to any one. We pay our own way and are under obligations to nobody and are responsible to nobody." The *Chronicle* need not have worried, for beneath her support of union organization, of strikes, and of immediate union goals lay a vision of society in basic conflict not only with the socialists, but even with Samuel Gompers.[7]

For Jane Addams was far from being a militant trade unionist, far from devoted to the bread-and-butter issues of hours, wages, and working conditions. On the contrary, in her first grappling with the labor question she was a Christian humanitarian. Later the specifically Christian terminology dropped out, but the attitudes remained. Mary Kenny, finally, was correct in her first suspicions: Miss Addams did not understand, or if she understood she did not approve of, what the union movement was about. When Samuel Gompers was asked what he wanted, he gave the classic response: "More, more, more, now!" Jane Addams acknowledged that workers needed more and should have it. "The labor movement is bound," she said, "to work for shorter hours and increased wages." But a more important way of putting the question was, for her, "Are you content that Christianity shall have no place in trade?" Like many Christians, she meant Christianity not as a theology, but as synonymous with the golden rule.[8]

Her support for the trade-union movement and her criticism of it were both based on a refusal to treat class conflict as a normal part of the social system. Trade unions often softened class consciousness and class conflict. They provided, she felt sure, that sense of brotherhood among workers which could be the beginning of a sense of a wider brotherhood. They gained human dignity for their members by allowing them to escape dependence on their employer. They provided a mechanism whereby the fruits of industrial change could be spread widely through society. In 1894 she felt that the labor movement was in danger of losing sight of these broad ethical goals, the origins of the social ethic, in a quest for victory in a class war. This class war was "negative," she felt, and revealed the "present undeveloped condition" of the labor movement. Some few labor unions, it was true, kept higher goals in mind, but most were locked into that "primitive" state of class warfare.

In a similar way, writing just after the Pullman strike, she sympathized almost entirely with the demands of the workers: lower rents, higher wages, the opportunity to bargain collectively. She was wholly out of sympathy with George Pullman's "There is nothing to arbitrate." She compared Pullman to King Lear, kind only as a despot, and the workers to Cordelia, basically right but inadequately aware of kindness received. Yet in doing so she pictured the workers in a way they would certainly have rejected. They were not children, owing gratitude to their employer for decent housing—which returned 4 per cent on costs. They would not, as Jane Addams thought they should, include in their vision of a just society benevolent co-operation with

George Pullman. She might have thought their union was the beginning of a new co-operative commonwealth, but they wanted more money and more self-determination. In this George Pullman had no place, for he already had too much of both. In asking the workers to be more mature, she was condescending.[9]

In fact she argued that the unions should not concentrate too much on the "fleshpots" or the "sordid" aspects of unionism, by which she presumably meant money, and thereby develop a "group morality" by which they would have loyalty to their own group as against loyalty to the larger society. In 1904, she argued, as she had ten years earlier, that strikes and class warfare were indicative of a barbaric sort of primitivism still extant in the labor movement and proposed some method of arbitration.[10]

These views were in sharp opposition to the president of the A.F. of L., who regarded arbitration as a dirty word meaning surrender, and who thought labor had to rely on its own economic power. Nor was Miss Addams a good prophet in this case. In hoping for a co-operative society free of class consciousness, she wanted to eliminate social conflict. It was not part of her vision that conflict could be institutionalized and regularized; she could not conceive of union leaders, with the power of a mass of workers behind them, sitting across a table from management, with the power of ownership behind them, and the two sides bargaining as equals, but equals in a conflict.

To her it was deplorable that unions had to be the ones working for shorter hours, decent pay, healthy conditions, prevention of child labor. These things were the responsibility of all society.[11] So in a sense she became more radical than the trade unionists. When Gompers said he wanted "more," he may have been rude, but he was not radical, for what he clearly meant was "more of the same." Miss Addams argued, in the portion of *Democracy and Social Ethics* devoted to labor, a more startling proposition. She proposed that corporations should no longer be regarded as private property, that they were in fact public institutions subject to public control, and that in this control the employees ought to have a major share. Had a bearded radical on a street corner argued for this sort of end to the privateness of corporations, the idea would not have been out of place.

To be so concerned with eliminating class conflict was not, of course, to deny its existence. Miss Addams was acutely aware of the importance of social class and economic forces in historical development. She pointed out that the most brutal of criminal punishments were always meted out "for crimes which a so-called lower class has committed against its superior." In 1780, she noted, a Frenchman was executed for stealing some linen, "not because of the value of the linen but because he had dared to touch the property of the class above his own." More generally, "The king attempted to control the growing power of the barons as they wrested one privilege after another from him. . . . The barons later successfully established themselves in power only to be encroached upon by the growing strength and capital of the merchant class. These are now, in turn, calling upon the troops and militia for aid, as they are shorn of a pittance here and there by the rising power of the proletariat."[12] Here was gentle Jane Addams speaking the language of Karl Marx, probably as taught to her by Florence Kelley.

American society, too, Jane Addams thought, was shaped by class considerations. The makers of the Constitution took their model from English law, which was concerned "more with guarding of prerogative and with the rights of property than with the spontaneous life of the people."[13] The result was a government based on coercion by an elite, covered over with a thin layer of apparent democracy. Miss Addams wanted to change all that. If history was the story of class war, she wanted no return to a past stage of the struggle. King versus baron, baron versus merchant, merchant versus proletariat: all were equally detestable. On the contrary, her whole aim was to end the continual struggle, to establish a co-operative society, a peaceable kingdom, in which the factory owner would lie down with the worker. She wanted, in a word, to transcend history.

Businessmen at the turn of the century also spoke much of a classless society, and it is important not to confuse their view with hers. When manufacturers and owners testified before the National Industrial Commission in 1900 they insisted that *their* workers were free of class antagonism, that *they* dealt with the workers on a basis of mutual respect, and that it was the "walking delegates," as union organizers were called, who disturbed this relationship. To this kind of an employer, and George Pullman was certainly one of them, a strike was not only an economic threat but more importantly a threat to his self-image as a kind, humane, and understanding manager of men. When such businessmen insisted, as they did, that the United States was a classless society, they were really crying out against a threat to their self-image. Jane Addams, on the other hand, no matter how much she may have disagreed with Samuel Gompers, had no illusions about what American society was like in 1900. She knew that a class war was going on; she knew it had always gone on; and she knew which side she favored.

She knew pretty clearly too with what she wanted to replace it. "I suppose I am sort of a socialist," she once said, "because I believe in a good deal of collectivism."[14] But her rejection of a victorious proletariat as a goal kept her out of the socialist ranks. Although she told Sidney Hillman that she admired men who worked for goals that were "immediately useful and practically attainable," she was herself a Utopian, albeit a practical Utopian. She had a flash of enthusiasm for Tolstoy, who renounced wealth and position to work in the soil like a peasant—though she rejected this alternative as too interested in individual rather than social salvation. She admired the co-operative communitarian life of the Doukhobors, and tried to help them settle in the United States. Had there been a Brook Farm available, she would have sympathized. She would not have joined, however, because her aim was far more ambitious: to make the nation, and then the world, into one co-operative Utopian community. She was a Utopian, but not a come-outer. She wanted not to establish a city upon a hill, but to bring the Kingdom down from the hill to all humanity.

Although this theme is the common thread which runs through all her writing, speeches, and testimony before congressional committees, the most explicit statement occurs in *Democracy and Social Ethics,* published in 1902 but given as a course of lectures in the 1890's before Hull House was a decade old. Her argument was basically an ethical one, clearly Christian in origin though cast entirely in secular terms. Over the centuries human beings have developed codes of individual morality and internalized them. After so many generations, these rules are easy to follow. "It is as easy for most of us to keep from stealing our dinners as it is to digest them, and there is quite as much voluntary morality in one process as in the other." Similarly, a strong sense of family obligation is deeply ingrained in most people.

Perhaps kindness, consideration, and generosity extend to a relatively small circle of friends. This sort of morality was both too easy to be virtuous and increasingly inadequate for the industrial situation. "To attain individual morality in an age demanding social morality . . . is utterly to fail to apprehend the situation." The new age demanded a new ethical sense: a social ethic. It was now necessary to apply the dictum that all men are brothers to daily situations. To do so, one must first become dissatisfied about "the dreary round of uninteresting work, the pleasures narrowed down to those of appetite, the declining consciousness of brain power, and the lack of mental food" which was the lot of increasing numbers of people. This concern had to transcend class lines. Indeed the purpose of founding Hull House was to re-establish communication and moral commitment across barriers of economic class. Jane Addams believed that there was no barrier between human beings that their common humanity did not transcend.[15]

To make a plea for Isaiah's heaven was, in the 1890's, nothing more nor less than the Social Gospel. One minister suggested, only half facetiously, that Miss Addams should be ordained. She rejected the idea, but did so with more seriousness than she did, for example, the suggestion that she run for mayor of Chicago.[16] Like Miss Addams, the ministers of the social gospel rejected any distinction between sacred and secular ethics, asserting that individual salvation was not enough, that Christian ethics now demanded social salvation. No major misinterpretation would be involved in calling Jane Addams a part of the social gospel, though at the more secular end of the movement. The social gospel did not necessarily lead to governmental action, however. Here Miss Addams was influenced, apart from the practical necessities as she saw them, by German historical economics, through her friendship with Richard T. Ely. Ely was one of a handful of American economists who received their graduate training in Germany in the 1870's and 1880's just as that country was developing a theoretical challenge to the dogmas of nineteenth-century British laissez faire. Laissez faire was fine for continued British economic dominance, but Germany needed a doctrine to justify a program of industrial development based on tariffs, subsidies, and other types of state intervention. The result was the assertion that free trade, untrammeled competition, and the "iron law of wages" were not natural laws, but reflections of particular historical circumstances. Other circumstances would produce different "laws" of economics. Ely brought this radical idea to an America where devotion to laissez faire was the determinant not of whether one were an orthodox economist, but of whether one were an economist at all. In 1885 he helped found the American Economic Association, which, for its first few years, was committed to promulgating the German school.

Ely was also influenced by social Christianity, and he was an admirer of Hull House. Miss Addams taught him about the day-to-day problems of industrial poverty; he taught her what might be done through the application of German economic analysis. He published inexpensive editions of *Democracy and Social Ethics* and *Newer Ideals of Peace* in a series he edited for Macmillan, "The Citizen's Library of Economics, Politics and Sociology." The series included E. A. Ross, Albion W. Small, Florence Kelley, Charles Zeublin, Delos F. Wilcox, and Ely himself.

To the desire for a co-operative society and a conviction that government was the best agent for creating it, Jane Addams added an almost mystical Rousseauan sense of government as the will of all. Miss Addams was an admirer of Mazzini. She ignored his violent methods—perhaps she did not know of them—and endorsed his romantic nationalism. The state, as Mazzini pointed out, represents "no more than the mass of principles in which the universality of its citizens were agreed."[17] She had no idea of government as an institution in society with interests of its own which might conflict with the general welfare; no idea of the state as oppressor; no fear of too much power lodged in one place. Nor did she see the state as performing the Madisonian function of mediating among conflicting interest groups. Here again she was not willing to contemplate the institutionalization of inevitable conflict. Instead, the state was to be the mechanism through which the consensus could be effected.

Thus when Jane Addams called for a redefinition of the role of government in American society, she joined a rising chorus of political analysts, economists, Christian ministers, sociologists, and day-to-day reformers, all of whom insisted that human intelligence could control human destiny, that the old dogmas were irrelevant, and that bold new experiments should be tried. Instead of drifting in the currents of laissez faire, Walter Lippmann was to assert, Americans should use their intelligence to master their fate.[18]

* * *

In no industrial society had laissez faire ever taken the extreme form it did in the United States. Even in England, the home of laissez-faire economics, factory legislation went on simultaneously with the repeal of the Corn Laws. Herbert Spencer found his most enthusiastic following in the United States. While England may have had a higher percentage of her population in abject poverty, there was never a very strong commitment to the idea that society had no responsibliity for them. Indeed, the stratified nature of British society led to one type of responsibility, exemplified by the Earl of Shaftesbury. The assumption of easy mobility and classlessness in the United States, even though false, meant that each man was responsible for himself and himself alone. As de Tocqueville pointed out, equality of condition put a great load on each individual, and individualism tended to drown community.

The need for community in the sense of a general responsibility for the welfare of each individual became more insistent in an industrial society. As Jane Addams asserted again and again, a city made the social nexus of a village, whose interpersonal relationships provided community, impossible. Yet the American commitment to the ideology of individualism was so strong that the need for community was admitted with tortuous slowness and grudging bad temper. A great army of reformers had to pound for decades on gates locked by conviction, and what had started in the depression of the 1890's had to wait until that of the 1930's for even the beginnings of fruition. For the reformers to be heeded, a major ideological reorganization in popular thought was necessary, an ideological change involving a redefinition of the nature of man; of his relationship to his fellows; and of his relationship to his environment.

To assert that an acceptance of the collective-welfare ideology demands an acceptance of the basic goodness of man sounds like no transformation at all, for in a sense Americans had always regarded mankind as good. Was this not the basis of the Jeffersonian image in the American mind? Does not democracy itself demand an acknowledgement of human goodness? There is a difference, however, between the eighteenth and early nineteenth-century acknowledgement of human goodness and that of the late nineteenth and twentieth century. Locke—and at base the traditional America position was Lockean—never went so far as to call mankind basically good. He merely insisted that men were in general capable of rationally perceiving their own self-interest, and of rationally pursuing it. Men were not so much good as capable. Put in even more negative terms, Locke simply said that no man was good enough to govern other men without some form of consent. After all, the very reason for having a social contract was because men could not be trusted to abjure injuring others. All men were endowed by their creator with certain inalienable rights, not with certain inalienable virtues. The basic constitutional theory of Hamilton and Madison alike was that government is to be an arbiter among the competing selfishness of various groups or "factions." The traditional American position was not that all men were good but that all men, including elites, no matter how defined, were rationally self-interested.

The counterargument relevant to the American experience was never the Hobbesian absolutism which Locke felt himself to be combating, but rather a type of romanticism with its modern roots in Rousseau which found its way to America by various paths, some direct, some via German or English romantics. The ideas found their most congenial home among the Massachusetts transcendentalists. The ideas themselves are complex enough, or vague enough, that one could find in them almost anything one wished. What appealed most to Americans, perhaps, was the idea of the natural man. Nothing was more internally contradictory in Rousseau, for example in *Emile,* than his use of the term Nature. Yet out of the midst of vagueness and contradiction emerged the clear idea that "Everything is good as it comes from the hands of the Author of Nature," including human beings. If human beings were somehow left free to express their natural essence, if they were not encrusted with the impediments of civilization, evil actions would disappear. Evil, according to this view, included the rational selfishness at the base of Locke. Man was not merely reasonable; he was naturally kind and productive.

The idea of the natural man appears in Jefferson; Jackson made it part of his campaign oratory in 1828; Lincoln played upon the theme in every one of his campaigns. Jefferson, Jackson, and Lincoln all asserted the inherent virtue of the natural man, but it was in the Lockean, not the Rousseauan sense. Jane Addams and other welfare proponents felt they had to convince the nation that men were more than competent, and that institutions based on that assumption could, indeed must, be changed.

A second idea which had to be transformed dramatically in the twentieth century was that of environmentalism. Here again a similarity of words between older and newer traditions masked a dissimilarity in essence. In a way, Americans had always been environmentalists. Indeed, faced with the overwhelming wilderness they could hardly have avoided it. Leo Marx has recently shown with enormous insight how Americans coped ideologically with this environment. To most Americans the environment, in its raw state, was too wild, too savage. Men living in it would become subhuman savages. Yet cities, like those of Europe. were too civilized, too remote from nature. Men living in them became either effete or another kind of savage. The solution lay in the "middle distance," or garden. A garden was, after all, not a forest. It was nature tamed for man's purpose, but nature still. The garden could be a formal one, as at Monticello, or it could be a farmer's field. In either case, the environment of a garden would produce people who were wise, upright, and virtuous.

When Jane Addams and others like her looked into urban slums, they saw an environment which clearly was molding human beings. The naturally good and generous human being was being pushed and squeezed into all sorts of distorted shapes. Reformers had to revive environmentalism to argue that this vast mass of people could only retain its inherent goodness if its environment was improved. The reformers had to argue that where men did not appear to be as good as they were supposed to be, the cause could be found in an inhuman environment. They had to reassert in an urban context an environmentalism which had hitherto seemed relevant only in confrontation with nature.

Politically what appealed to the transcendental mind, whether in 1840 or 1890, was the rejection of egoism and the rediscovery of community. In 1863, the Homestead Act created what was surely the largest symbol of individualism the world has ever seen: half a continent. Mile after mile, individual families set to farming isolated rectangles of soil. There was virtually no thought of community, no consideration of the sort of social or psychological relationships that might, or ought to, exist on the vast expanse of prairies and plains. The land could have been divided so that people would live close to each other. Towns could have been part of the plan, perhaps even with commons as in the Puritan villages. But the Homestead Act simply established innumerable individual economic units; and every time that a group of people challenged that basic individualism, whether Amish or Doukhobors, that group came into conflict with the larger society.

Individualism was so strong that it crushed not only any incipient communitarianism, but environmentalism as well. For if each man were responsible for his own fate then he could not be shaped by his environment; if he were shaped by his surroundings, he was not responsible for his own fate. The three ideas thus form a nexus: man is rational, therefore he is responsible for his own fate, therefore his environment is his own fault. Against this nexus, people like Jane Addams had to oppose their own nexus: man is good, therefore appearance of evil has a social cause, therefore mankind has a responsibility toward each man to allow his natural goodness to flourish. Jane Addams was only partially successful in convincing the nation that the social ethic was a natural next step for democracy, but even that partial acceptance was a major transformation.

The romantic assumption of man as basically kind and productive, received from her father's Quakerism and reinforced by the combination of Puritanism and transcendentalism at Rockford, was at the base of Jane Addams' ideology. A glorification of the "primitive," if it meant natural rather than bestial, was inherent in her Tolstoyism, for it was not first his pacifism which she admired, but his living the life of a peasant. Indeed, this "back to the people" impulse appeared frequently in the thinking of many reformers of the progressive years.[19] Whereas Tolstoy and the Massachusetts transcendentalists found salvation in attempting to put a brake on history, however, Jane Addams knew that history had no brakes. The old ways were both irretrievable and irrelevant, though the old values might still be honored. Factories could not be dismantled, but children must be kept out of them; cities could not be plowed back under the sod, but they must include art museums and playgrounds.

Laissez-faire economics assumes a cosmic mechanism regulating the historical process. To intervene with human intelligence is implicitly to deny any invisible hand. Jane Addams, in proposing intervention, assumed an orderliness in human behavior and adequate intelligence to control it. In short, we could be masters of our fate, and if we could, we must. To neglect the task would be morally horrendous. It was precisely this assumption which produced works like Ross' *Social Control.* Yet it is important to understand the differences between Jane Addams and the rationalistic social engineers. "Efficiency and Uplift" was their cry, not hers. To others she left the calculation of the long-term economic costs of child labor or neglect of the delinquent. She might use their argument to convince a legislator, but her own appeal was different. She deplored these things, not for their calculable waste but for their incalculable inhumanity. A single underfed child was to her the most potent argument.[20]

Likewise, though she favored a children's bureau, a women's bureau, an investigation of working conditions, factory inspection, and regulatory commissions, they were for her manifestations of an emotion—the oneness of humanity—not of social analysis. All the scientific study, all the most rational organization were as nothing unless they served that end.

The tools she chose to achieve her essentially romantic ends placed Jane Addams in the camp of the radicals. Eclectically, she drew upon British *noblesse oblige,* Bismarckean domestic *Realpolitik,* and the Socialist doctrine of class conflict; welding them into a creed which rejected individualism, the self-made man, and the congruity of wealth with virtue. Instead she proposed a view of man as naturally virtuous and creative, and a thoroughgoing collectivism in which these benign human beings would express their will through the democratic process, and have their will carried out with the technical aid of sociologists, economists, and settlement workers. But it was not only this collectivism which made Jane Addams a radical. She was, in her own way, even more radical than the Marxists. Where they asked for changed institutions and assumed that a new morality would follow, she asked for moral and institutional renewal simultaneously. She wanted not only governmental protection of the weak; she also wanted to substitute a social ethic for an individual ethic. If radicalism means a desire to change many fundamental aspects of life rapidly, one would be hard put to find a more radical posture than this.

By about 1910 Jane Addams had essentially made her arguments about children, immigrants, the poor, class conflict, and the role of the state. She had written and spoken intensively during the previous dozen years or so. Most people who were alert to such questions knew where she stood on them. Just as, in the late 1890's, Jane Addams began to reach out from Hull House toward a wider audience, so in 1910 or 1911 she seemed to feel that the time for speaking had passed and the time for action had arrived. For her the road to effective political action lay not back through Hull House and Chicago, but through the nationwide woman's movement, particularly woman suffrage. Through suffrage she was led to participation in the Progressive party of Theodore Roosevelt.

PART III

Jane Addams and National Policy

13

Suffrage and the Bull Moose

THERE was a feminist strain in all of Jane Addams' activities, and in her choice of life style. Her desire for a bachelor's degree rather than a mere seminary certificate, her attempts at medicine, and her choice of "career" all were in part assertions of women's abilities and women's rights. At times, as when her class chose a motto at Rockford, she seemed to assert the primacy of the female as against the male—as indeed the redoubtable President Sills of Rockford believed.

Yet her work in the suffrage cause was much more than an assertion of feminist arguments. In fact feminism and suffrage were merely devices by which Jane Addams tried to bring to reality the social vision she had been formulating. She wanted to enfold the poor, immigrants, children, Negroes, and women to full participation in American life not only because as a matter of right they deserved it, but because all of society would be redeemed by their inclusion. The poor had an ethic which all society needed; immigrants and Negroes brought cultural richness; children could redeem society with their moral purity. Women, finally, would confront and solve the problems of the new industrial age.

Miss Addams was concerned with the poor, immigrants, and children simultaneously; and simultaneously she seemed to regard all of them as sources of the social salvation which she continuously sought. Therefore in no sense did disappointment with one cure lead to faith in another. Yet her suffrage activities did gain momentum after about 1910. If not exactly disappointed in the results of her work for other groups—for, after all, results did not yet exist—she may well have felt that working for women's rights offered more far-reaching possibilities of achieving the co-operative commonwealth than more piecemeal attempts in behalf of children, immigrants, and the poor.

By the time Hull House opened, pioneer women B.A.'s, M.D.'s, and other professionals had convinced most Americans that women were not inherently the intellectual inferiors of men. With the basic issue of equality out of the way, the suffrage movement could shift to what the practical results of the feminine franchise would be. Rather than arguing abstract rights or abstract equality, as they had during the nineteenth century, women now argued that social justice would be served by giving women the vote. The liquor interests would be routed; child labor would cease and prizefighting would disappear; long hours of overwork would be eliminated, along with the bitterness of labor relations; government would be run without corruption. Whereas women had once been regarded as simple-minded sources of evil temptation, the suffrage forces argued that women possessed the virtues necessary to correct all injustice in America.[1] Carrying this argument one step further, Jane Addams thought that the quickest way to achieve the kind of society for which she had been arguing for two decades was through woman suffrage.

Inevitably Miss Addams' opinion of the nature of human females carried heavy emotional weight by its being an inextricable part of her view of herself. Her insistence, for example, that a college-educated woman had a responsibility to society which could not be met merely through home and family was as much self-justification as social analysis. She almost argued that women had a *duty* to become settlement house workers. As one reads her analysis of prostitution, one cannot but notice that the girls were always victims, set upon in their innocence by evil men. Behind every tree, around every corner lurks that fearful creature, a man, ready to snatch the pure young girl for his own evil purposes. Immigrant girls just off the boat, rural girls coming for the first time to the city, young working girls thirsting for a bit of glamour, shop girls in constant contact with strangers, domestic help imprisoned and dependent on a single family for human contact: all were set about with dangers every day and every evening. There was the saloon, the dance hall, the dark streets, and above all, scheming men.

While these problems were no doubt real, her virtual panic

about sex was at least partially a reflection of Jane Addams' own fears. In a sense she started from an older view of women. For her they were not able to take care of themselves in an equal battle. They were fragile creatures needing the protecting help of society. But if, like the poor, the immigrants, and children, they were victims because of their weakness, they were also, like the other victimized groups, sources of social redemption, and in part because of their weakness. Although she might deny thinking that women were better than men, she did believe that they possessed more human sympathy and appreciation for suffering than men.

On the other hand, Miss Addams wanted women to vote, to be doctors, lawyers, college professors, legislators, and policy makers in the executive departments of government. Years later, the first woman cabinet member was asked whether being a woman was a handicap. "Only in climbing trees," Frances Perkins snapped back. And while Frances Perkins was more of the Florence Kelley type than the Jane Addams type, Miss Addams admired both of them. How could women be on the one hand pure and weak, and on the other supremely competent? Miss Addams, it seems clear, was making an implicit class distinction. It would be unfair to say that she wanted votes only for middle-class women, but she did share at least a portion of the middle-class outlook of suffragism generally. Certainly she did not regard the strong Anna Howard Shaw, or the blunt Carrie Chapman Catt, as set about with temptations to a life of vice.

Well-to-do-women should vote as a matter of right. Poor women should vote for the same reason that poor men should vote—they needed the franchise for their own protection. *All* women needed the franchise in order to bring their natural human sympathies more effectively to bear on the problems of industrial America. For after all, she argued, were not most of these problems in fact simply extensions of the primordial female task of protecting her children? Women, like men, came to their role "not in entire forgetfulness" of their evolutionary development. Where men were warriors and hunters, women were nurturers and protectors of the young. To Jane Addams, the stream of girls entering a biscuit factory was a continuation of tribal breadmaking. In fact, this primordial role when translated into an urban environment inevitably involved women in public affairs.

> From the beginning of tribal life women have been held responsible for the health of the community, a function which is now represented by the health department; from the days of the cave dwellers, so far as the home was clean and wholesome, it was due to their efforts, which are now represented by the bureau of tenement-house inspection. . . . Most of the departments in a modern city can be traced to woman's traditional role.[2]

The city, she argued, was only in part analogous to a business corporation; it was also analogous to a home and therefore women should naturally play a part. Nor was she willing to have the participation confined to educated women, for the questions on which women's judgment was needed were "far too primitive and basic to be largely influenced by what we call education."[3] These views in balance outweighed whatever class distinctions may have been implicit in her attitudes, and in fact she acted as a counterweight in the National American Woman Suffrage Association (N.A.W.S.A.) leadership to the more explicit snobbery and nativism of someone like Carrie Chapman Catt.

Thus Jane Addams became involved in the suffrage campaign not on the basis of any doctrine of natural rights, or even legal rights, but as a continuation of her work for social justice. In June of 1912 she was scheduled to give a talk in Cleveland on modern charity during the Ohio suffrage referendum. Word leaked out that she would speak on suffrage and the antis protested that they had been tricked. Miss Addams said, "Of course I shall speak on suffrage. The topic on which I was invited to speak by the Chamber of Commerce on Tuesday, The Trend of Modern Charity, could lead me to no other subject. Charities are being taken rapidly by the state, and I intend to show that by giving women the vote, charities as state organizations would be much better cared-for and there would be better organization when women are allowed a voice in legislation."[4] Jane Addams, then, wanted two things from the movement for women's rights: social justice for *women,* particularly working women; and social justice for *society* through the operation of the particular virtues possessed by women.

To achieve social justice for women required solid knowledge. She knew from her experience with reform in Chicago that there was nothing like a mass of evidence to convince legislators. In Chicago this had meant surveys of garbage in alleys and tours of milk-bottling plants. Collecting evidence on the plight of women in industry was much too ambitious a job for any private group, however. Jane Addams knew what such evidence would show, but merely reciting anecdotes from her own experience would not get protective legislation, or get it approved in the courts. It was clear that the federal government would have to collect the information. In February of 1905, Jane Addams, Mary McDowell, and Lillian Wald were received by President Theodore Roosevelt in Washington where they urged upon him the formation of a commission to investigate the condition of working women. In the fall Miss Addams wrote renewing the suggestion. In his annual message for 1905, Roosevelt recommended the commission and a few days later he wrote Miss Addams: "Will you let me say a word of very sincere thanks to you for the eminent sanity, good-humor and judgment you always display in pushing matters you have at heart? I have such awful times with reformers of the hysterical and sensational stamp, and yet I so thoroughly believe in reform that I fairly revel in dealing with anyone like you."[5]

Roosevelt's enthusiasm for Miss Addams was to have its ups and downs over the next few years, but the commission did in fact come into existence after a two-year delay, and published the results of four years of investigation in nineteen volumes dealing with both women and children workers. The report provided much of the data for state protective legislation for women, which was the leading edge of regulation for all workers.

Actually, for a person so concerned with women's rights, needs, and duties, Jane Addams came late to organized suffrage work. Although she gave a rather mild suffrage speech in Boston in 1904, she attended her first national convention of the National American Woman Suffrage Association in 1906 as a result of losing a battle for municipal suffrage in Chicago. This 1906 Baltimore convention was the last which the old warrior, Susan B. Anthony, attended; she died a few months later. She and Miss Addams were guests of the same Baltimore family, and in their meeting the generation which raised the issue symbolically met the generation which was to bring it to fruition. The speech Jane Addams delivered at this convention was her statement that traditional women's concerns had now become public policy. Reprinted in many forms, delivered on many occasions by Miss Addams and others, the speech became part of the standard literature of suffrage. Yet for the next five years she played only a minor role in suffrage activity, being more concerned with her writing than with political activity.

In March, 1908, at the invitation of the College Suffrage Association, she spoke at the major women's colleges in Massachusetts—Radcliffe, Smith, Mt. Holyoke, Wellesley—as well as Boston University, urging the suffrage cause as the natural extension of the feminine role in industrial society. This was simply an added wrinkle on a type of activity she had long been doing. In 1909 Miss Addams organized another campaign for the municipal suffrage and took a group of ladies to Springfield to testify before the Illinois legislative committee. Again the campaign lost.[6] In about 1910 or 1911, however, a more active phase of her life seems to have superseded a decade during which she concentrated on persuasion, either through writing or speaking. As ten years earlier the day-to-day activities of Hull House seemed to offer too narrow a realm of activity and she turned to writing, so by the end of the first decade of the twentieth century she seemed to feel the need of a more active phase, of wider fields. Suffrage work brought her back to activity, and on this more national level. Between 1911 and 1914 her life was dominated by suffrage work, of which the Bull Moose campaign was the high point. This was, of course, not any abandonment of the goals toward which she had been working for twenty-two years. Through suffrage she was convinced these goals could be achieved.

In 1911 she began regular active attendance at the N.A.W.S.A. conventions. Though she had attended most of them since 1906, she had taken no very active part in the proceedings. From 1911 to 1913 she was a vice-president of the organization and was often the principal speaker at the public mass meetings held in conjunction with the convention.

In 1911 Jane Addams and Catharine Waugh McCulloch ran a campaign in Illinois for not merely municipal, but total, suffrage. They made their 1909 efforts look like an amateurish experiment. The ladies hired a special train and filled it with three hundred suffragettes, decorated it with banners, and made a slow journey punctuated with whistlestop speeches between Chicago and the state capital. In Springfield they had an hour-and-a-half hearing before a committee at which Miss Addams acted as mistress of ceremonies. If the legislators thought they would get off after an hour and a half they were sadly mistaken, for during the next three days the ladies worked in platoons, meeting legislators for breakfast, collaring them in the halls, and altogether doing an effective job of lobbying. They got the bill placed on the calendar, but again they lost the vote.[7]

At the mass meeting in 1912 during the Philadelphia convention of the National American Woman Suffrage Association, she shared speaking duties with W. E. B. DuBois. He urged "Democracy of Sex and Color," while she said that suffrage would end the white slave trade. Each of the speakers asserted, in effect, that suffrage would end the degradation of the group they represented, and the juxtaposition was an interesting survival of the connection between suffrage and abolitionism—a connection which did not often survive into the twentieth century. Only a year later, for instance, Carrie Chapman Catt was to argue before a congressional committee that native white American women should be given the vote as a counterweight to all the male members of "undesirable" groups who were getting it.[8]

Taking advantage of being so near Washington, the N.A.W.S.A. convention sent a large delegation to testify before the House Judiciary Committee in favor of a federal suffrage amendment. Jane Addams' experience in Springfield made her the natural one to lead the delegation of more than a thousand women. Only a few, of course, testified before the committee. Jane Addams ran the testimony, chose speakers, allotted time. The committee did not treat the matter as a joke or comic opera. Most of the members were present most of the time. They listened seriously and asked serious questions. Members of the House not on the committee, who had been co-sponsors of the amendment, also testified; but, as Miss Addams noted with a smile, the women were allowed ten minutes and the men only five.

Miss Addams opened the testimony by arguing that government was taking over many of the traditional duties of women. When government was entirely a male function, these female duties would not be performed well, as demonstrated by deterioration in the quality of children's court and public nursing activities in Chicago when women volunteers ceased to have a part in the activities. Ida Husted Harper, one of the early woman lawyers, argued the case on constitutional grounds, a tack followed by some of the male witnesses as well, some of whom came from suffrage states and presented evidence on the benefits of women voting.

While the Judiciary Committee agreed to print and frank 16,000 copies of the testimony to be distributed by N.A.W.S.A., it made no report and the amendment did not come before the House or Senate in 1912.[9]

That same year Jane Addams, Catharine Waugh McCulloch, and Ella S. Stewart, head of the Illinois Equal Suffrage Association, organized the Mississippi Valley Suffrage Association. Since most N.A.W.S.A. conventions were held on the east coast, midwestern women came only in small numbers. The M.V.S.A. was supposed to give them more opportunity to develop plans and leadership beyond the state level. It met regularly until 1917, apparently as an effective body. For the final three years before the federal suffrage amendment, national activity took place in the midwest, obviating the need.[10]

Miss Addams' activities in 1912 were not confined to testimony before congressional committees, speechmaking, and organizational work. In that year she did two things she had never done before: she appeared on the vaudeville stage, and she acted in a movie. On April 1, she was the headliner at the Majestic Theater in New York, giving what was described as a "witty monologue" on the suffrage issue, though unfortunately the full record has not survived. Nor can a print be located of Miss Addams' only appearance in a movie, though a still photograph survives and the plot has been preserved.[11] Jane Addams and Anna Howard Shaw played themselves. The intricate plot revolved around sweatshop labor, which suffrage would eliminate. Suffragettes take an "anti" to the home of a widow who, with her two small children, is sewing into the night for a pittance. The "anti" is converted, and persuades her fiancé, who owns the shop where the widow works, not only to raise wages, but to contribute $5000 to the cause and march in a suffrage parade. Even this movie could not save the election, however, and Illinois defeated suffrage by two to one in 1912.

Continuing her deep involvement with woman suffrage in 1912, Jane Addams was the inevitable leader of the N.A.W.S.A. delegation to the Republican National Convention in Chicago, June 16–20, to try to persuade the G.O.P. to adopt a platform favorable to suffrage. National politics in 1912 was dominated, as it had been since 1901, by the comic, serious, enigmatic, charismatic figure of Theodore Roosevelt. Even when he was off on a safari in Africa ("The poor lions," commented Mr. Dooley), his spirit was ever present. William Howard Taft was hardly allowed to have a policy in his own right: he either "followed Roosevelt" or "broke with Roosevelt." When Roosevelt returned from safari, it appeared that the breaking would predominate over the following. Then the question became whether or not Roosevelt would seek the 1912 Republican nomination. Taft, of course, would want renomination, and would have the backing from Republicans not in sympathy with the progressive trend. In the absence of any announcement by Roosevelt, Robert La Follette sought the nomination at the head of Republican progressives. Competition between the two wings of the party was intense and bitter. La Follette had virtually been read out of the party by Taft two years before, and felt he was fighting not only for the progressive policies which Taft had betrayed, but also for his very political life. Taft, on the other hand, quite rightly regarded La Follette as a dangerous schismatic as well as a radical on policy. The Wisconsin Senator had wide popular support, but Taft had the party machinery and appeared to be in clear position to win. Then, on February 25, Roosevelt announced his candidacy. La Follette was finished, for Roosevelt took most of his support out from under him, and from February to the convention Republican progressives under a former President battled Republican conservatives under the incumbent President. Not since the Civil War had matters of such fundamental principle seemed to turn on a political convention.

Mr. Dooley predicted that the Republican Convention would be a combination "iv the Chicago fire, Saint Bartholomew's massacre, the battle of the Boyne, th' life iv Jesse James, and th' night of the big wind." Certainly there was a lot of wind, and the Roosevelt forces insisted that the Jesse James spirit was very strong. Taft knew that the best way of getting a nomination as President of the United States was already to be President of the United States. He had a firm control on the organization of the convention and of the credentials committee. Roosevelt, on the other hand, had vast numbers of enthusiastic supporters, both inside the convention and in the Chicago streets. One such was reputed to have circulated a handbill saying:

At Three o'Clock
Thursday Afternoon
THEODORE ROOSEVELT
will walk on
the waters of
LAKE MICHIGAN.

Roosevelt knew perfectly well, however, that adulation counted no delegate votes. The Taft forces seated their own and threw out contesting Roosevelt men from a number of delegations. Taft was nominated 561 to 107, and with cries of foul play, the Roosevelt delegates walked out.[12]

Jane Addams and the suffragettes watched the proceedings closely. She had led a committee to press suffrage on the platform committee, but had been given only seven minutes to present her case, which was listened to politely but ignored in the platform. When the Roosevelt supporters announced they would hold a convention for the formation of a new party in August, it was natural that Jane Addams should be elected one of the Illinois delegates.

Roosevelt's strategy for the new party was clear. He concluded that his only hope for success was to be just as radical as political realities would permit; that is, to adopt in full measure the aims of the social justice movement, the antitrust movement, and the movement toward direct democracy. He correctly reasoned that the country wanted a reformer in the White House, so he staked out his claim to everything to the left of Taft. In July he wrote to Owen R. Lovejoy, who was secretary of the National Child Labor Committee and chairman of the Committee on Standards of Living and Labor of the National Conference of Charities and Correction: "I want to make my platform, as far as I have any say in it, primarily a platform for social and industrial justice, dealing in just the manner that your conference dealt with the very problems affected."[13] Just before the convention he wrote his managers in Chicago to make sure that Paul Kellogg, editor of the *Survey*, got a good seat.[14]

If this was the tack he was going to take, Roosevelt clearly needed Jane Addams and others like her on his side. By 1908 his earlier appreciation of her as a sane and sensible reformer, not given to hysteria, had changed when he came up against her pacifism in *Newer Ideals of Peace*. "Foolish Jane Addams," he now called her, blaming it all on the "mischievous effect produced by the teaching of a man like Tolstoi upon a mind without the strength, training and natural ability to withstand them."[15] In 1912, however, he needed not only foolish Jane Addams but all the help he could get, even from "reformers of the hysterical and sensational stamp."

Suffrage was one crucial issue. Roosevelt tried to temporize by proposing that the platform plank endorse suffrage only after a national referendum of women indicated that they wanted to vote. The Resolutions Committee of the National Progressive party, of which Jane Addams was a member, quickly brushed aside such half-hearted endorsement. Even though the platform had been released to the press, they substituted the plank which was finally adopted: "The Progressive Party, believing that no people can justly claim to be a true democracy which denies political rights on account of sex, pledges itself to the task of securing equal suffrage to men and women alike."[16] Although Theodore Roosevelt later telegraphed Jane Addams that "without qualification that I am for Woman Suffrage," the hastiness of his conversion led to a certain amount of suspicion. Ida Husted Harper, long-time leader of suffrage forces, insisted that he had tricked the suffragettes, most notably Jane Addams, into supporting him.[17]

For Jane Addams, the Bull Moose Convention was a heady experience. After years of laboring along the slow path of piecemeal reform, her ideas seemed now to have been adopted by a new national party which was to achieve instant power through the instrument of the most popular leader in the nation. In her home city of Chicago, virtually every reform she had worked for year after year was to be part of the platform of a major party. No longer would she have a polite seven minutes to testify before an indifferent platform committee. Now she would be an influential member of the platform committee. Triumph seemed imminent.

Indeed, the convention in many ways resembled a reunion of all the organizations of which she was a member. In one corner of the hall, she might imagine herself at a meeting of the National Federation of Settlements; in another at the National Conference of Charities and Correction; in yet another at the meetings of the American Economic Association, or the National Child Labor Committee, or the Mississippi Valley Suffrage Association, or the

Playground Association of the United States. Thousands of reformers of every stripe shared enthusiasms, hardly daring to believe what was happening. "It was a curious moment," she recalled, "of release from inhibitions, and it did not seem in the least strange that reticent men and women should speak aloud of their religious and social beliefs, confident that they would be understood. Because we felt so at home in that huge Coliseum, there was a quick understanding of those hidden scruples which we were mysteriously impelled to express."[18]

They had come, of course, to cheer the platform and to nominate Roosevelt. William Prendergast, at the end of a short nominating speech, mentioned the magic name at 2:22 P.M. on August 7, and the Coliseum went wild. Men, and even some women, paraded in any and all directions. Flags were waved, including a huge one from the upper reaches of the girders supporting the roof. A large brass band manfully played "The Battle Hymn of the Republic," but the delegates could not hear themselves, much less the triumphant music. A frenzied Texan climbed up to the first balcony and kissed the head of a bull moose placed there for decoration, and in his excitement Thomas Pfeiffer, an alternate from Kansas, threw a ham sandwich at the chairman. Senator Dixon, looking down at the crowd from the speaker's platform, said in awe and perhaps disgust, "This is not politics, this is religion." The permanent chairman, Senator Albert Beveridge, tried to quiet the crowd after twenty minutes, but the demonstration lasted a full three-quarters of an hour. Finally, Beveridge restored order and the seconding speeches began.

Ben Lindsey gave the first speech, damning the two old parties, then Beveridge introduced Jane Addams who was herself greeted by cheers which very nearly became a demonstration. To the reformers in the hall, she symbolized the spirit of social justice which the platform proclaimed. In her seconding speech Miss Addams said:

> I rise to second the nomination stirred by the splendid platform adopted by this convention.
>
> Measures of industrial amelioration, demands for social justice, long discussed by small groups in charity conferences and economic associations, have here been considered in a great national convention and are at last thrust into the stern arena of political action.
>
> A great party has pledged itself to the protection of children, to the care of the aged, to the relief of overworked girls, to the safe-

guarding of burdened men. Committed to these humane undertakings, it is inevitable that such a party should appeal to women, should seek to draw upon the great reservoir of their moral energy so long undesired and unutilized in practical politics—one is the corallary of the other; a programme of human welfare, the necessity of women's participation.

We ratify this programme not only because it represents our earnest convictions and formulates our high hopes, but because it pulls upon our faculties and calls us to definite action. We find it a prophecy that democracy shall be actually realized until no group of our people—certainly not ten million of them so sadly in need of reassurance—shall fail to bear the responsibility of self-government and that no class of evils shall lie beyond redress.

The new party has become the American exponent of a world-wide movement toward juster social conditions, a movement which the United States, lagging behind other great nations, has been unaccountably slow to embody in political action.

I second the nomination of Theodore Roosevelt because he is one of the few men in our public life who has been responsive to the social appeal and who has caught the significance of the modern movement. Because of that, because the programme will require a leader of invincible courage, of open mind, of democratic sympathies, one endowed with power to interpret the common man and to identify himself with the common lot, I heartily second the nomination.[19]

At her last words some women rushed to a yellow banner emblazoned VOTES FOR WOMEN, and as Miss Addams descended from the speaker's platform and walked up the aisle, an impromptu parade swung in behind her. Beveridge, pounding with his gavel and showing his watch, managed quickly to restore order. After a few more seconding speeches. Roosevelt was nominated by acclamation, and Hiram Johnson of California was named as Theodore Roosevelt's running mate. Finally, worn out by their enthusiasm, the delegates rose, solemnly sang the old Puritan hymn, "Praise God From Whom All Blessings Flow," and disbanded.

Jane Addams had chosen the words of her seconding speech very carefully. Her emphasis was as much on the platform and as little on the candidate as common courtesy would permit. Her first sentence could indeed be read as seconding the nomination which the platform had thrust forth. Later she made the same point when she remarked that "I was there, and I think the same was true of many others, because the platform expressed the social hopes so long ignored by the politicians; though we appreciated to the full our good fortune in securing on their behalf the magnetic personality of the distinguished candidate."[20] A close look at the platform and at Roosevelt's major speech to the convention reveals that her support was even more partial. Roosevelt devoted not more than one quarter of his written remarks, and (since he departed from his text to make a long defense of his policy on Southern Negro delegates) considerably less of the address he actually delivered, to social justice. The platform devoted not more than the same proportion of its length to the issues which Miss Addams had at heart, and about which she had spoken from the podium. Probably no national political convention ever had a seconding speech which was so lukewarm about the nominee. Just as Roosevelt was attempting to use reformers of the "hysterical and sensational stamp" for his ends, so they were attempting to use him for theirs. Probably both were successful to a degree.

There were deep and important differences between the candidate and the woman who seconded his nomination. The radicals could push Theodore Roosevelt into support of suffrage, the initiative and referendum, and a long list of social-welfare measures, but they could not talk him out of his battleships. After a brief flurry of opposition, the platform committee endorsed the building of two. Jane Addams later admitted "that I found it very difficult to swallow those two battleships."[21] But swallow them she did, along with a recommendation to fortify the Panama Canal.

Perhaps harder yet for her to swallow was Theodore Roosevelt's decision on the seating of Negro delegates from the Southern states. A number of Northern states had Negroes among their delegations, and Southern delegations to Republican conventions frequently included Negroes. Some of these had actually bolted the convention to support Roosevelt. Between the Republican and Bull Moose conventions, four Southern states elected contesting delegations, one all white and one racially mixed. Before the convention met, and during its first day, the question of whether the "lily-white" delegations would be recognized received more press attention than any other issue. By the end of July, Roosevelt had made his position clear. He would go for the lily-white delegates. If he was to stand any chance of winning, he would need some Southern support, which in 1912 meant white, racist support. He tried to soften the opposition by insisting that he was against discrimination and that each man must be treated "on his worth as a man." However, he argued that attempts to base a Republican party in the South on Negro support had failed and had, in fact, led to increased discrimination. The best road to advancement for Negroes, he argued, was through the election of progressive-minded white men. The argument that the road to racial equality lay through a Jim Crow political party, however, could hardly be expected to please the Negro delegates. As one said, "there will be a lot of Negroes hoeing corn this election day."[22]

Jane Addams led the fight against the lily-white policy in the Resolutions Committee. She and Henry Moskowitz of the Madison Street settlement in New York were the only ones to speak against Roosevelt's position. Miss Addams said: "Some of us are much disturbed that this Progressive party which stands for human rights, should even appear not to stand for the rights of the negroes. It seems to us to be inconsistent when on one page of our newspapers we find that this party is to stand for the working man and the working woman, and to protect the rights of the children, and to prevent usurpation of the voters' rights by special interests, and on the next we find that it denies the right of the negro to take part in this movement." She added that she believed Colonel Roosevelt could easily "clear up" the misunderstanding without compromising his "statesmanlike plans . . . for breaking the Solid South." But Roosevelt had his way at the convention, and the Negroes went home in disgust.[23]

Although Jane Addams had not concentrated either in word or deed on racial equality, anyone who followed her career with care would have expected her position. Relatively few Negroes lived in the area around Hull House, and the great migration northward of Southern Negroes had not yet created northern urban ghettos. Yet Miss Addams was well ahead of most whites and even of many Negroes in her views on race relations. It was perhaps fitting that in 1912 Booker T. Washington endorsed Wilson, while Jane Addams broke with Roosevelt over the issue of race. To the extent that she was involved, Miss Addams was among the radicals. She insisted against the vicious racism of turn-of-the-century America that lynching was both horrible and criminal, and that Negroes should have precisely the same rights, politically, economically, and socially, as whites. In 1909 she signed the public appeal which led to the creation of the National Association for the Advancement of Colored People, and she was a permanent though not a very active member. Without equivocation or reservation she maintained that the blame for the Negro's condition lay at the door of white America, North and South. Nor was she content with the terms of the Atlanta Compromise. She wanted to confront discrimination squarely and move against it rapidly.[24] Since 1954, to be sure, the NAACP has been superseded by other organizations as spearhead of the Black Revolution. But in 1912 it was too radical for many Negroes and for most whites, and in participating in the NAACP Jane Addams came very close to sacrificing her claim on "respectability."[25]

Henry Moskowitz was also a founder of the NAACP, so Roosevelt was probably not surprised when Moskowitz and Jane Addams opposed his lily-white policy. But Colonel Roosevelt stuck to his guns, since he felt that political necessity required it, and Miss Addams swallowed Jim Crow in the southern delegations as she had swallowed the two battleships and a fortified canal. Indeed, all differences of opinion were soon submerged beneath the rolling, swelling enthusiasm for a new party, a new cause, and a candidate who, if not new, at least appeared reborn.

Meanwhile, at Hull House letters were piling up, either in support or disagreement. A telegram of thanks from the nominee said, "I prized your action not only because of what you are and what you stand for, but because of what is symbolized for the new movement."[26] Negroes flooded her with letters of thanks and support for her standing up to Roosevelt. Some said they would support him anyway. "It is an error of judgement, not of conscience," argued the business manager of Howard University. Others damned the candidate, and occasionally one asked how Miss Addams could, after disagreeing with Roosevelt on such an important issue, then second his nomination. Robert A. Woods endorsed Roosevelt, arguing that slow progress was the only way.[27] Socialists wrote of their sense of betrayal at her supporting the Bull Moose when they, the socialists, had been fighting for social justice since before Roosevelt had even heard of it.[28] Pacifists and members of the old anti-imperialist league, of which Jane Addams was a member, could not understand how she could have supported so warlike a candidate.[29] One anonymous correspondent who claimed to have been a Rough Rider said that Roosevelt was not any good at *that* either. Even some of the suffrage workers did not like the idea of her tying suffrage to the star of a particular party. Only to this last did Miss Addams reply, arguing that for years she had been working to prevent child labor, improve working conditions for girls, obtain suffrage, and the like. "They are now taken up systematically by the Progressive Party. It seems to me quite as consistent that I should advocate them there as that I should have appeared before congressional committees." Being an officer of N.A.W.S.A., she went on, should not limit her own political activity. Most suffragettes supported Miss Addams even if they did not support Theodore Roosevelt.[30] Some were unable to choose between Roosevelt and Woodrow Wilson.

Many people found themselves in a similar dilemma. In fact, Roosevelt himself recognized that Wilson's nomination on a progressive platform had pre-empted much of the political area he himself had hoped to occupy. The progressive vote would be divided, with probably most of the Southern part of it going to Wilson, along with Populist remnants in the South and the Midwest. All three candidates expected a Wilson victory. Yet the Bull Moosers would fight on. Jane Addams' seconding speech had made her a national political figure, so with some reluctance she agreed to serve on the executive committee of the new party, in charge of organizing women, or "Moosettes" as they were to be called.[31] She also agreed, with perhaps less reluctance, to a major speaking tour, concentrating in the northern midwest and plains states.

First, however, she took a six-week working vacation at the Bar Harbor home of Mrs. Bowen. Vacations in Maine were to be, for the rest of her life, a regular part of most years. At Baymeath, as the house was called, she arranged her speaking schedule, helped get names of women to act as women's organizers in Illinois and neighboring states, and worked on a series of articles to be distributed to various newspapers as Bull Moose propaganda. These put her views on child labor, labor unions, industrial safety, and other progressive tenets in simple newspaper style and showed how the program of the Progressive party would solve each problem. In addition, her seconding speech was reprinted and used as a campaign document, especially with women's groups.[32]

On September 27 she returned to Chicago and almost immediately plunged into a suffrage campaign in Wisconsin. Although not officially partisan, the fact that the Bull Moosers were the only ones backing suffrage made the implication clear. On October 10 she spoke in Detroit on her way to the official opening rally of the presidential campaign in New York on October 11. She was also to have spoken at the University of Michigan, but at the last moment the hall was refused her on the grounds that her speech was partisan. After the October 11 rally she went to Worcester, Massachusetts, for a debate with her friend Rabbi Stephen S. Wise, a Wilson man, and then left to spend the rest of campaign time in the midwest. The total number of her speeches in behalf of the Progressive party cannot be determined, but in the days between October 13 and the election, she covered Oklahoma City, Wichita, St. Paul and Minneapolis, Fargo, Denver and Colorado Springs, and ended up with her sister Alice in Kansas City.[33] She also spoke in dozens of little towns in those states as well as in Iowa, Nebraska, and Missouri. "The Progressive Party campaign remains in my mind," she later recalled, "as a wonderful opportunity for education not only on the social justice planks in the platform but on the history of the ideology behind them." In Leadville, Colorado, for instance, a group of miners expressed surprise that politics could have anything to do with what interested them most, hours and wages. In city after city she had a chance to argue her position before thousands of people who were eager to be convinced.[34]

As a campaign device, the Progressive party launched a series of "Jane Addams Choruses" made up of young ladies singing campaign songs, especially "Roosevelt, My Roosevelt" to the tune of "Maryland, My Maryland." Elgin, Illinois; Washington, D. C.; Chicago, Kansas City, and Indianapolis were blessed with these organizations. There was also something called the "Jane Addams Salute," performed with red bandannas; but no precise description of its execution survives.[35]

At Alice's on election eve, Jane Addams was exuding an optimism she had not felt earlier. The huge crowds and enthusiastic receptions which had greeted her wherever she went ran counter to her earlier judgments. "At that moment we believed that we were witnessing a new pioneering of the human spirit."[36] She was brought back to political reality by the election returns which showed Roosevelt a strong second, but second nonetheless to the governor of New Jersey.

The campaign had exhausted her, and she returned not to Hull House but to Mrs. Bowen's home on Astor Street, where Mrs. Bowen nursed her back to health. The defeat, however, did not discourage her. In a post-election interview, she said: "I had expected from the beginning that Mr. Wilson was to be the next President of the United States. The candidacy of Mr. Roosevelt and the principles enunciated in the Progressive platform afforded the opportunity for giving wide publicity to the necessity for social and industrial reforms, and it is my belief that Mr. Wilson as President of the United States will give heed to the necessities of the people as they have been so plainly apparent."[37] Roosevelt wrote an effusive note of thanks for her help, and promised, "I shall conscientiously do my best so as to act in the future that you shall not feel regret that you supported me."[38]

The picture was by no means hopeless, she felt. In addition to Wilson's progressive outlook, her old friend William Kent—the one who had given the playground to Hull House many years before—was elected as Bull Moose congressman from California, and A. A. McCormick won his first fight for president of the City Board in Chicago. The suffrage cause triumphed in Michigan, Arizona, and Oregon. Most important, as Jane Addams wrote Theodore Roosevelt, was the "tremendous impulse the campaign has given to social reform measures in which I have been interested for many years, but which have never before seemed to become so possible of fulfillment as at the present moment."[39] Nor was the Progressive party dead. No one yet knew that it was never to run another presidential candidate, never again be a force in national politics. The party's leader was proclaiming the permanence of the party and denying any plans of fusion with either Republicans or Democrats. In a doomed search for longevity, the party organized a Progressive Service Department to prepare carefully researched proposals for carrying out the planks of the 1912 platform. Jane Addams was to head the Department of Social and Industrial Justice.[40]

Besides, suffrage work would not end merely because of one election. Only three weeks after the campaign was over, she was again giving speeches for the cause. Three months later she left for an extended vacation in Europe and the Near East with Mary

Smith. Even on this journey there was suffrage work: a convention of the International Woman Suffrage Association in Budapest and the Woman's International Congress in Paris, where she was the most celebrated delegate. In July of 1913 she was back in America, testifying before congressional committees and working for women's organizations. In 1914 she spoke for the increasingly successful cause in New York City, Boston, and various cities in Georgia and Alabama, North and South Dakota, Missouri and Kansas. As one of the antis said, "It was an ill day when Jane Addams took up the cause."[41]

Triumph for her ideas had seemed so near in 1912. The next year and a half were not discouraging. The suffrage cause was winning victory after victory, including her own Illinois in 1913. Woodrow Wilson, after some initial caution, seemed to be increasingly sympathetic to the need for federal action to promote social justice. Poverty, conflict, the individualistic ethic still existed, but perhaps she could hope that the social ethic was gaining strength.

The victory which seemed—and perhaps only seemed—so near was snatched away by the war and by postwar reaction. Only partially sensing the impact that war would have on domestic reform, Jane Addams nevertheless found herself by early 1914 speaking as much on the war in Europe as on suffrage at home. Soon the mounting horror in the trenches gave work for peace an urgency which overwhelmed all else. From mid-1914, Jane Addams became primarily a pacifist.

14

Pacifism

WHEN Jane Addams first came to Chicago, she carried with her all the prejudices and blindnesses of her upbringing. A score of years living on Polk and Halsted streets taught her a good deal. Thus when she spoke about working conditions in the needle trades, or garbage collection in Chicago slums, she spoke out of the daily experience of knowing seamstresses and living by filthy alleyways. When she argued for a national policy to end cruel working conditions, she had long experience with governmental action and its effectiveness. When she testified before a congressional committee or a city council meeting, she usually knew what she was talking about. When she turned to international relations, however, she came to the subject without the toughening of years of experience; directly, as it were, from Rockford Female Seminary. On domestic politics she had not only been an effective force for change, but also a farsighted prophet of historical developments relating to the welfare philosophy. She was neither effective nor a good prophet on the "passing of the war virtues." For Jane Addams, active pacifism seemed a natural continuation of what she had been doing all along. In evaluating her place in history, however, it must be said that her engrossment in pacifism marked her departure from the mainstream of American liberalism into what must still be counted a back eddy.

She had always been a pacifist. Her Quaker background tilted her in that direction, though her father had supported Lincoln and the Civil War. At Rockford she had taken Christianity to mean an absence of hatred, and accepted woman's role as "bread giver," not destroyer. She had been interested in Tolstoy primarily because of his back-to-the-people philosophy, and they both saw pacifism as a natural outgrowth. In spite of her longstanding Republicanism, she had followed Bryan in his opposition to imperialism in 1900 and been a member of the Anti-Imperialist League. Her predisposition toward pacifism shaped her perception of the Hull House experience well before pacifism became the all-absorbing influence in her life.

Perhaps the matter ought to be put in even broader terms. She saw her efforts at Hull House not so much as relating to international peace, but relating to the absence of conflict in all human relations. Worker and manager would be harmonized; white and black would cease to hate and fear; native-born would welcome immigrant; nation would co-operate with nation. War seemed to her to be the supreme form of wasteful, inhuman conflict, so its ending seemed to follow naturally from her efforts to alleviate other, more limited forms of conflict. Like all social conflict, war was for her a matter of misunderstanding: the people of one nation did not realize their essential similarity to and community of interest with people of another nation. Once they realized these things, wars would cease.

She thought she saw among her neighbors the beginnings of this new international unity, these *Newer Ideals of Peace* as she called them. War was a survival into the modern age of virtues which, though once necessary for individual or tribal survival, were now vices. Unquestioned loyalty to one's own tribe, necessary under "primitive" (this time a pejorative) conditions, became a crime if it meant warfare. Surrounding Hull House in the first years of the twentieth century were colonies of people from a great many different European tribes which often had a tradition of mutual hostility and warfare. Yet, under the extreme conditions of urban poverty, and after the emotional shock of leaving the Old Country with its familiar associations, common humanity asserted itself as more important than any tribal loyalties. "It is possible," Jane Addams ventured "that we shall be saved from war by the 'fighting rabble' itself, by the 'quarrelsome mob' turned into kindly citizens of the world through the pressure of a cosmopolitan neighborhood."[1] She, like so many others in the first years of the century, was convinced that war was diminishing as "society progressed." "At the bottom is the small savage community in a perpetual state of warfare; at the top an orderly society stimulated and controlled by recognized ideals of social justice." One way she thought of her work at Hull House was as helping to move society from the former to the latter by substituting a moral equivalent for war—social reform—for surviving militaristic traits.

One example of such survivals was the exclusive right of men to participate in government. When the chief aim of a community was its own protection, it seemed natural that a voice in government should be limited to those who could bear arms. But the modern city was a different sort of organism. "To test the elector's fitness to deal with this situation by his ability to bear arms" was now ridiculous, Jane Addams said. Military virtues should not be taught in the schools; the analogy of battle should be banished from the trade-union movement; and, of course, money badly needed for social services should not be spent on battleships or cannons.[2] She argued that in the modern age of 1907, war was simply out of date; that in fact, those who argued the value of war quoted past achievements: "We may admire much that is admirable in this past life of courageous warfare, while at the same time we accord it no right to dominate the present, which has traveled out of its reach. . . ."[3] Feeling this sense of constant progress toward the newer ideals of peace, feeling that mankind was on the verge of abolishing war, Jane Addams was overcome by a sense "of desolation, of suicide, of anachronism" when the first news arrived from Europe in the summer of 1914.[4]

Her devotion to suffrage had also helped to bring her to pacifism. Suffrage was an attempt to extend normal female instincts into an industrial age. Care for children meant child-labor laws; housekeeping meant tenement-house regulations; feeding a family meant supervision of urban milk supplies. Women were the natural protectors of human beings. Men might build machines and businesses, but women literally bore and brought up humanity. They would not sit by and see it torn apart by high explosives. Therefore, it seemed merely an extension of all she had been working for when she became the head of the Women's Peace Party.

Perhaps other motives were operating as well. She was, after all, a national figure whose mere appearance on a stage could set an audience cheering. She had become a national symbol for human kindness. She had a public role to fulfill, and one which, if the truth be known, gave her deep satisfaction. After the excitement of the Bull Moose campaign, the peace movement offered her an alternative to merely returning to her position as head resident of a settlement house.

In reacting against the war, and even more against American participation in it, Jane Addams did not set herself apart from her countrymen as either a radical or a crank. Though few Americans shared her principles of nonviolence, or Tolstoyan nonresistance, the organized peace movement had a long and respectable history in the United States. In the years just before the outbreak of the World War, a number of new societies had been formed: The New York Peace Society, the World Peace Foundation, the Church Peace Union. These and others had large and in some cases rather distinguished memberships. Their programs tended to concentrate on political arrangements for settling disputes without violence: arbitration, a world court, disarmament agreements, international government. None challenged the basic concepts of nationalism; none believed that economic systems were at the basis of war; none carried pacifism to the point of believing that all war was sinful. And, as it turned out, virtually all of them ended up supporting Woodrow Wilson when he led the nation into war. Jane Addams was not a member of any of them.

It was not, in any event, a group of self-deluded outcasts who met at the Henry Street Settlement on September 29, 1914, only a few weeks after the European war broke out, but one of many groups of respected and influential people trying to keep their own country out of war and, if possible, to bring an end to the war itself. Organized by Paul Kellogg of the *Survey,* the group included, besides Miss Addams, Lillian Wald, John Haynes Holmes, Florence Kelley, Hamilton Holt, and other domestic reformers and pacifists. Many were, as Paul Kellogg noted, new to peace work, so he asked George Nasmyth of the World Peace Federation to address them.[5] Although it was not organized immediately, this meeting was the origin of the Women's Peace Party, later the U. S. branch of the Women's International League for Peace and Freedom.

The impulse toward the organization of a purely feminine peace group came from two traveling European pacifists and feminists: Rosika Schwimmer of Austria-Hungary, and Emeline Pethnick-

Lawrence of England. Along with Miss Addams, these two addressed a peace meeting in the Garrick Theater on December 5, 1914. Following the meeting, a small group called the Chicago Emergency Federation of Peace Forces was organized, with Jane Addams as chairman.[6] With the strong support, almost the leadership, of Carrie Chapman Catt, this group decided to organize a large peace demonstration in Washington in the first month of 1915. Miss Addams herself had some doubts about a purely feminine movement, and Lillian Wald did not really like the idea at all; but as Jane Addams said, "In this case the demand has been so universal and spontaneous over the country that it seemed to me best to take it up."[7]

Mrs. Catt's organizational ability must have been phenomenal, because on January 9, 1915, more than three thousand "women pacificators," as the *Washington Herald* called them, convened at the New Willard Hotel in the nation's capital to hear speeches and organize as the Women's Peace Party. Mrs. Pethnick- Lawrence was the most dramatic speaker. Calling on her experience as a militant suffragist, with years of stored-up indignation behind her, she poured scorn on war and on those who made it: "If men will tolerate this thing, women will not." Miss Addams' speech was more moderate in tone, arguing that patriotism had reverted to chauvinism, and that women must fulfill their traditional role by nurturing life, not destroying it.

Then the delegates got down to the hard work of hammering out a platform. In the over-all desire for a permanent organization, differences were easily overcome and most clauses of the platform were adopted by acclamation. The preamble condemned war—"legalized, wholesale, human slaughter"—as "the sum of all villainies," and demanded that women, as "half of humanity," as those who built "the basic foundation of the home and peaceful industry," be consulted on war and peace in the name of sovereign reason and justice. The first item of the program was the immediate calling of a convention of neutral nations in the interest of early peace. The idea that a convention of neutrals might mediate the war was much in the air in 1915. One form of the plan had been passed by the Wisconsin legislature and sent as a petition to Congress, and such a convention was considered by President Wilson as a possible course of action.

Other items in the Women's Peace Party platform included

arms limitation, woman suffrage, a world organization with law as a substitute for war, a police force to enforce the law, open diplomacy, and a vaguely worded plank calling for the "removal of the economic causes of war." With the adoption of the platform, the Women's Peace Party came formally into existence and, as no surprise to anyone, Jane Addams was elected chairman.[8] From this time until the Armistice, Miss Addams was involved almost totally in the peace movement.

The Women's Peace Party was, for the first few months of its existence, one of many groups urging neutrality and non-intervention on the President. It was given an international character when on March 20, 1915, Jane Addams received an invitation from Aletta H. Jacobs of Holland to attend an international congress of women at The Hague. This conference was to have been the biennial meeting of the International Woman Suffrage Association—a sequel to the Budapest meeting which Jane Addams had attended in 1913—and was to have been held in Berlin. The war caused the German suffragists to withdraw the invitation, but various national leaders of the suffrage cause were unwilling to allow the meeting to disappear. In fact, Carrie Chapman Catt voiced the feeling of many women that the war was incompatible with suffrage assumptions, and that the biennial meeting should be an international plea from women to end the slaughter. The suffragists of Holland took the initiative.[9]

"The undertaking, of course, offers many possibilities of failure; indeed, it may even do much harm," Jane Addams wrote Lillian Wald. "The whole enterprise has about it a certain aspect of moral adventure, but it seems to me to be genuine. I think, too, that women who are willing to fail may be able to break through that curious hypnotic spell which makes it impossible for any of the nations to consider peace."[10]

If she, herself, was filled with such doubts, it is no wonder that more belligerent Americans were sharply critical. Theodore Roosevelt thundered that the whole thing was "silly and base." He found it repulsive that the ladies would criticize evil in the abstract, but not the wickedness of Germany in particular. Let them, he said, specifically denounce the invasion of Belgium by Germany. The *New York Times* editorialized more moderately and more wisely that if the ladies proclaimed the superiority of peace to war, "everybody, including all the contestants in the great conflict will readily admit everything except the timeliness of their contentions. Each of the belligerents claims to be fighting for peace."[11] Harsh criticism was nothing new to Jane Addams, for she had endured the *Chicago Chronicle* for years, and she still had the support of many of her old friends and colleagues; but these were the first murmurs of what, within two years, would become a roar of disapproval unlike anything she had ever experienced.

In spite of any doubts she had, Jane Addams and forty-one other Americans left for The Hague aboard the Holland American line *Noordam* on April 21, armed with letters of introduction to American diplomats from the Secretary of State. The trip was uncomfortable physically; huge following seas caused the ship to pitch, and for the first day or two Miss Addams felt not only seasick, but lonely and discouraged as well. Here she was, setting out on a trying journey to a warring Europe overcome by passion. Was it simply a bizarre initiative as silly, if not as base, as Roosevelt said? Gradually a sense of camaraderie grew among the delegates which provided the warmth to melt her loneliness. Every day at 11:00 they had a class on international problems. "It was interesting to see the party evolve from a chaotic lot of half-informed people and muddled enthusiasts and sentimentalists with a few really informed ones, into a docile teachable coherent body," Alice Hamilton reported to Mary Rozet Smith. But Alice Hamilton, too, had doubts. She would be quite absorbed in the discussions, and then all of a sudden "the whole thing looks absolutely futile." By the twenty-fifth of April they were past the stage of enthusiasm and were working on what seemed to them a feasible plan. Perhaps it would not be so futile after all.[12]

Their surprise and anguish were therefore intense when, on the morning of the twenty-sixth, they found themselves stopped by a vessel of the British Navy and forced to anchor off the British coast. The Admiralty had stopped all shipping to Holland. Were they to be stopped after crossing the entire Atlantic, here, only a few hours from their destination? Miss Addams telegraphed Walter Hines Page, the American ambassador, pleading with him to intercede with the Admiralty. Page deeply regretted the delay, he said, but he could do nothing. The Admiralty had acted as a war measure, and a neutral could hardly interfere. The ladies became more frantic. Could nothing be done? More telegrams were sent. Finally after some personal unofficial words from Page, the British government allowed the *Noordam* to sail, after it had lain at anchor for parts of three days. The Americans arrived at The Hague in time for the opening speeches of the Congress on the evening of April 28.[13]

The Congress of Women did not get off to an auspicious start. The French and the English were prevented by their own governments from attending, although a few of the latter found their way to The Hague. Germany would not allow the Swiss to come. There was, moreover, an echo of disruptive nationalism when a Belgian woman pleaded for justice to her country while the Germans insisted that they were fighting in self-defense. Yet the hundred-odd delegates did manage to find some common ground and to arrive at common recommendations.

With Miss Addams presiding, the evenings were devoted to public addresses by ladies from the various countries, appealing for an end to the madness of war. During the day, the conference worked out its basic platform. Essentially there were only two planks: continuous mediation by a conference of neutrals, and universal woman suffrage. However, a more elaborate set of resolutions was passed in an attempt to stop future wars, including self-determination of all areas and open diplomacy. After a good deal of disagreement, the Congress decided to try to send delegations to the various European capitals to discuss the idea of continuous neutral mediation. With the promise to convene again concurrent with the peace conference after the war, the Congress established an executive board, headed by Jane Addams, and adjourned.[14]

One week after the Congress adjourned, at 2:10 P.M. on May 7, U-boat 20 fired one torpedo at the liner *Lusitania* just off the Irish coast. The ship sank within eighteen minutes, carrying down 1,198 passengers and crewmen.

If Jane Addams had doubts about the Congress itself, these were redoubled about the wisdom of actually approaching heads of state and foreign ministers of nations at war. The whole thing seemed mad—yet the world itself was mad in 1915, and perhaps something could be gained. Here was truly a bizarre initiative: a woman of fifty-five, with no experience in international affairs, with no official standing, journeying from warring capital to warring capital, from London to Budapest, pleading with heads of state to come to their senses and accept neutral mediation. Jane Addams was not—or had not, at least, seemed to be—a fool. Though she had appeared on a vaudeville stage once, part of her strength had lain in her dignity and good sense. That she carried the mission off was a tribute to her courage, which was in no way diminished by the mission's futility. Yet neither was the futility diminished by her courage.

The official delegates to the capitals of Europe were Miss Addams and Aletta Jacobs. In addition, a German lady and Alice Hamilton went along, more or less as aides. They warmed up for the difficult countries by visiting the Dutch Foreign Minister —who was, after all, near at hand—and the British government, where they felt they could count on at least a polite reception. "I have not lost my head," Jane Addams assured Mary Smith as she set out, "There is just one chance in 10 thousand. . . . You can never understand unless you were here, how you would be willing to do anything."[15] Miss Addams was received politely by Foreign Secretary Edward Grey and Prime Minister Herbert Asquith, and she lunched with Ambassador Page. Grey, however, said that mediation at that time was hopeless. The war must go on. By the time she returned to Holland, Alice Hamilton felt that the trip which had seemed hopelessly melodramatic and absurd might not be so bad after all. People did seem to be taking Jane Addams seriously.[16]

On the front lines this was perhaps the most horrible war ever fought. Tactics appropriate for muzzle-loading rifles were used against high explosives and machine guns, the result being that in some battles as many as half the men engaged were casualties. Yet there was still a distinction between a battle zone and an area that was not a battle zone. Not until the next war would technology—rather than declining morality—allow the obliteration of the distinction between combatants, and noncombatants. Thus, the physical problem of traveling within Europe was not particularly difficult, and Jane Addams found it almost possible to imagine that this was just another European trip. The trip consisted of many hours on trains, seemingly infinite hours in consular offices waiting for forms, visas, passports and permission, and a few—very few—hours with leaders of nations.

Berlin, their first stop, was outwardly much as it had always been. Public transportation functioned smoothly, and private citizens went about their business. Then the travelers noticed that there were no young men around, save those in uniform, and that the walls and shop windows were filled with posters appealing for money for the relief of widows, orphans, and the wounded. A few of the Germans they met were pacifists; but most were absolutely convinced that Germany was fighting for self-defense, and most were very bitter about the United States and the Allies.

The American Ambassador easily obtained appointments for them with Foreign Minister Gottlieb Von Jagow and Chancellor Theobald Bethmann-Hollweg. The former told them that he thought mediation by neutrals might be some use, but that he hardly regarded the United States as neutral. The Chancellor took their mission somewhat more seriously, and tried to explain how Germany had to fight to keep from being crushed by England. Jane Addams' attempt to convince him that England did not want to crush Germany made no impression at all. The Chancellor did say that Germany certainly could not ask for negotiations to begin; that would be a sign of weakness.[17]

After these rather unsatisfactory interviews, the ladies spent an evening with Maxmilian Harden, editor of *Die Zukunft* which, before the war, had bitterly attacked the Kaiser, militarism, and the Junker class. He had now gone over completely to the war party, poured contempt on Germany's enemies, and said Germany was going to remake the continent of Europe.[18] On May 24 the delegation left Berlin for Vienna. That very day Italy declared war on Austria-Hungary.

Vienna was harder hit by war than Berlin. Even bread was in short supply. People were underfed and the horses were starving. Wounded soldiers were far more in evidence. As in Berlin, the American ambassador thought the ladies to be somewhat cracked, but he did arrange an interview with Prime Minister Carl Stürgkh. They presented him with their proposal and made their plea. Stürgkh said nothing, but his hard, overbearing eyes stared at and through them. Made nervous by his silence, Miss Addams stammered, "It perhaps seems to you very foolish that women should go about this way; but after all, the world itself is so strange in this war situation that our mission may be no more strange nor foolish than the rest."

Another silence. Then the prime minister banged his fist on

the table. "Foolish?" he said. "Not at all. These are the first sensible words that have been uttered in this room for ten months." Then he pointed to the panelled door of his office and said, "That door opens from time to time, and people come in to say, 'Mr. Minister, we must have more men, we must have more ammunition, we must have more money or we cannot go on with this war'. At last the door opens and two people walk in and say, 'Mr. Minister, why not substitute negotiations for fighting?' They are the sensible ones." Miss Addams could hardly believe her ears, and was ushered out much encouraged. In fact, Stürgkh had virtually no influence on policy, and Austria-Hungary was to fight on until it had totally destroyed itself.[19]

The atmosphere in Budapest was again entirely different. There was no food shortage. Newspapermen asked them questions without restraint, like American reporters. An energetic group of pacifist ladies took them in tow, and arranged for interviews with Prime Minister István Tisza, and for a large public meeting. The prime minister, as well as various minor governmental officials, told Miss Addams that Hungary was getting nothing out of the war and was, in fact, being forced to fight Prussia's war. At an evening public meeting, the audience was sympathetic to Jane Addams' speech on the senselessness of battle and the need for negotiation.

The visit to Berne, on June 1, was perfunctory. The president of Switzerland gave them only a hurried interview and said that while neutral mediation had some merits, the Swiss confederation could not take the initiative. In Rome, officials of the Italian government responded similarly, saying no more than that they would not regard an offer of mediation as a hostile act. Italy had just entered the war, and populace and government alike were filled with the gay confidence with which every nation entered the holocaust. Much to the excitement of their Italian friends, however, Jane Addams and Alice Hamilton were granted an audience by Pope Benedict XV on June 8. There was fussing over veils and tucking of scarves; the Americans were instructed on how to kneel and kiss the Pope's ring. When in fact they met him, the Pope greeted them simply and asked them to sit down. Benedict XV seemed genuinely excited about their plan and asked eagerly about the response of various statesmen. He encouraged them to pursue their efforts, especially with their own president.[20]

Paris was the most discouraging capital. Not only had French women been refused permission to come to The Hague, but the most important French women's organization had also denounced the Congress and called for the complete defeat of Germany—a sentiment vigorously reiterated by Théophile Delcassé, the foreign minister. Even more distressing, many former pacifists whom Jane Addams had known as supporters of suffrage had become ardent for a military victory. The French leaders were not leading their nation into war against the desire of the people; they were going exactly where the people wanted them to go. After a brief visit with the Belgian government in exile, which was bitter over the failure of the allies to drive out the Germans, the little group went back to London. There they found, if anything, a hardening of attitudes against Germany, though a pacifist meeting, with Bertrand Russell and Jane Addams sharing the speaking, gave them some encouragement.[21] On June 24, after over five weeks of continual travel, Jane Addams and Alice Hamilton left Europe, planning to return whenever the postwar peace conference convened.

As their vessel steamed westward toward New York, Jane Addams and Alice Hamilton tried to sort out their impressions of their journey. Alice Hamilton had perhaps expected less, and so had been less disappointed. The Congress itself, they agreed, had been a stimulating experience and one with great potential for constructive change. The war thundered on as before, but no one at the conference had expected anything else, and the emergence of a permanent women's peace organization gave hope for the future. The trip to the war capitals, however, left Jane Addams frustrated and disappointed to the point of anger. She had expected, of course, nothing more than lack of opposition to neutral mediation from the national leaders, and received what she expected. What came as a shock to her was popular opinion. In each nation they heard the same atrocity stories about the enemy, with the nationalities of the participants reversed. In each nation they heard how all the other nations were aggressors, but this one was fighting purely for defense. There was no question of scheming leaders pushing a war on a reluctant populace; the people themselves were screaming for blood. Equally frightening, perhaps, was the fact that the war seemed to have generated its own reasons for existence. Whatever reasons there may have been for inaugurating the war in the first place, they were no longer relevant. Germans were now fighting to hold off "Slavic barbarism," the English to avenge "crimes of Teutonism." There was no end to such reasoning, no termination date for such a war, short of the extermination of one side or another. On the battlefields of Europe all the carefully nurtured humanitarian feeling which had been built up over half a century was being buried in a blind rage for revenge and destruction.

Yet Jane Addams never for a moment considered altering her basic attitudes about the nature of human beings. What she saw did not move her one iota toward the view that men were inherently passionate, irrational creatures with an inborn drive to kill, maim, and blow up their fellows. The assumption of potential human goodness was so deeply a part of her that it could never come up for re-evaluation. In fact this assumption had been the basis for her life's work, and to give it up would have meant denying virtually everything she had done and believed. Many Americans did experience just that sort of disillusion, and thereby perhaps helped to create one of the more reactionary periods in American history. Miss Addams did not join that disillusion, but insisted with Anne Frank that "I still believe that people are really good at heart." How then could she explain what she had seen? How were these essentially benign creatures marshalled into a bayonet charge? If the leaders were not villains, who then was leading mankind astray?

Miss Addams found an answer, but it was not a very satisfactory one, not even for herself, and it showed the weaknesses rather than the strengths in her intellect. For she was not very good at thinking analytically in larger theoretical terms. From her day-to-day experience at Hull House she could extrapolate perceptive and effective generalizations. When it came to thinking analytically about nationalism, public opinion, the relationship between leaders and the led, the power of irrationality, or competing economic and political systems, her intellect simply proved inadequate. Nor had anything in her education given her training in that sort of thinking. The best explanation she could offer for the popularity of the war was to find and blame a culprit: the press. She came back, she said, convinced "that the next revolution against tyranny would have to be a revolution against the unscrupulous power of the press." The press, she said, had "assumed the power once exercised by the church when it gave the people only such knowledge as it deemed fit for them to have."[22] If the people of Europe only possessed sufficient knowledge, they would perceive their common interest and lay down their arms.

The simplicity, the innocence of this judgment suggests very strongly that it was formulated principally to rescue her belief in humanity in the midst of a world gone berserk. She did not seem to wonder why the press had done this terrible thing, or how the press decided what to print, or why people chose to believe it. In the spring of 1915 the theoretical basis of her life's work was badly shaken, and she was using weak reeds to try to prop it up.

A huge welcome was arranged for Jane Addams when she returned, capped by an address by her at Carnegie Hall on the evening of July 9. Theodore Roosevelt, though invited, refused to attend. To an audience of three thousand Miss Addams related the story of her trip and her conclusions: The war would be a long one, and no one was ready for peace. In the course of perhaps a forty-five-minute address she mentioned in passing that she had heard that troops of both sides were given stimulants before going "over the top." It was as if the rest of her speech did not exist, for with a whoop and a holler the American press, in apparent confirmation of her opinions of the fourth estate, seized upon two sentences of her address. Within three days she personally felt the force of a war hysteria she had merely observed in Europe. Richard Harding Davis picked up the story and then wrote in ringing phrases of the courage of a French or English—not German—soldier who had been killed in a bayonet charge defending their home and country after preparing himself by months of discipline:

> Miss Addams denies him the credit of his sacrifice. She strips him of his honor and courage. She tells his children, 'Your father did not die for France, or for England, or for you; he died because he was drunk.'

Miss Addams had a generally good press as her European tour came to an end, but the opinion expressed by Davis swept everything before it, and for weeks hundreds of newspapers echoed his charge that Miss Addams was a self-satisfied woman who had flung a grievous insult at brave men. In fact, she had brought up the incident to show that the men preserved their humanity to the point of not wanting to stick bayonets in their fellows—but no one noticed that.[23] Later she quietly gave her sources and reiterated her position. The criticism raged on. In America, as in the European countries she had visited, public opinion was more belligerent, more intolerant of alternative views than were the national leaders. The furor over the drugged infantrymen was a hint of the way her countrymen, who had cheered for her in 1912, would reject Jane Addams by 1915, if she stood against war.

After New York she went to Washington where President Wilson asked her to confer with him. She and Lillian Wald, who had not gone to The Hague, spent over an hour telling Wilson in effect that they saw no immediate prospect for peace. Then she returned to Chicago to an enthusiastic welcome. At a speech to some four thousand in the Auditorium Theater, she again told the story of her journey and pleaded for neutral mediation as the only way to end "this curious spell in inflamed Europe." She did not repeat the sentences relating to drinking and the bayonet charge.[24]

The summer of 1915 was not a good time to plead for forbearance, patience, or peace. The sinking of the *Lusitania* dominated public opinion. In mid-summer came sensational revelations of German propaganda and espionage activities within the United States, including the arrest of one superspy as he was trying to return to Berlin from New York. Then, on August 19, a German submarine sank the British freighter *Arabic,* with the loss of forty-four lives, including two Americans. Wilson had taken such a stiff position on the *Lusitania* that he had very little room left for belittling the *Arabic* sinking. As Colonel House wrote him, "Our people do not want war, but even less do they want you to recede from the position you have taken."[25] Although there was no widespread agreement on exactly what policy the country should follow toward Germany, with some segments of opinion being more belligerent than others, anything which smacked of weakness was taken as pro-German by an indignant public. The "pacificators" had to walk softly.

In point of fact, Jane Addams could hardly walk at all. As in the campaign of 1912, she had exhausted herself. The latter part of the summer of 1915 she spent resting in Maine. Then exhaustion turned into a poorly defined over-all deterioration in her health. When Maine got too cold, she continued resting in

Atlantic City, then in late October in Chicago. Every time she tried to resume an active life, she would have a relapse. In Chicago she tried to live at Hull House, but realized that she could not do it, and so retreated to Mrs. Bowen's house on Astor Place where she could be taken care of.[26]

Her illness had the one happy result of preventing her from going to Europe on Henry Ford's Peace Ship. Rosika Schwimmer, the impetuous, cranky, brilliant pacifist from Hungary, had persuaded Ford that a dramatic demonstration for peace might do some good. The plan was to have a shipload of distinguished Americans travel to Europe on a special peace vessel. What they were to do on arrival was unclear. The whole effort was poorly thought out, badly organized, and subject to much ridicule. By November, Jane Addams thought she was regaining her health, and that although the peace ship was unpopular and anyone sailing on it would become unpopular, there was no way for her to refuse to go. Three days before the sailing date, however, she entered the hospital and her doctors refused to consider any talk of a journey. Rosika Schwimmer, who saw the entire world in terms of conspiracies and counterconspiracies, was certain that Miss Addams had deserted the cause. And no amount of public or private statements could get rid of the idea, assiduously promoted in the newspapers, that the Ford Peace Ship was so ridiculous that even Jane Addams would not co-operate.[27]

Her illness was not feigned, however. Between the tour of war capitals and the American break with Germany in April, 1917, she was constantly ill. Any activities were merely brief, uncomfortable interludes in a long attempt at regaining a health which seemed shattered. First it was pneumonia, then a kidney infection which led to the removal of one kidney. She was left weakened for many months.[28]

One interlude of activity involved the "preparedness" controversy. The question of how much military strength the United States ought to have in the face of the European war had been simmering almost since the war broke out. From the outset, Theodore Roosevelt and Henry Cabot Lodge had led a small but effective group pressing for large increases in both the army and navy. This group was influential enough that Wilson felt he had to respond to them in his annual message on December 7, 1914. As emphatically as he could, the president took the opposite position: "We are at peace with the world. . . . We are the champions of peace and of concord." In this situation, no increased military effort was necessary. To build up a huge army, he said, would mean only that the United States had been thrown off balance "by a war with which we have nothing to do, whose causes cannot touch us, whose very existence affords us opportunities of friendship and disinterested service."[29] The sinking of the *Lusitania* had changed the war from something far off, with which the nation had nothing to do, into a spreading holocaust which might even leap the Atlantic. Not only did the advocates of increased military force gain popular strength, but preparedness advocates within the administration felt that the president was swinging away from his earlier position. Less than a year after his 1914 message, Wilson opened the preparedness controversy in earnest with a speech before the Manhattan Club in the Biltmore Hotel in New York on November 4, 1915. There he announced plans for what seemed at the time the creation of a major military force—the heart of which was to be a continental army of some 400,000 men—and a speed-up in naval procurement. A month later he placed the program before Congress.[30]

Wilson knew that his proposals would occasion a fight in the country and in Congress, and he resolved that although he would be flexible on details of his program he would flatly insist on increased military strength and ride out the storm of protest. Support, as the president well knew, was widespread; and it was expressed quickly in the eastern press, among business and patriotic groups. But opposition was also widespread. A number of Christian groups spoke out in opposition and joined a virtually solid bloc of farm leaders. Some labor unions and various socialist splinters also made themselves heard. These views had spokesmen in Congress, with a core of about thirty Democrats from farm areas in the south and west. Inevitably, leadership in the anti-preparedness crusade fell to the greatest spokesman for the cause, William Jennings Bryan. Bryan's resignation from the state secretaryship because he thought Wilson too harsh in the *Lusitania* crisis made him the great hope of peace forces. Ever since his resignation he had been touring the country giving pacifist speeches, and Wilson's program crystallized a group of followers behind Bryan's leadership.[31]

The preparedness debates which raged over the next few

months showed clearly how foreign policy issues split the reform coalition. On one side were Theodore Roosevelt and Woodrow Wilson, who had been calling each other vile names in the previous election campaign; and on the other were William Jennings Bryan and Jane Addams, one a former cabinet member of Wilson, the other a prominent Roosevelt supporter. Naturally, the Women's Peace Party opposed preparedness. On January 11, 1916, the House Committee on Foreign Relations heard from the Women's Peace Party for one hour, with Miss Addams running the hearings and alloting time. The ladies urged an international police force, a world organization, and no preparedness. Miss Addams urged particularly that the United States, as "outside of the war fever," had a duty to try to mediate the conflict. She insisted, in answer to a question, that though the European governments had regarded the Women's International League for Peace and Freedom as feeble, they had taken seriously the organization's proposal of neutral mediation.

Two days later she gave a more detailed statement of her position in extended testimony to a hearing on preparedness before the House Committee on Military Affairs. While she was really in favor of disarmament—as some of the committee tried to get her to admit—she asked only for a delay in armaments increases, and no increases until after a thorough study of existing strength and potential enemies. Her basic contention was that the war had nothing to do with the United States, and was, indeed, a kind of epidemic which this country should make every effort to avoid catching. The war fever was being spread by newspapers, with perhaps some backing from interests who stood to make money from armaments. Armaments themselves would cause an increase in the war spirit and make war more likely, as they had done in Europe. She reiterated that in Europe the common people had not been adequately consulted, and that the same thing was now happening in the United States. After all, various nationalities in the Hull House neighborhood had worked out their own cosmopolitanism, and the countries of Europe could do so too. War was disappearing as morality improved. Then, with perhaps some faltering of logic, she argued that no military build-up should be commenced until the European war was over and we knew who our enemies might be. Then our arms might be built up, so that they might subsequently be reduced in pursuit of an international program to limit arms and eliminate war.

"As I understand it," a committee member asked her, "you supported Mr. Roosevelt in the last presidential campaign?"

"Yes; I did," she answered. Then, in apparent forgetfulness of the two battleships, she added, "But we had nothing about preparedness in our platform. I am a Progressive because the Progressive Party has a program of what seems to me to be a very remarkable political expression of social justice."

"But as you understand it," the committee member pressed on, "a great many other citizens supported Mr. Roosevelt—"

Almost poignantly, Jane Addams interrupted, protesting, "He was not talking as he is now."

"But he was the same Roosevelt."

"But he was talking minimum wages, the protection of children and women in industry, and things of that sort."

Other committee members probed the obvious weak points in her remarks: Could not the war, which might seem distant, suddenly involve the United States? Was not some means of defense necessary? Was not defense prepared ahead of time better than a hastily thrown-together force when danger was at the doorstep? Would not our moral force have more influence if we were not defenseless? Was she not really taking a position of nonresistance to evil and total nonviolence? In general, the committee was more critical than receptive.[32]

There was, of course, also critical newspaper response to her testimony. One editorial suggested darkly that Congress investigate Jane Addams and others to "compel them to state why they desire the country to remain defenseless."[33] But this was mild compared to what was to come in later years. Miss Addams was standing with a large body of American opinion—a minority, and a losing minority at that—but she was still in the area of legitimate political combat. When she spoke as an out-and-out pacifist, she was in a tiny minority, but mere opposition to preparedness provided a roomier platform. On it could stand western and southern farmers, essentially isolationist, who thought that the United States ought to let Europe go hang, but who were not pacifists. It also had room for Jane Addams the pacifist, though not the isolationist. The latter wanted the United States to intervene, but *morally* instead of militarily: she wanted Wilson to go to a postwar peace conference with clean hands and a pure heart. Later, when she maintained her pacifism during the war, she would be vilified, but during the preparedness controversy, criticism remained relatively polite. She even continued cordial relations with the White House. With the controversy at its height, Woodrow Wilson maintained a solicitous interest in her health and once even sent her roses.[34]

Miss Addams differed with the administration in only a limited area, and even there differences were not complete, for some sort of neutral mediation was always an alternative in Wilson's mind. More important in Jane Addams' view was the president's rapid progress toward the domestic program advanced by the Progressive Party in 1912. Jane Addams said in 1912 that she expected Wilson to lead the country in a progressive direction. During the election year of 1916 Wilson seemed to be trying hard to enact not only the Democratic, but also the Bull Moose platform of 1912. Louis D. Brandeis was seated on the Supreme Court over serious opposition, through strong pressure from the president. A workmen's compensation bill for federal employees became law in the summer. In the early fall, Wilson signed an effective child labor act.

Jane Addams would vote for President for the first time in 1916, and it was news when, in mid-October, she announced that her first vote would go to Wilson. She was only sorry, she said, that she was too ill to participate actively in the campaign. Just before the election, she issued a detailed statement of her reasons for supporting the Democratic candidate: the provision of the Clayton Act declaring that labor was not a commodity; the LaFollette Seamen's Act; the Keating-Owens Child Labor Act; the Workmen's Compensation Act for federal employees; support for the eight-hour day; and the Rural Credits Bill. She included foreign policy in her endorsement, too, speaking highly of the Bryan arbitration treaties, repeal of toll exemptions for American ships in the Panama Canal, restraint in dealing with Mexico, a strengthened Pan-American Union, and lowered tariffs. Her endorsement was merely symptomatic of the swing of a great many Roosevelt progressives to support for Wilson in 1916.[35]

The pacifist forces were encouraged that the man who had "kept us out of war" could win at least partly on that very issue. They were further cheered by his "peace without victory" speech in January, 1917. Their hearts fell when, only a few days later, he boasted that the United States would have the biggest navy in the world and when, a few weeks later, he personally led a preparedness parade in Washington. Although pacifists still had access to Wilson, they knew they were on the outside of events, and getting ever further from the center where policy was made. They feared the worst when the German government announced, on January 31, 1917, the resumption of unrestricted submarine warfare. When, four days later, Wilson broke diplomatic relations with Germany, Jane Addams telegraphed him pleading once again for a conference of neutrals. But she must have known that it was too late. Congress had burst into applause when Wilson announced the break, and the country was clearly behind him.[36]

There was still no declaration of war, however, and Jane Addams dared hope that some way might be found to keep the nation from that last fatal step. At the end of February she went to New York, first for an executive committee meeting of the Women's Peace Party, then for a combined meeting with all the leading peace societies. Then a delegation from the combined groups journeyed to Washington for an appointment with President Wilson on February 28. Probably no time could have been worse for a delegation of pacifists to urge moderation on Wilson. Just four days earlier he had learned of the so-called Zimmerman telegram, in which Germany offered Mexico her lost territory in the southwestern United States in return for Mexican aid in a war against her northern neighbor. The telegram had not yet been made public, but Wilson was seething with fury. He had lost all faith now in any German protestation of good will. Jane Addams' account of this last interview with the president before the United States entered the war is vague, but she did remember that Wilson was stern and unimpressed by any plea for patience with Germany. He did not reveal the contents of the Zimmerman note, but he said to the pacifists, "If you knew what I know at the present moment, . . . you would not ask me to attempt further dealings with the Germans." The next day the note was made public in eight-column banner headlines all over the country.

On March 18, three American ships were sunk without warning by U-boats. The next day the Czar was overthrown, making Russia "a fit partner for a League of Honor," in Wilson's words. On April 2, the president asked a joint session of Congress for a declaration of war against Germany. "What does it all mean?"

Helena Dudley wrote to Jane Addams. "It is almost demoniacal, this sweep toward conscription . . . and labor so passive and the Socialists broken up and the social workers lining up with the bankers! . . . I feel as if a reaction must set in but now the Russian Revolution is put down to the credit of war and by war we are to 'democratize the world'! What folly and blindness—And Wilson! I feel sometimes as if I must be mad—or else the world is mad!" Vachel Lindsay wrote in a similarly despairing vein: "What shall I do? This war breaks my heart. . . . I would rather be shot than shoot anybody." And Jane Addams could only respond in kind: "I feel as if a few of us were clinging together in a surging sea." One by one her former allies in the peace and progressive movements fell into line behind President Wilson. The Church Peace Union, the League to Enforce Peace, even William Jennings Bryan accepted the argument that the shortest road to peace lay through war. When she learned that Robert A. Woods had pledged the Boston settlement-house movement to aiding in army enlistments, she sadly commented that the hardest thing was "that I seem to stand aside not only from a community demonstration, but from my old friends and comrades." Increasingly she found herself on the radical fringe of society, a troubled outcast.[37]

Despair or not, there was still work to do. An Espionage Act and a Conscription Act were before Congress, and Jane Addams testified against both. Her testimony, and that of other persons who feared restraints on expression of opinion, produced some changes in the former act. She asked the committee pointedly whether, under the proposed law, she would be permitted to express her internationalist position. When asked if she would agitate against the Conscription Law once it was passed, she calmly answered that she had alway agitated against laws that she did not like and hoped to continue. Her testimony had no effect whatever on the Conscription Bill. While in Washington, she unsuccessfully pressed on Newton D. Baker her plea for draft exemption for conscientious objectors, even those who were not formal members of a pacifist religion.[38]

Miss Addams returned to Chicago and was virtually silent for two months. She did urge, in vague terms, that women should hold to their ideals, and she announced that she would be willing to take part in work to relieve the suffering of war. In early summer, she began to accept invitations to speak before Chicago groups. She found that the Chicago City Club had trouble finding anyone to preside at the meeting she addressed because no one wanted to be identified with pacifism. On June 10 she spoke at the First Congregational Church in Evanston on "Pacifism and Patriotism in Time of War." She had a kind word to say for Americans who had emigrated from Germany, protested the allied blockade, and insisted that pacifists were not cowards. As newspapers all over the country reported the next day. "Profound silence followed." After a lengthy, embarrassed pause, Judge Orrin N. Carter of the state supreme court rose to speak. "I have been a life-long friend of Miss Addams," Judge Carter began. "I have agreed with her on most questions in the past, but—"

"That 'but' sounds ominous," said Miss Addams, smiling. "It sounds as if you were going to break with me."

"I am going to break," the judge answered, not smiling. "I think anything that may tend to cast doubt on the justice of our cause in the present war is very unfortunate."

Hastily the meeting adjourned.

SOME TOOLS OF KAISERISM AND OTHERS, thundered the *New York Herald* the next day: "Evidently the Teutonic oligarchy in control of the Socialist party's organization counts that day as lost which does not add to the accumulation of evidence of its Teutonism. . . . There is little difference between the Teutonism of Socialism and the Teutonism of pacifism." The next day the paper added that pacifism was not cowardice. "It is infinitely more despicable. It is bordering on treason." Other newspapers agreed, and a landslide of criticism rolled down upon Miss Addams. "The Hun is at the gate," a Chicago clergyman wrote, "and this is no time for criticism." Once in a while a newspaper might point out that "Her record at Hull House stands," but usually she was classed with the "pacifists, slackers, objectors and sleepy heads" who continued to trouble Uncle Sam. "Any spoken or written word," wrote a Chicago businessman, "that lessens the strength of the arm of the Government is a disloyal act." "Have you forgotten," a letter writer to the *Chicago Tribune* asked Chicagoans, "that Mrs. Catt and Dr. Shaw have both been officers in the Woman's Peace Party. . . ? Is there not a serious menace in this close alliance between socialist and suffragist, pacifist and feminist?" To make matters worse, if possible, the *Staats-Zeitung,* the city's leading German-language newspaper, printed a poem in praise of Jane Addams.[39]

This storm of abuse, when added to the criticism which had already rained down upon her, disturbed Jane Addams—more, perhaps, than she knew. She went though a period of self-doubt unmatched since the ennui that followed her father's death. Speaking essentially of herself, she said that the pacifist in war time "finds it possible to travel from the mire of self-pity straight to the barren hills of self-righteousness, and to hate himself equally in both places." She had, after all, committed herself to the broadest possible definition of democracy: popular impulses were in their general tendency good and progressive and should be followed. Yet here she was standing against what was undoubtedly a popular impulse. "In the hours of doubt, and self-distrust the question again and again arises, has the individual or a very small group, the right to stand out against millions of his fellow countrymen? Is there not a great value in mass judgement. . . ?"[40] She longed, at times, to feel more a part of the community. "Solitude has always had its demons, harder to withstand than the snares of the world, and the unnatural desert into which the pacifist was summarily cast out seemed to be peopled with them." There was, for her, a terrible mental strain, which had physical counterparts, in standing apart from her fellows. She attributed the deaths of several older pacifists—Kier Hardy, Jenkin Lloyd Jones, Washington Gladden—in part to this strain. And though she did not say so, she may well have partly attributed her own semi-invalidism to it also. She had shown over the years since 1889 that she could stand outside society as a pioneer, breaking trail and making paths. She could not stand outside society as a rebel, moving on well-traveled highways but against traffic.

In these months of agony, her occasional meetings with other pacifists were like water to a thirsty man. At meetings of the Women's Peace Party, she could, for a moment at least, forget somewhat "the sense of social disapprobation and of alienation of which we had become increasingly conscious." To make such meetings more numerous, she joined the Fellowship of Reconciliation, a newly formed group without rigid doctrine, but essentially of Christian pacifists, close in spirit to the Quakers. In fact, she turned more explicitly than she had for many years to Christian terminology, and had nothing but amazed contempt for a minister who could say, "If Jesus were living today he would be fighting in the trenches of France." Rather, Jane Addams was sure, he would be under surveillance by the Justice Department—as was the Fellowship of Reconciliation. She also turned for comfort and support to books by pacifists and those who favored some sort of world government, to convince herself that, after all, she was not mad and the rest of the world sane. She had to constantly reassure herself that "the moral changes in human affairs may also begin with a differing group or individual, sometimes with the one who at best is designated as a crank and a freak and in sterner moments is imprisoned as an atheist or traitor."

Though she did not realize it, during the course of the war the nation was not only rejecting Jane Addams as a pacifist, but also the entire reform impulse which she represented. A reaction was gathering force which would sweep away as much of progressivism as it possibly could, and would firmly resist pressures of the type which led to child-labor laws, the Clayton Act, and the children's court.

She longed for some way she could hew to her ideals and yet return from her position of pariah. She was unwilling to remain "alienated"—to use her own word—to stand on a position even if the heavens fell. She had not the strength of the young men who went to prison rather than register for the draft; Hull House even housed a local draft board. She had not the strength to stand with Norman Thomas and tell her countrymen they were wrong. As a matter of fact, at the 1917 meeting of the Women's Peace Party, a forlorn gathering in a Philadelphia Friends meeting-house so innocuous that even the Department of Justice only glanced in at the door, she tried to resign her chairmanship, saying she was sick of the very term pacifist. She felt herself an outcast, and she did not have the strength to stand it. In her search for a way of being both principled and popular, she read in James Frazer's *The Golden Bough* of the universal symbol of the corn mother, the nourishing mother, the earth and her daughter which might be corn, rice, or wheat, whatever was staple in a given part of the world. She was reminded of the motto of her Rockford class, and knew that war provided many opportunities for the primordial task of "bread giving" with which she had identified herself for decades.[41]

The solution she found, and which almost miraculously seemed to provide the cure for her lingering invalidism, was to join enthusiastically in the efforts of the U. S. Food Administration, under Herbert Hoover. She had all along taken the position that no group, no matter how convinced of the evils of war, should do anything to obstruct the war effort, and she had indicated that she would be willing to help in some form of relief work. Before the United States entered the war, Hoover had done yeoman's work organizing relief for the Belgians. He had applied the organizational logic that came from his engineering background to relieve suffering—just that application of intelligence and knowledge to social problems which many progressives had been urging. With America's belligerency, he turned his efforts to food conservation at home. Jane Addams disagreed with the editors of the *New Republic,* who thought that the necessities of wartime efficiency might lead to rational central planning in peace, for she believed that the rational planning for war would terminate with the hostilities. But she welcomed any step toward the efficient use of resources, even on a short-term basis.

Her reading of Frazer convinced her again of the mystical importance of bread. "To every man his measure of grain," she quoted a Russian peasant greeting, "and may every man in the world be a Christian." She found similar statements or poems in France, England, and the Scandinavian countries. She therefore felt a great sense of relief when the Food Administration was formed, for she was convinced that going around the country speaking for food conservation, or "Hooverizing" as it was called, was the beginning of a new internationalism. She had, to this point, been suspicious of panaceas, but in these days when her faith in human goodness was challenged, when she was oppressed by her alienation from her fellows, she seized upon Bread as a new savior for humanity. Her reasoning was that just as women had been brought into domestic politics because their household duties had become matters for public policy, so the need to feed the world might bring them into international life. Their entrance into domestic affairs had led to laws against excessive hours and child labor, among other things. Perhaps their entrance into international affairs could lead to an ethic which might end war.

"I believed that a generous response to this world situation might afford an opportunity to lay over again the foundations for a wider international morality . . . a new powerful force might be unloosed in the world when the motive for producing and shipping food on the part of great nations was no longer a commercial one, but had for the moment shifted to a desire to feed the hungry."[42] Tariffs would evaporate, an acknowledgement of interdependence would grow, and the social ethic would take on world-wide dimensions.

Having thus deluded herself, Jane Addams could in good conscience throw herself into work that was respectably patriotic. She toured thousands of miles between November of 1917 and May of 1918, making scores of speeches on food conservation and trying to persuade her audience that a world-wide effort to feed the hungry was a major step on the road to an internationalism which would make future wars impossible. Once again she was on the platform with a chance to use her oratorical skills; once again she received public applause. The devils of solitude were banished.[43] When at last the war ended Jane Addams could reconvene the Congress of Women without any sense of discontinuity between her wartime and peacetime selves. True, she had not held out totally against the war. True, she could almost be said to have served the national effort. Yet always she felt that her service had been in the cause of humanity, of feeding the hungry, and not in the service of victory.

The reconvened Congress met in Zurich in May of 1919, and what Jane Addams saw in Europe reinforced her views that a peaceful world lay by way of an international effort to relieve human misery. On the way to Zurich the American delegation, smaller this time than in 1915, stayed for three weeks in France. Since they were not making any useful contacts with diplomats, Lillian Wald arranged for two cars and Red Cross drivers to take them through northern parts of the country. The April weather was overcast and cold, with intermittent rain keeping the fields sticky with mud. Neither news pictures nor the written word had prepared them for the nightmare scenes they encountered. At Vimy Ridge, where casualties had been heavy even for World War I, the car in which Alice Hamilton, Jeanette Rankin, Lillian Wald, and Jane Addams were riding broke down. While the other two remained with the car, Alice Hamilton and Miss

Addams walked along the ridge in silence. Rolls of barbed wire rusted in the rain, shell-shattered trees stood in haphazard shapes, and the earth was crisscrossed in some places by trenches and in others plowed by shells. A little way below them, Chinese laborers were exhuming the hastily buried bodies of Canadian soldiers for proper and lasting burial. Nothing grew in that barren earth. A cold wind blew through the ladies, and the clouds hung like funeral crepe above them.

The next day, in Lille, they saw a doctor examining emaciated children for Hoover's relief organization. As a doctor, Alice Hamilton was shocked to see shoulder blades protruding like wings beneath their nearly fleshless skin—but what they saw later in Germany made these French children seem reasonably well-off. The doctor had lost his voice during the war, and talked only in whispers. The children, thinking that something was secret, whispered back, and the whole pitiful scene was wrapped in an unnatural hush. After a day with the Quaker relief organization, Dr. Hamilton and Jane Addams went in search of John Linn's grave.

> We reached the road that turned off from the highway to the Chadrun farm where he is buried, our car sank deep in mud. The snow had stopped and we climbed out and started off on foot. It was a muddy road, winding up over the ridge with desolate stretches on either side covered with all sorts of debris from the Army and dug up to make 'fox holes' where the soldiers sheltered themselves. It was on his return from a trip to take food to the boys in their holes that the shell struck John.

They hardly knew where to look for the grave in the large temporary graveyard marked with crude crosses with metal identification tags, but they finally found it, and paid brief last respects.[44]

The American women had known that war was like this, so in a sense they did not learn anything from the trip, but they arrived in Zurich for the conference on May 6 with a heavier sense of tragedy. The conference itself, while an intense emotional experience for those attending it, was of virtually no importance for the wider world. War had led to just the kind of bitterness and vengefulness that Wilson himself had predicted in 1917, and the president was unable to seriously modify the claims of the victors. One hundred twenty-six lady pacificators, no matter how distinguished they might be as individuals, simply did not constitute a significant force. The conference received far less notice in the American press than The Hague conference, and even these reports were more interested in the doings of famous women than in programs they represented.

None of this meant that the pacifist assessment of the peace settlement was mistaken. The details of the treaty were revealed while the conference was in session, and as clause after clause was published the pacifists reacted with stunned horror. Their worst fears of a victors' peace were not nearly harsh enough to predict the reality. Colonies were transferred from defeated to victorious nation with never a thought of asking the inhabitants; a euphemistic "mandate" system was invented, also with no shred of self-determination; huge indemnities were required from the Central Powers. The ladies condemned the settlement and asked for a return to Wilson's fourteen points. Jane Addams applauded, with reservations, the establishment of the League of Nations. No one can say what a more lenient settlement might have prevented twenty years later; but certainly later analysis does not leave the Women's International League for Peace and Freedom in the position of hopelessly naive "Alices in Blunderland," as one newspaper called them. Their conclusions were at least as sound as those of presidents and prime ministers.

For Jane Addams personally, the conference was an emotional feast after years of inadequate sustenance. She was surrounded by like-minded women, and lapped around with that devotion which since 1912 she had come to need. The scars and cuts made by her war years as an outcast, which the speeches for the Food Administration had not fully healed, finally disappeared. Florence Kelley was deeply affected too. She had gone as a skeptic, simply as an act of faith, "to black Jane Addams' boots and lug her suitcases." "Next time I would go on my knees," she said. "It was unbelievably wonderful." Alice Hamilton was impressed by how little radicalism and how little nonsense was talked. There were emotional scenes, as when a German woman and a French woman shook hands, then embraced, or when Jane Addams preached internationalism from a pulpit eighteen feet high. The conference passed resolutions condemning the peace treaty and asking for an immediate end to the Allied blockade, which was keeping food from Germany. The Zurich Conference also established the permanent organization of the Women's International League for Peace and Freedom.[45]

Jane Addams returned to Paris feeling that the Zurich Conference had been even better than the one at The Hague four years previous. In the French capital she was approached by Carolena Wood, an English Quaker, who asked her to join a Quaker delegation which was going into Germany to investigate the condition of children suffering from long years of underfeeding. She checked with Hoover, who told her he hoped she would indeed go. "Germany needs not only food," he said, "she needs people of good will to bring her back to normal relations with the rest of the world." With the response set in those terms Miss Addams had to go. With Hoover's support, they thought all things would be easy but the delays were interminable. First Hoover encouraged them; then he told them they would have to wait until the peace treaty was signed—and no one knew how long that would be. They waited for a while in Paris. Impatience drove Alice Hamilton to England to pursue her special field of industrial medicine, and two weeks later, near the end of June, Jane Addams joined her in London. As usual Miss Addams was buried by invitations in that city, so there was no danger of their impatience being turned into boredom. At the end of June, permission came—the first civilian passports issued after the war for travel in Germany.

Carolena Wood, Dr. Aletta Jacobs, Alice Hamilton, and Jane Addams, guided by two German Quakers, were in Germany for just over two weeks, from July 6 to 23, and went to Berlin, Halle, Leipzig, Frankfort am Main, and several outlying small villages. Since the blockade was still functioning, they had to eat the wartime food: heavy, soggy black bread composed in part of sawdust and bark, cabbages, turnips, and various ersatz. The ersatz coffee was drinkable, but ersatz meat—soft, gooey and dyed red—was too much for even Alice Hamilton's stomach. Often this was supplemented by "war soup," made from who-knew-what and water—mostly water. Aletta Jacobs had brought a huge handbag stuffed with cheese, bacon, crackers, and some chocolate. While it lasted, this supplemented their diet.

They visited chiefly institutions caring for children and saw not only physical starvation but emotional starvation too. These children had never been treated like babies and infants, with the solicitous cuddling and mothering that new human beings needed. They were listless and without spirit. Jane Addams had seen careworn and overworked children in Chicago and youngsters with more responsibility and independence than they could shoulder. She had worked for years to improve their lot. Yet here, her own country was helping to drive children into a state far worse than anything she had seen in Chicago. The nationalism which had seemed such a constructive force in the Europe she had seen in 1885 had gone sour. In the eighties she thought that unity, coming together, finding common traits among Slavs, Germans, Italians, had overcome socialism. After all, *Deutschland, Deutschland über alles* had originally meant a united Germany superseding the little Germanic states. Nationalism then had burned with a fervent humanitarianism. Now, however, nationalism had become exclusive and dogmatic, dividing people instead of uniting them, demanding worship, tribute, and now retribution.

These thoughts drew her closer to the two international ideals of Quakerism and the League of Nations. The American Friends Service Committee had allowed Miss Addams to buy $30,000 worth of food for the Germans, and this was but the beginning of a large Quaker effort to feed a whole nation. So widespread was the practice that the Germans invented a new verb, *quackern,* which meant to be fed by Quakers. Perhaps this sort of humanitarian effort could break down the exclusive dogmatism of nationalism and lead to a continuation of the trend toward unity.[46] Perhaps, too, the saving remnant in the peace treaties might be the League of Nations. Imperfect though it was, the League offered an instrument through which a larger humanitarian effort, far larger than the American Friends Service Committee could ever undertake, might be organized. If the League, instead of devoting itself to mandates and reparations, could concentrate on feeding the hungry and rebuilding a shattered world, a higher internationalism might grow out of nationalism. Jane Addams returned to the United States in late August resolved to put her efforts into these twin campaigns: to feed the hungry and to make the League an agency for international social welfare.

When she spoke about working conditions in the needle trades or garbage collection in Chicago slums, she spoke from firsthand experience. As a legislator in Springfield who often opposed her position said, "She always knew her stuff." When Jane Addams dealt with international relations, however, she spoke out of no experience, no data, no knowing her stuff.

While her hopefulness was surely naïve, she was more realistic than many progressives that the war effort would lead to progressivism triumphant. As she recognized, the war had shattered the coalition which produced the stupendous reform achievements of Wilson's first term. At the very moment of the progressive payoff came the war and the end of the coalition. The suffrage movement split; the trust-regulation movement split; the former Bull Moosers split; and each splinter fell away from the other. When the final vote for war came, the leading congressional spokesmen for reform was on the opposite side of the president who had done the most to put the reform into national law. The first congresswoman, Jeanette Rankin, cast one of the handful of votes against the declaration of war; Anna Howard Shaw, for many years the leading suffrage advocate, eagerly joined the Committee for National Defense and was annoyed when she was given only minor responsibilities. The editors of the *New Republic* decided that intervention might, all things considered, be the best course for the nation; Randolph Bourne, who had been a contributing editor, resigned and savaged his former colleagues, especially John Dewey, from the pages of the *Dial* and *Seven Arts*. There was virtually no relationship between one's position on domestic issues and one's position on entry into the war. In the small minority of opponents of the war were men and women who, under other circumstances, would have been bitter political enemies, while the antiwar progressives looked across a great chasm to see their former colleagues supporting Wilson and the war.

A hopeful progressive might find glimmers of what he wanted to see in the wartime nationalization of railroads, in rationally planned housing developments near military bases, in military insurance which might be a start toward broader social insurance. But as Jane Addams recognized, railroads nationalized to carry troops and ammunition were likely to be denationalized when the need for troops and ammunition disappeared.

The war did help to produce the closely related reforms of woman suffrage and prohibition. Whether the latter was "progressive" depends on one's definition of that variously defined term. Prohibition was pushed by a coalition which existed virtually for that single issue: rural fundamentalist groups, usually considered conservative, and urban reformers, usually thought of as liberal or progressive. Its parentage was, in these terms, ambiguous. Suffrage was more clearly a part of the over-all progressive program and may well be the clearest domestic reform which the war produced. For many people, of course, the war was viewed as a continuation of the reform idea, transferred to international politics. For Jane Addams, however, war was a major step backward along the road she wanted America to travel. Where in 1915 everything had seemed possible, by 1919 everything seemed difficult.

15

After the War

THE difficulties stemmed from what Jane Addams called the "post-war psychology," which flourished so luxuriantly after 1919. De Tocqueville had noted nearly a century before that dissent had a hard row to hoe in a land dominated by equality of condition. He had also said that democracy would have a bad time at the beginning and at the end of a war. But these two insights do not fully explain either the virulence or the character of wartime and postwar repression. The United States was actually at war a short time and was physically damaged not at all; yet the nation succumbed to a rather extreme form of hysteria, and the war was clearly a traumatic experience for a nation which had become accustomed to picturing itself as immune from the petty squabbles of a distant and decadent Europe. During the war German was dropped from the curriculum of high schools and colleges, the Espionage and Sedition Acts were enforced with a rigor amounting to repression, and the nation as a whole seemed eager to find dissenters and keep them in their place. This hysteria survived the war, and even increased after the armistice. If war produced hysteria, war plus the Bolshevik Revolution produced panic. "The blaze of Revolution is sweeping every American institution of law and order . . . licking at the altars of the churches, leaping into the belfry of the school house, crawling into the sacred corners of American homes, seeking to replace marriage vows with libertine laws . . .," cried A. Mitchell Palmer in 1920.[1]

Jane Addams found that she was attacked more frequently and more angrily in the 1920's than she had been during the war itself. No longer was she voted the greatest woman in the nation or honored as a modern saint. The settlement-house movement, the entire quest for social justice were nearly forgotten in the attacks on her pacifism and radicalism. Similarly, but on a larger scale, the 1920's saw a turning away from humanitarian social reform in general. While individuals and organizations continued to struggle for progressive programs during the decade, it was, as one of them said, "Uphill all the way."

Jane Addams understood the nature of the postwar psychology and could look back on it from the end of the decade with a certain degree of detachment. The fear of Bolshevism after World War I was, she felt, parallel to the "cold fear which held Europe in its grip during the three decades following the French Revolution."[2] She noted with a touch of bitterness the way all proposals for change were discarded not after careful analysis, but merely by labeling them Bolshevik. She felt that she and her ideas would simply have to wait until the illness passed, when they could once again continue where they had left off in 1917.

Yet while she was willing to wait, albeit impatiently, for the mood to pass, hysteria would not leave her alone. In January of 1919 a Senate committee investigating German propaganda during the war released a list of "Radicals and Pacifists" with the clear implication that their activity had aided the enemy. Beside Miss Addams, the list included Roger Baldwin, Charles A. Beard, Elizabeth Gurley Flynn, David Starr Jordan, and a long list of others of varying shades of opinion. Lillian Wald, also on the list, shot a telegram to Miss Addams asking if she and "our comrades" were planning any protest. Jane Addams consulted with Sophonisba Breckinridge and answered that probably a protest would make matters worse. Newton D. Baker pooh-poohed the list and the issue quickly passed.[3]

The next controversy, almost exactly a year later, did not pass quickly. On January 2 and 6, 1920, Justice Department agents carried out a dragnet raid all over the country against presumed members of the Communist and Communist Labor parties. Thousands were arrested, some not members of either party, and the abuse of due process was widespread.[4] These were the Palmer Raids, organized mainly by J. Edgar Hoover, and the high point of the postwar Red Scare. The illegality of the government's procedures was so flagrant that even men in general sympathy with Hoover's purpose were moved to protest. Most Americans, however, applauded the raids. As one angry patriot wrote to Jane Addams, "Our government has been too patient and waited altogether too long in taking action against the scum of Europe."[5]

Miss Addams addressed a meeting in Recital Hall on February 22. Her subject was Americanization, and at the end of her remarks she noted that the immigrants around Hull House had been very uneasy about their position since the Palmer Raids and had lost confidence in the evenhandedness of American justice. The course of events after this remark was predictable. The Chicago newspapers rained abuse on her head. In rolling prose the *News* thundered that "so called defenders of American institutions, some of whom have degenerated into philosophical anarchists without knowing it, continue to denounce the deportation of alien apostles of sedition in a spirit of sublime detachment from the truth."[6] An anonymous correspondent sent her a clipping from California about a *social and charity worker*—the correspondent had underlined those words—who had just been sentenced to fourteen years in prison on charges of criminal syndicalism. Pencilled across the clipping were the words, "It is sometimes well to read 'the handwriting on the wall.' "[7]

In a long reply to the newspapers, Miss Addams defended herself with more anger and passion than she normally showed. She said that she had "contended that while many of those arrested aliens might be legitimately liable to deportation, that the methods employed were not those to give them an impression of even-handed justice and lawful procedure; that the entire situation was a dangerous departure from the Anglo-Saxon tradition of arresting a man for his overt act and not for his opinions." She closed her vigorous letter with: "We come around to the old situation, that an injustice against the most wretched man in the community is in the end an injustice against all of us."[8]

She had had "questionable associations" before the war; she had been a pacifist during the war; now she had associated herself with anarchy and red revolution. To Americans who were prone to this sort of thinking, there was no contradiction in accusing a person of being simultaneously a Bolshevik and a Prussian sympathizer, for in truth many Americans greeted the Russian revolution as a German plot to weaken the allies. Jane Addams had now placed herself squarely at the bullseye of the target of intolerance. Attacks on her continued throughout the decade, with scarcely a year passing without some new accusation. Immediately after her protest of the Palmer Raids an invitation to speak at the University of Toronto was withdrawn because of the possibility of "disturbance or protest."[9] About a year later the Lusk Committee of the New York legislature issued a four-volume, 5000-page report on *Revolutionary Radicalism: Its History, Purposes and Tactics.* Clayton Lusk was a vigorous politician building a career on saving his nation from dire distress. He was alarmed at declining morality, and proposed movie censorship as a cure. He was more alarmed at sedition and disloyalty which he found creeping into settlement houses, churches, schools, and colleges; it is Lusk whom all New York teachers have to thank for instituting the loyalty oath in the state. His *magnum opus,* parts of which were leaked to the press for about a year, finally appeared in full in the spring of 1921. In it, virtually every liberal organization was accused of being seditious. Prominent among the accused organizations were the various peace groups of which Jane Addams was a member. There were even photographs of letters proving without a doubt that Jane Addams knew Sophonisba Breckinridge. The Lusk Report was the most important basis for accusations against Jane Addams in the early 1920's; it was to be referred to by newspapers and individual patriots for years to come.[10]

The middle years of the twenties were the high point of accusation against Miss Addams. By that time the American Legion seems to have discovered how dangerous she was. At an Armistice Day meeting in Boston in 1926 a group of school children gave patriotic speeches, then were spirited away secretly so that subversives would not get their names. Next a veteran attacked the subversives of the Women's International League for Peace and Freedom, the Fellowship of Reconciliation, and the American Civil Liberties Union, ending with the pointed question of these pacifists, "Which is the greatest menace, khaki or love of Lenin and Trotsky?" Although Jane Addams was a member of all three groups, she did not answer the question directly. In a long letter to the Boston *Herald,* however, she defined her position:

> I am not in any sense a Socialist, have never belonged to the party and have never been especially affiliated with them. I am certainly not a communist or a bolshevik. I am, of course, president of the Women's International League for Peace and Freedom and we have advocated

recognition of soviet Russia, not because we have been in favor of the government any more than we were with that of the Czars. I did not go to Europe with Mr. Ford on his peace ship, although I am generally credited with having done so.

I do not know why I am called a bolshevik except as a term of opprobrium that is easily flung about.[11]

To people who could believe that the Women's International League might plot revenge on children who made patriotic speeches, no such denial would be convincing. The accusations continued, including a particularly harsh one from the head of the Illinois American Legion.[12]

In 1927 the Daughters of the American Revolution discovered with some consternation that they were harboring a viper in their midst—that in fact Jane Addams was a life member of the organization. In 1895 she had been a juror at an exposition in Paris which awarded the grand prize to the D.A.R. for an exhibit. In gratitude the patriotic society made her an honorary member. "I thought it was for life," Miss Addams remarked, "but it seems it was only during good behavior." A heresy trial was held in San Francisco:

First of all a great slab of the constitution was read to me, and I was asked if I was loyal to that. Then I was asked if the International League for Peace and Freedom members took any vow against participation in war. We have not, and I told the women that.

Then I was asked if a member of the League could be loyal to the United States. I told them that as postmaster at Hull House every year I renewed my vow of loyalty to the United States of America, and that answered that.

She was not excommunicated, and the incident was greeted with a saving remnant of mirth by at least some of the San Francisco press.[13] This incident may have signaled the beginning of the end of "post-war psychology," for silly attacks against Jane Addams declined sharply after 1928. Things went so far that by 1931 the Kansas American Legion awarded a medal to a young man for a patriotic essay which mentioned, among other great Americans, Jane Addams of Hull House.[14]

In spite of this constant criticism throughout the 1920's, she continued to urge internationalism on her countrymen. During the winter of 1919 she spoke throughout the midwest in support of the League of Nations. Even after the Treaty of Versailles and the Covenant of the League were defeated by the Senate, she continued to urge the virtues of the League. Always her message had the same thrust: political internationalism, of which the League was the first manifestation, should be the basis for a broader humanitarian internationalism. Jane Addams knew from her trip to Europe that hundreds of thousands of people, including Germans, were destitute and starving. Americans must join with people of other nations to end this suffering, not only for the sake of their fellow human beings, but because the effort itself could lead to a new international spirit. Again and again she drew the parallel between domestic American experience and the international situation. Humanitarian impulses had led Americans to oppose child labor, filthy streets, dangerous machinery. In the course of dealing with these specific problems a new spirit of co-operation, the "social ethic" was encouraged. In the same way, an international effort to succor German children could lead to a social ethic in international terms. As she entitled one of her talks, the United States should "Feed the World and Save the League."[15] She continued, until her death, to speak for the League, the World Court, and the recognition of Soviet Russia.

While Miss Addams favored diplomatic recognition of the U.S.S.R., she did not fall so heavily under the spell of the Soviet experiment as did some of her friends. Her first reaction to the revolution was to applaud those Russian soldiers who simply refused to fight—the reaction of a pacifist, not a social reformer. While she was interested in the spectacle of a great nation seeming to function in part as a social laboratory, she was suspicious of the fanaticism of the Bolsheviks. By 1920 she was already worrying about a nation governed "by any creed so firmly held that for its sake men are willing to inflict widespread misery." She quoted with approval Romain Rolland's wry comment that "there is no danger in any state as great as that of men with principles."[16] Rather than placing her faith in continuous revolution, she placed it in continuous persuasion by pacifist and international organizations, chiefly the Women's International League for Peace and Freedom, and during the 1920's she devoted enormous effort to this squabbling, impoverished group whose chief claim to public notice was that she was its president. Each year there was an international conference to arrange, money to solicit, and personal quarrels between members to adjudicate. The problems were many, the aims noble, the correspondence endless, and the effects negligible.

She also delivered her message as a private ambassador of international good will. In 1923 she circled the world: Europe, India, the Philippines, China, Japan, and home. At each stop she was lionized by women's and peace groups, and she gave speech after speech on the virtues of internationalism. As a premonition of things to come, she had to stay briefly in the hospital in Tokyo for the removal of a tumor from her breast. She recovered quickly, however, and resumed her trip. In 1925 she went to Mexico; in 1928 she attended the Pan-Pacific Conference of Women in Honolulu. All this in addition to regular attendance at W.I.L.P.F. congresses in various European cities.

She also lent her aid to relief organizations: for German prisoners of war still in Siberian camps, for Russian women and children, for Lithuanian refugees, for victims of British atrocities in Ireland. She received frequent letters from individuals either destitute or caught in the meshes of the bureaucracy that always afflicts refugees in a postwar period. She could do little more than allow her name to be used on appeals for money, but she was eager to do that, and to speak in behalf of these relief organizations when she was asked. The movement to outlaw war, which culminated in the Kellogg-Briand Pact of 1928, of course asked for and received her support. S. O. Levinson, the moving spirit of the movement, frequently consulted with her, and when the treaty was finally signed Miss Addams, with unconscious irony, pronounced it the "most significant event since the promulgation of the League of Nations Covenant."[17]

The most notable facet of Jane Addams' internationalist activities in these years was their sense of remoteness, of detachment from what was really happening. Contrast the Jane Addams who visited an anarchist in the cells beneath city hall with the Jane Addams who wrote letters to "sections" of the W.I.L.P.F. In the one case she was in the midst of the daily turmoil that was Chicago, in the other she was in a sort of self-created world which could have continued to function even if every other person had vanished from the face of the earth. Jane Addams had become at best a person whose name liberal organizations wanted on their letterheads. She was no longer in the thick of battle. Much the same thing could be said of her activities in behalf of domestic reform. Of course she supported her old friend Robert M. La Follette when he ran for president in 1924; of course she worked for a new trial for Sacco and Vanzetti; of course she supported the child-labor amendment to the Constitution. But all these were endorsements of other people's battles. She had not known it at the time, but her turning to peace work in 1915 had marked the end of her leadership in domestic reform.

It was not simply that she was aging. Clearly the mood of the 1920's was not hers. She was very mild in her criticism of the younger generation and was surprisingly open to changing attitudes toward sex, yet that generation danced to a drummer she did not hear. Significantly, the book she worked on in these years was on Julia Lathrop, and it concentrated on the early days at Hull House—those days when if one wanted to know where the most important social experiment was in progress, one simply asked where Jane Addams was. Significant too was her vigorous endorsement of prohibition. She found the work at Hull House much easier when drunkenness was so decreased. If only, she thought, the laws had been adequately enforced, alcoholism might have been permanently eliminated. Likewise, her support of Herbert Hoover for President—not only in 1928 but 1932 as well—indicated that one old progressive had not kept pace with what was going to produce the New Deal. The ideas she had formulated before the war still had currency and applicability, but perhaps she herself did not keep pace with them.

After all, she was sixty-five years old in 1925, and her health was beginning to fail. One could hardly fault her for spending her last decade in quietness rather than on the firing line. During that entire decade she was in extremely poor health. In 1924 she tried to recuperate by spending an extended vacation in Maine, but her strength would not return. In 1925 she had to cancel most of a European lecture tour, and in 1926 she had a heart attack which made her a semi-invalid the rest of her life. Beginning in 1929 she spent many of the winter months in an Arizona hotel, where her needs could be met with a minimum of effort on her part. What was remarkable was that, in spite of her votes for Hoover, she did not turn either senile or conservative. "In my travels around the world," she said in 1931, "I have been much impressed with the power of old women for making mischief. They always want to hang on to things as they were."[18] She was not going to let that happen to her. As late as the end of 1934, when she was already in her final illness, she indignantly denied the accusation that Hull House had opposed a federal program because it would interfere with Hull House activities. Hull House had always been glad, she insisted, to relinquish programs to public agencies, thus freeing the settlement for new directions.[19]

To be sure, she might criticize the younger generation for inadequate devotion to social causes, but she would not condemn the morality of young people. "There is no real difference between the modern girl as compared to the girl of my own time," this heir of Quaker and New England Puritanism could claim, "except the modern girl is franker and more open in her views."[20]

In spite of her experience with World War I, she remained optimistic. "Life improves," she said in a 1930 birthday interview. "Human beings are becoming more humane to their fellows; the great causes, the persuasive war cries of yesterday are submerged, forgotten or transformed today. Some of them have been won entirely, some only in part, some not at all, some have been abandoned." Then she added: "But always there are new causes, new slogans to work for, new conflicts to be solved and settled, another foot of progress to be made." She stoutly refused to predict the future, confident only that problems would be solved in unsuspected ways. Whether the optimism would have been shaken by another world war, which made the one she had lived through seem like a mere rehearsal, cannot be said. Certainly few more difficult tasks of historical imagination could be invented than to picture Jane Addams as a pessimist.[21]

As her health declined so that she was no longer a threat to anyone, and as the virulence of the Red Scare faded, the nation once again turned to honoring rather than excoriating her. Although only one institution of higher learning saw fit to tender her an honorary degree between 1920 and 1928, she received nine such degrees during the last seven years of her life. In that same period, every year saw dinners in her honor, votes as one of the world's greatest women (once even as one of the world's greatest *men*), and awards from every kind of organization from the Greek government, Bryn Mawr College, and the League of Women Voters to the *Pictorial Review* and a manufacturer of perfume.

The culmination of all these honors came one day in November of 1931. Miss Addams was lying ill in Mary Rozet Smith's home in Chicago. Her nephew, James Weber Linn, visited to inquire about her health.

"I have something to tell you, but I'd better not," his aunt said to him. "It is strictly confidential."

"About your operation?" he asked.

"Oh, that. No, that will come along presently. This is something nicer."

"What is it?"

"I am instructed to tell nobody."

"Then tell me."

"Go over to the bureau and open the second drawer on the left. There is a telegram on top of things. You can read it, but you must be quiet."

James Linn did as he was told. There he found a telegram from the Norwegian Minister at Washington, informing Jane Addams and Nicholas Murray Butler that they had won the Nobel Peace Prize for 1931.

The award was officially to be presented on December 10 in Oslo, but of course she would not be strong enough to go in person. Telegrams of congratulations nearly drowned her in the Johns Hopkins Hospital in Baltimore, where she was moved for still another operation. President Hoover, senators and congressmen, even General John Pershing sent telegrams. All the old Hull House people were delighted, and many of them added some sort of a clause indicating that they wished "Nick" had not been included. Ultimately the prize amounted to some sixteen thousand dollars of which, as might be expected, Jane Addams gave twelve thousand to the Women's International League for Peace and Freedom.[18]

She never really recovered from those operations in 1931. She could still attend occasional dinners in her honor, including a huge one in Washington as late as the spring of 1935. She could still work on her biography of Julia Lathrop, and even attend a meeting of relief organizations, "as a moral force on the Federal government," she said. Yet she was in fact an invalid.

On the morning of May 15, 1935, she had a sudden attack of pain, low down on the left side. Alice Hamilton and another doctor examined her and found evidence of an acute infection, but could offer no clear diagnosis. Her condition remained the same through the next day, and on May 17 a surgeon was called in. He advised an operation. On May 18 she was driven to Chicago's Passavant Hospital in an ambulance, with Alice Hamilton beside her. The doctors operated at 11:15 in the morning and found to their surprise an advanced cancerous condition. Their fear now was that she would recover for what could only be a few months of agony, and a lingering death. She came out of the anesthesia slowly, but seemed to be reasonably alert. Her condition remained static the next day, but on the afternoon of May 20 it was clear that she was slipping away. Dr. Hamilton and Ida Lovett, another old friend, spent what they knew was to be Jane Addams' last night in the hospital with her. Most of May 21 she was in a coma, and in the evening, just after six o'clock, she died.[23]

One can recount her obituaries, which were many, long, and unstinting in their praise. One can tell of her funeral in the Hull House courtyard, jammed with friends and neighbors, with thousands more in the street unable to get in. One can tell of her ride back to Cedarville, and of her burial near the home she grew up in. But these are merely obituaries, a funeral, a burial, and they were much like many others. Perhaps the best obituary was in fact delivered four years before she died. Fittingly enough, it was Frances Perkins who said:

> It was not mere coincidence that the span of Jane Addams' adult life is identical with the period in our national life which has seen our progress from a highly individualistic conception to a service conception of human relations in a democracy.[24]

AFTERWORD

IF one considers victories won and goals achieved, Jane Addams' ideas must be regarded as only partially successful. Perhaps of the triple nexus of virtuousness of mankind, environmentalism, and community, the second has received widest acceptance. Only in small segments of the extreme right wing of the American political spectrum do men seriously deny the enormous importance of environment as a determiner of human potential, and most people probably acknowledge that the largest portion of the environment is man made. The consequent, that if man made it it can be altered by men, is the basis for nearly every social innovation from urban renewal to mental-health clinics.

The inherent virtuousness of mankind is certainly more controversial. The Lockean postulate that men are "good" only in the sense of knowing their own self-interest is still widely accepted. Surely the "social ethic" has not replaced self-interest, any more than a sense of community has replaced a basic individualism. Yet if one looks carefully at important segments of recent reform tendencies, one can find a strong strain of the sense of community which Jane Addams asked for. This strain is in no danger of achieving victory, or even of growing very strong, but it continues to constitute a platform upon which critics of the way things are can stand. It continues, too, to take the roughest edges off of individualism and to provide much of the impetus toward humanizing contemporary society.

The place to look first is in the Black Revolution, the spearhead for so much mid-twentieth-century reform. As the largest group still left out of those who matter, black people are finally insisting that they too be included in the process of infolding out-groups. Yet it is in their method, even more than their goals, where one finds the social ethic. The young heroes from North Carolina Agricultural and Technical College who started the sit-ins; Miss Rosa Park and the Birmingham bus boycotters; the black and white young people who went to Mississippi for the COFO summer of 1964—all were engrossed in a cause larger than themselves and in a quest for, or the creation of a sense and reality of, *community*. Partly, of course, all these people were simply demanding that black people be included in American individualism; but partly, too, the very act of demanding created, as it once did for organized labor, something more than individualism.

Similarly, at the very center of a major federal program was something called a Community Action Agency. What it became in practice is a complex question. At base it was supposed to be, and in some cases for a brief while actually was, the rallying point around which neighborhoods, often urban and often black, could coalesce as functioning mutually responsible communities. Even without Community Action Agencies, a demand for community control and the consequent creation of a community occurs in places like the Ocean Hill-Brownsville section of Brooklyn; and it seems on the verge of being imitated in other black neighborhoods where the demand for control of schools, police, welfare, governmental services, and the economy is increasingly heard.[1]

Part, though only a part, of the student rebellion at universities from New York to California is likewise directed against an individualism which seems to some as having reached the point of dehumanization. Students should not, these people say, be embroiled in a system which needs high-speed computers to know even the basic question of who is enrolled in what course. Under such circumstances there is no human contact whatever between teacher and student, and very little among students, all of whom are simply being shuffled along a path they did not choose toward a goal they do not seek. Was there not some of the same desire for community evident in the esprit of the young people who worked so hard, and really so successfully, for Eugene McCarthy in 1968?

Finally, if one wants to move further toward the periphery, the flower children, the communal living, and the hippie culture generally, at least where it is genuine rather than a put-on, explicitly rejects individualism for a social relationship based on love.

So, from rather central concerns of American life like the Black Revolution and the war on poverty, all the way to the fringes of hippiedom, critics of American society are insisting that traditional American individualism be abandoned, that a sense of co-operation, of community, of a social ethic be established in its place. Those who search for radicalism in America, those who deny Louis Hartz's formulation of centrism, need look no further. What could be more radical *in the United States* than a challenge to individual self-seeking? What could be more radical than a challenge to Lockean liberalism?

It is worth repeating that this challenge is not on the brink of success. We are talking, after all, about radicalism, and that cannot by definition be a majority position. But the challenge to individualism constitutes a stance, an attitude, a frame of mind out of which the most cogent criticisms of American society seem to grow. Eventually the criticisms bear some fruit in the form of programs, institutions, laws, or ideas which are infolded by more centrist groups. The sum total of these halting, partial, sometimes subverted victories is never the kind of co-operative society that the radical critics would like; but the victories seem nevertheless to produce an improving society.

Thus those who seek an American radical tradition in the imitators of European Marxism are looking for the wrong thing in the wrong place. The search itself, in fact, constitutes a kind of romantic attachment to a political world that is of another time, another place. The tortured twisting of history which the search entails, for example insisting against all the evidence on the essential unity of the black and white poor, is the best manifestation of its futility. Of course there is an American radicalism, but it must be defined and studied in terms which are relevant to it, not those which are relevant for nineteenth-century England or Germany. When one approaches the matter correctly, one finds radicalism in the most unlikely of places: within the American liberal tradition.

NOTES

Except where noted, manuscripts are in the Jane Addams Papers, Swarthmore College Peace Collection; newspapers are from the clipping collection, Swarthmore College Peace Collection.

Introduction

[1] Jane Addams to Paul Kellogg, March 6, 1929, Survey Associates Manuscripts, Social Welfare History Archives, University of Minnesota.

[2] I am thinking here of people such as Gabriel Kolko, Norman Pollack, and Richard D. Abrams, among others. Their position is more apparent in papers delivered at professional meetings than in their published work. The basis for this view is Richard M. Hofstadter's *The Age of Reform: From Bryan to F.D.R.* (New York, 1955) and George E. Mowry's statistical work in *The California Progressives* (Berkeley, 1951), though neither Mowry nor Hofstadter necessarily agrees with the younger men. The literature is examined in Irwin Unger, "The 'New Left' and American History: Some Recent Trends in United States Historiography," *American Historical Review,* LXII (July, 1967), 1237–1263; and John Braeman, "The Wisconsin School of American Diplomatic History: A Critique," delivered at the meeting of the Organization of American Historians, April 27, 1967.

Chapter 1: Childhood

[1] Account of the journey is from John Addams' Journal, Swarthmore College Peace Collection.

[2] Genealogy from Edwin B. Yeich, "Jane Addams," *Historical Review of Berks County,* XVII (October–December, 1951), 10–13.

[3] Description of death is from George Weber to brother and sister, January 17, 1863.

[4] Marcet Haldeman-Julius, "The Two Mothers of Jane Addams," typescript in the Swarthmore College Peace Collection; James W. Linn, *Jane Addams* (New York, 1935), 1–40; Jane Addams, *Twenty Years at Hull-House* (New York, 1910); Jane Addams to Alice Haldeman [?], November 2, 1870; George Haldeman to Alice Haldeman, December 10, 1871 (the latter in the Stephenson County, Illinois, Historical Society).

[5] The name is spelled Halderman in newspaper accounts in the 1860's, but family sources spell it without the "r" and I have adopted the latter version.

[6] Jane Addams to Sister, December 3, 1871.

[7] Addams, *Twenty Years at Hull-House* (Signet Edition, New York, 1961), 25.

Chapter 2: Rockford

[1] Photostats of Anonymous, *History of Rockford and Winnebago County* (n.d., n.p.), 287–295; Charlotte W. Smith, "Historical Sketch of Rockford College"; and Hazel P. Cedarborg, "History of Rockford"; all in the Rockford College Archives.

[2] Rockford *Register,* June 28 [?], 1873.

[3] Transcript of Laura Jane Addams, Rockford Female Seminary, 1877–1881.

[4] *Rockford Seminary Magazine,* VII (July, 1879), 239; IX (March, 1881), 86.

[5] Jane Addams to Alice Haldeman Addams, January 23, 1880.

[6] *Rockford Seminary Magazine,* VIII (September, 1880), 235–237; IX (April, 1881), 97–100, 115.

[7] Jane Addams to Ellen Gates Starr, August 11, 1879; May 15, 1880; and January 29, February 13, March 10, 1881.

[8] Jane Addams to Ellen Gates Starr, July 11, 1883, in the Starr Manuscripts, Smith College; Jane Addams to George Haldeman, December 21, 1890, in the Stephenson County, Illinois, Historical Society.

[9] Ernest Rose, *A History of German Literature* (New York, 1960); Oskar Walsel, *German Romanticism* (New York, 1932); Thomas Carlyle, *Sartor Resartus* (Boston, 1896); John Ruskin, *Works,* ed. by E. T. Cook and Alexander Wedderburn (London, 1905), XVIII, 166, 182; and XVII, 21–23.

[10] *Rockford Seminary Magazine,* IX (July, 1881), 193–194.

Chapter 3: Uncertainty and the Scheme

[1] Freeport *Weekly Journal,* August 24, 1881.

[2] Ernest Earnest, *S. Wier Mitchell, Novelist and Physician* (Philadelphia, 1950).

[3] Jane Addams, *Democracy and Social Ethics* (New York, 1902), 87.

[4] Return to Cedarville from Linn, *Jane Addams,* 68–69.

[5] Mary P. Elwood to Jane Addams, July 30, September 1, 1882; Sarah F. Blaisdell to Jane Addams, August 29, 1882.

[6] Alice Haldeman to Jane Addams, September 10, 1882; Ellen Gates Starr to Jane Addams, October 22, 1882.

[7] Linn, *Jane Addams,* 178.

[8] Jane Addams to Ellen Gates Starr, January 7 [1883].

[9] Sarah Blaisdell to Jane Addams, January 26, 1886; Jane Addams to Ellen Gates Starr, April 24, July 11, 1883, in the Starr Manuscripts.

[10] Report of the Administrator of the Estate of John H. Addams, filed January 5, 1885, in the Stephenson County Courthouse, Freeport, Illinois. Jane Addams received lands valued at $22,848; a portion of John Addams' personal estate amounting to $22,994; fifty-two shares of the Second National Bank of Chicago; twenty-five shares of Northern Pacific preferred; seventeen shares of Northern Pacific common stock; and chattel property valued at $800.

[11] For the itinerary: Jane Addams to George Haldeman, January 4, October 8, November 30, 1883; and February 2, March 21, October 17, December 28, 1884; all in the Stephenson County, Illinois, Historical Society. Also Jane Addams to Ellen Gates Starr, November 3, December 2, 1883; March 9, 1884; and February 21, March 30, 1885; all in the Starr Manuscripts. Also Jane Addams to Sarah F. Blaisdell, March 15, April 26, 1884. For the itinerary, plus evidence of Miss Addams' state of mind: Jane Addams to George, March 8, 1884, in the Stephenson County, Illinois, Historical Society; and Jane Addams to Ellen Gates Starr, June 8, June 22, December 7, 1884, in the Starr Manuscripts.

[12] Jane Addams to Mary Rozet Smith [1909?].

[13] Marcet Haldeman-Julius, typescript recollections of Jane Addams in Swarthmore College Peace Collection (1939), 5. Jane Addams to Alice Haldeman, July

5, 1890; Jane Addams to George Haldeman, December 21, 1890; both in the Stephenson County, Illinois, Historical Society. Also Jane Addams to Alice Haldeman, August 12, November 9, 1891; May 19, 1899; September 25, 1903; March 16, 1913. Also Jane Addams to "Ma," December 22, 1903, and to "Mother," August 10, 1913. Also Alice Haldeman to Harry Haldeman, June 13, 1897.

[14] On the Negro orphanage: Jane Addams to Alice Haldeman, December 28, 1886. For the pattern of their lives in general: Jane Addams to Ellen Gates Starr, December 6, 1885; February 7, July 17, 1886; all in Starr Manuscripts. Also Jane Addams to Alice Haldeman, January 22, 1887; and *Rockford Seminary Magazine,* XVI (April, October, 1886), 134, 260.

[15] Jane Addams to Alice Haldeman, February 25, March 2, May 31, September 24, 1887. Also Jane Addams to Ellen Gates Starr, April 3, 1887, in the Starr Manuscripts.

[16] Addams, *Democracy and Social Ethics,* 73, 74, 82. The same material appeared first as "The College Woman and the Family Claim," *The Commons,* XXIX (September, 1898), 3–9.

[17] Jane Addams to Alice Haldeman, January 6 [1888].

[18] Mary Addams Linn to Jane Addams, January 31, 1888; Jane Addams to Mary Addams Linn, February 5, 1888.

[19] For itinerary, sciatica, and death of Mary: Jane Addams to Alice Haldeman, December 2, December 23, 1887; and January 10, January 29, March 3, April 6, 1888. Also Jane Addams to "Ma," December 27, 1887, and March 15, 1888 (the latter in Stephenson County, Illinois, Historical Society). Also Jane Addams to "My brother and sisters," January 20, 1886. Also Ellen Gates Starr to Anna H. Addams, February 23, 1888, and to Eliza Allen Starr, March 6, 1888. Also Mary Linn to Jane Addams, March 6, 1888.

Chapter 4: Hull House: Its Context

[1] Jane Addams to Mary Linn, March 13, 1889.

[2] Ellen Gates Starr to Mary Blaisdell, February 23, 1889.

[3] Jane Addams to Ellen Gates Starr, May 31, 1889 [?], in the Starr Manuscripts. The search for Hull House is from the same letter. See also Sarah Blaisdell to Jane Addams, January 5, 1889; Jane Addams to Ellen Gates Starr, January 24, June 4, June 7, June 14, 1889 (the latter four in the Starr Manuscripts); Jane Addams to Mary Linn, April 12, 1889; and Jane Addams to Alice Haldeman, March 31, August 6, 1889. For Miss Addams' expenses: Hull House "Donors Book," 2, in Hull House.

[4] Ellen Gates Starr to Mary Blaisdell, February 23, 1889, in the Starr Manuscripts.

[5] Jane Addams to Alice Haldeman Addams, September 13, 1889.

[6] Frederick Jackson Turner, "The Problem of the West," *Atlantic Monthly,* LXXVIII (September, 1896), 297.

[7] Edward C. Kirkland, *Industry Comes of Age: Business, Labor and Public Policy, 1860–1897* (New York, 1961); Harold U. Faulkner, *Politics, Reform and Expansion, 1890–1900* (New York, 1959); Richard M. Hofstadter, *Social Darwinism in American Thought* (Boston, 1955); Robert H. Wiebe, *Businessmen and Reform: A Study of the Progressive Movement* (Cambridge, 1962); Arnold M. Paul, *Conservative Crisis and the Rule of Law: Attitudes of Bar and Bench, 1887–1895* (Ithaca, 1960); John P. Roche, "Entrepreneurial Liberty and the Fourteenth Amendment," *Labor History,* IV (Winter, 1963), 3–31; Edward C. Kirkland, "The Robber Barons Revisited," *American Historical Review,* LXVI (October, 1960), 68–73; Henry George, *Progress and Poverty* (New York, 1880); Henry Demarest Lloyd, *Wealth Against Commonwealth* (New York, 1894).

[8] Blake McKelvey, *The Urbanization of America, 1860–1915* (New Brunswick,

1963); Morton and Lucia White, *The Intellectual Versus the City: From Thomas Jefferson to Frank Lloyd Wright* (Cambridge, 1962).

[9] Robert H. Bremner, *From the Depths: The Discovery of Poverty in the United States* (New York, 1956), 60–66; Allen F. Davis, *Spearheads for Reform: The Social Settlements and the Progressive Movement, 1890–1914* (New York, 1967), 3–40.

Chapter 5: The Daily Round

[1] Jane Addams, "Why the Ward Boss Rules," *Outlook,* LVIII (April, 1898), 880–881.

[2] Jane Addams to Mary Linn, February 19, 1889; Jane Addams to Alice Haldeman, February 19, 1889, in the Stephenson County, Illinois, Historical Society.

[3] Jane Addams to Alice Haldeman, October 8, 1889.

[4] Robert Woods to Jane Addams, September 4, 1895.

[5] Jane Addams, *My Friend, Julia Lathrop* (New York, 1935), 53.

[6] Jane Addams to Mary Rozet Smith, October 6, 1898.

[7] *Chicago Post,* May 19, 1899.

[8] *New York Mail and Express,* September 13, 1901; *Central Christian Advocate,* September 18, 1901; Clarence Darrow to Jane Addams, September 11, 1901; Linn, *Jane Addams,* 217.

[9] The pledge, handwritten by Jane Addams and signed by Mrs. Dennis on November 15, 1907, is in the Swarthmore College Peace Collection.

[10] Interview with Jessie Binnford, December 14, 1961; Addams, *Twenty Years at Hull-House,* 127.

[11] Linn, *Jane Addams,* 114.

[12] Addams, *My Friend, Julia Lathrop.*

[13] Josephine Goldmark, *Impatient Crusader: Florence Kelley's Life Story* (Urbana, 1953).

[14] Alice Hamilton, *Exploring the Dangerous Trades: The Autobiography of Alice Hamilton* (Boston, 1943), 62.

[15] Addams, *My Friend, Julia Lathrop,* 119.

[16] David Donald, *Lincoln Reconsidered: Essays on the Civil War* (New York, 1956), 19–37.

[17] Hamilton, *Exploring the Dangerous Trades.*

[18] Edith Abbott, "Grace Abbott and Hull House," *Social Service Review,* XXIV (Fall, 1950), 374–394; Wilfred S. Reynolds to Sophonisba Breckinridge, January 14, 1926.

[19] Interview with Jessie Binnford, December 14, 1961.

[20] Hamilton, *Exploring the Dangerous Trades,* 61.

[21] Minutes of Residents' Meetings, 1893–1895. When I visited Hull House in 1961, these were in a closet on the second floor.

[22] Interviews with Jessie Binnford, December 14, 1961, and with Lea Taylor, Highland Park, Illinois, June 11, 1963. See also D. Moore, "A Day at Hull House," *American Journal of Sociology* (March, 1897).

[23] Abbott, "Grace Abbott and Hull House," 374–394.

[24] M. R. Werner, *Julius Rosenwald: The Life of a Practical Humanitarian* (New York, 1939), 91–92.

[25] Jane Addams to Alice Haldeman, January 8, January 22, April 20, 1890; Addams, *Twenty Years at Hull-House* (Signet Edition), 83–87.

[26] Jill Conway, "Jane Addams: An American Heroine," *Daedalus,* LXIII (Spring, 1964), 761–780; Lewis S. Feuer, "John Dewey and the 'Back to the People Movement' in American Thought," *Journal of the History of Ideas,* XX (October, 1959), 565–568; Linn, *Jane Addams,* 209.

Chapter 6: Hull House: Institutional Growth

[1] Hull House Account Book, 1889, p. 141. The record of net worth is in the Swarthmore College Peace Collection, under May 1, 1906.

[2] Louise DeKoven Bowen to Jane Addams, April 21, 1904; November 24, 1905; and May 6, 1906. Also *Chicago Chronicle,* January 13, 1907.

[3] Jane Addams to Mary Rozet Smith, March 3, 1894; Linn, *Jane Addams,* 126–127; Addams, *Twenty Years at Hull-House,* 205–207.

[4] Addams, *Twenty Years at Hull-House,* 113; Linn, *Jane Addams,* 122; *Chicago Tribune,* October 13, 1895.

[5] *Chicago Record Herald,* December 9, 1911; *Chicago Examiner,* June 21, 1909; Jane Addams, *The Second Twenty Years at Hull-House: September 1909–September 1929* (New York, 1930), 348; Jane Addams, *The Spirit of Youth and the City Streets* (New York, 1920), 10; Jane Addams, "Public Recreation and Social Morality," *Charities,* XVIII (August, 1907), 492–494; Jane Addams, "Child Labor and Pauperism," *Charities,* XI (October, 1903), 303; Jane Addams, "Problems of Municipal Administrations," *American Journal of Sociology,* X (January, 1905), 428.

[6] *Chicago Tribune,* August 31, 1912.

[7] Addams, *My Friend, Julia Lathrop,* 50–51; Addams, *Twenty Years at Hull-House,* 295, 299.

[8] Linn, *Jane Addams,* 209; D. Moore, "A Day at Hull House."

[9] Hull House activities are described in Addams, *Twenty Years at Hull-House,* and in Linn, *Jane Addams, passim.* See also Hull House *Yearbook,* 1910; and Jane Addams, "Julia Lathrop at Hull-House," *Survey Graphic,* XXIV (August, 1935), 373–377.

[10] Jane Addams to Alice Haldeman, September 29, 1899; *Chicago Tribune,* December 26, 1899.

[11] Hull House Donors Book, 1889–1894; Helen Culver to Jane Addams, March 3, March 15, 1890; Jane Addams to Helen Culver, March 7, March 11, 1890; and Helen Culver to Jane Addams, May 3, 1906. Also *New York Evening Sun,* June 4, 1909.

[12] Hull House list of Donors, 1910; Louise DeKoven Bowen to Jane Addams, June 1, June 19, 1905.

[13] Jane Addams to Anita McCormick Blaine, 1894 [n.d.]; December 11, 1895; December 22, 1897; December 25, 1899; all in the McCormick Manuscripts, State Historical Society of Wisconsin.

[14] Letters between Jane Addams and Mary Rozet Smith are too numerous to cite every one. The following indicate the points that I have made about their relationship: Jane Addams to Mary Rozet Smith, November 27, 1896; March 29, July 19, July 22, 1897; June 9, 1899; July 19, 1900; March 24, May 3, May 19, 1902; March 26, 1903; August 24, 1906; May 10, May 13, June 11, 1909; March 6, March 8, April 15, November 8, November 28, December 1, 1910; July 23, August 24, 1911; February 21, 1912; October 6, 1914; April 24, April 26, May 9, 1915; and April 14, April 18, May 1, May 3, May 23, 1919. See also Jane Addams to Alice Haldeman, July 23, 1905, and September 21, 1914; to Catherine D. Blake, April 10, 1926; to Ida Lovett, February 17, 1931; and to Lillian D. Wald, July 13, 1914, and March 12, 1919 (the latter two in the Wald Manuscripts, New York Public Library). See also Alice Hamilton to Mary Rozet Smith, May 19, May 30, 1919; Swarthmore College clipping collection, 1923; *El Universal* [Mexico City], March 18, 1925; and Lillian D. Wald to Mary Rozet Smith, January 12, March 9, and October 27, 1932 (the latter three in the Wald Manuscripts).

Chapter 7: Urban Politics

[1] Addams, *Twenty Years at Hull-House,* 202–205.

[2] Jane Addams to Mary Rozet Smith, February 24, 1895; *Union Advertiser* [Rochester, New York], August 12, 1895.

[3] Daniel Levine, *Varieties of Reform Thought* (Madison, 1964), 48–64.

[4] Minutes of Residents' Meeting, Hull House, 1893; Anonymous to Jane Addams, January 17, 1898; *Chicago Times-Herald,* January 28, March 6, 1898; Jane Addams to Mary Rozet Smith, March 20, April 3, 1898; *Chicago Chronicle,* December 6, 1899; *Chicago Tribune,* January 20, 1900; Ray S. Baker, "Hull House and the Ward Boss," *Outlook,* LVIII (1898), 769–771; Florence Kelley, "Hull House," *New England Magazine,* XVIII (1898), 565–566; Jane Addams, "Ethical Survival in Municipal Corruption," *International Journal of Ethics,* VIII (1897–1898), 273–291; *Democracy and Social Ethics,* 221–278, 222–224; Allen F. Davis, "Spearheads of Reform," Ph.D. dissertation, University of Wisconsin, 1959.

[5] Jane Addams to Henry D. Lloyd, December 22, 1895, in the Lloyd Manuscripts, State Historical Society of Wisconsin.

[6] Jane Addams to *Chicago Evening Post,* February 20, 1900.

[7] Addams, *Democracy and Social Ethics,* 222–223.

[8] Nancy P. Pottishman, "Jane Addams and Education," M.A. thesis, Columbia University, 1962, 61–63. Louis Post, "Living a Long Life Over Again," unpublished autobiography in Post Manuscripts, Library of Congress, 243–277.

[9] *Chicago Advance,* June 22, 1905; W. R. Mitchell to Jane Addams, July 3, 1905; Graham Taylor to Jane Addams, June 24, 1905 (the latter in Stephenson County, Illinois, Historical Society).

[10] Board of Education *Proceedings* (1905–1906), July 12, 1905; *Chicago Chronicle,* July 18, 1905; Board of Education *Proceedings* (1905–1906), September 13, 1905, p. 96; Edward Tilden to Jane Addams, August 29, 1905; *Chicago Post,* September 2, 1905; *Chicago Chronicle,* September 1, 1905.

[11] Board of Education, *Proceedings* (1905–1906), February 28, 1906, p. 552.

[12] Board of Education, *Proceedings* (1906–1907), November 21, 1906, pp. 491–512; *ibid.,* February 13, 1907, pp. 893–894; *New York Tribune,* January 14, 1907.

[13] Board of Education, *Proceedings* (1906–1907), May 22, 1907, p. 113; *Chicago Tribune,* May 26, 1907; *Chicago Examiner,* May 27, 1907; Chicago *Inter-Ocean,* May 30, 1907.

[14] Board of Education, *Proceedings* (1907–1908), January 15, 1908, pp. 397–400; *ibid.,* June 3, 1908, pp. 867–870.

[15] Board of Education, *Proceedings* (1906–1907), June 26, 1907, pp. 1188–1189; *ibid.,* May 29, 1907, pp. 1117–1119; *Chicago Tribune,* July 18, 1907.

[16] Board of Education, *Proceedings* (1906–1907), pp. 1188–1189; *ibid.,* July 17, 1908, p. 39; *Chicago Record-Herald,* July 4, 1907.

Chapter 8: Father of the Man

[1] Addams, *My Friend, Julia Lathrop,* 56–57.

[2] Mary B. Sayles, "Settlement Workers and Their Work," *Outlook,* LXXVIII (October, 1904), 305–311; Anonymous, "The Most Useful Americans," *Independent,* LXXIV (May, 1913), 958.

[3] Jane Addams, "Respect for Law," *Independent,* LIII (January, 1901), 19; *Twenty Years at Hull-House,* 179–180.

[4] Edwin G. Boring, *A History of Experimental Psychology* (New York, 1950), 506; William James, *Psychology* (New York, 1890).

[5] G. Stanley Hall, *Youth: Its Education, Regimen, and Hygiene* (New York, 1912), 1, 3.

[6] Margaret K. Smith, "Child Study in Connection with the Professional Training of Teachers," National Education Association, *Proceedings* (1893), 448.

[7] G. Stanley Hall, "Some of the Methods and Results of Child Study Work at Clark University," National Education Association, *Proceedings* (1896), 863.

[8] Addams, *Spirit of Youth,* 6, 52–54, 77.

[9] *Ibid.,* 25–26.

[10] Jane Addams, "Child Labor Legislation—A Requisite for Industrial Efficiency," *Annals of the American Academy of Political and Social Sciences,* XXV (May, 1905), 542–543.

[11] Nina C. Vandewalker, "Kindergarten," in Paul Monroe, ed., *Cyclopedia of Education* (New York, 1912), III, 598–606; *idem., Kindergarten in American Education* (New York, 1908); Elizabeth Jenkins, "Froebel's Disciples in America," *German-American Review,* Number 3 (1933), 15–18.

[12] Addams, *Democracy and Social Ethics,* 181, 180.

[13] *Ibid.,* 201-204; Lawrence A. Cremin, *The Transformation of the School: Progressivism in American Education* (New York, 1961), 34–57.

[14] John Ruskin, *The Nature of the Gothic,* quoted in Raymond Williams, *Culture and Society* (New York, 1958), 141.

[15] Addams, "Child Labor Legislation," 543.

[16] Jane Addams, "Humanizing Tendency of Industrial Education," *Chatauquan,* XXIX (May, 1904), 266–267.

[17] *Idem.*

[18] Richard M. Hofstadter, *Anti-Intellectualism in American Life* (New York, 1963), 299–392.

[19] Addams, *Democracy and Social Ethics,* 208–209, 211.

[20] Jane Addams, "Child at the Point of Greatest Pressure," National Conference of Charities and Corrections, *Proceedings* (1912), 28–29.

[21] Addams, *The Second Twenty Years at Hull-House,* 345.

[22] Addams, "Child at the Point of Greatest Pressure," 29.

[23] Jane Addams, "Toast to John Dewey," *Survey,* LXIII (November, 1929), 203–204.

[24] John Dewey, "Play," *Cyclopedia of Education,* III, 725–727.

[25] Clarence A. Perry, "Playground," *Cyclopedia of Education,* III, 728–730.

[26] Graham R. Taylor, "How They Played at Chicago," *Charities,* XVIII (August 3, 1907), 471–480.

[27] Luther H. Gulick, "Play and Democracy," *Charities,* XVIII (August, 1907), 481–486.

[28] Taylor, "How They Played at Chicago," 471–480.

[29] Jane Addams, "Public Recreation and Social Morality," *Charities,* XVIII (August, 1907), 492–494.

[30] Addams, *Spirit of Youth and the City Streets,* 17; Jane Addams, "The Public Dance Halls of Chicago," *Ladies Home Journal,* XXX (July, 1913), 19.

[31] Addams, *Spirit of Youth and the City Streets,* 58–70.

[32] *Ibid.,* 8.

[33] *Ibid.,* 96.

[34] *Ibid.,* 101.

[35] Graham R. Taylor, "Recreation Developments in Chicago Parks," *Annals of the American Academy of Political and Social Sciences,* XXXV (1910), 304–321; Montgomery H. Wright, "Give the Children a Chance to Play," *The American City,* II (March, 1910), 115–117; Jessie F. Steiner, *Americans at Play* (New York, 1933), 14–34.

[36] Jerome Bruner, *Toward a Theory of Instruction* (Cambridge, 1966); David Riesman, "Thoughts on Teachers and Schools," *Anchor Review,* Melvin J. Lasky, ed. (New York, 1955), 27–60.

[37] Cremin, *Transformation of the School,* 274–328.

Chapter 9: Environmentalism: Child Labor, Child Crime

[1] Jane Addams, *Newer Ideals of Peace* (New York, 1907), 170, 157; Addams, *Spirit of Youth and the City Streets,* 11, 118.

[2] Addams, *Newer Ideals of Peace,* 160.

[3] Eric F. Goldman, *Rendezvous with Destiny: A History of Modern American Reform* (New York, 1952).

[4] Addams, *Spirit of Youth and the City Streets,* 135.

[5] Addams, *Newer Ideals of Peace,* 158.

[6] *Ibid.,* 167; Addams, *Democracy and Social Ethics,* 169.

[7] Jane Addams, "Child Labor on the Stage," *Annals of the American Academy of Political and Social Sciences,* XXXVIII (July, 1911), Supplement, 60–65; "Stage Children," *Survey,* XV (December 3, 1910), 342; William P. Haladay to Jane Addams, April 21, 1911; Edward F. Brown to Jane Addams, April 29, 1911; Jane Addams to Owen R. Lovejoy, [May ?] 1911; John T. Denvir to Jane Addams, May 10, 1911; John G. Oglesby to Jane Addams, May 9, 1911; Illinois Senate Committee on Judiciary, "Hearings in the matter of Children on the Public Stage," transcript of March 8, 1911, pp. 17–26.

[8] Jane Addams, "Child Labor Legislation—A Requisite for Industrial Efficiency," 542–550; *Washington Star,* December 10, 1906; Albert J. Beveridge to Jane Addams, December 15, 1906; Jane Addams, "Operation of the Illinois Child Labor Law," *Annals of the American Academy of Political and Social Sciences,* XXVII (March, 1906), 327–330; Jane Addams, "National Protection for Children," *Annals of the American Academy of Political and Social Sciences,* XXIX (January, 1907), 57–60; Jane Addams, "Ten Years' Experience in Illinois," *Annals of the American Academy of Political and Social Sciences,* XXXIII (July, 1911), Supplement, 144–148.

[9] House of Representatives, Committee on Labor, *Hearings on HR 4694* (Washington, 1911); *Chicago Tribune,* April 3, 1912.

[10] Grace Abbott, *The Child and the State* (2 vols., Chicago, 1938), I, 265.

[11] Addams, *Spirit of Youth and the City Streets,* 70.

[12] Addams, *The Second Twenty Years at Hull-House,* 362–364.

[13] Jane Addams, "The 'Juvenile-Adult' Offender," *Ladies Home Journal,* XXX (October, 1913), 24; Addams, *The Second Twenty Years at Hull-House,* 366.

[14] Jane Addams, *A New Conscience and an Ancient Evil* (New York, 1912), 108.

[15] *Idem.*

[16] *Idem.*

[17] Addams, *The Second Twenty Years at Hull-House,* 317.

[18] Jane Addams, "Respect for Law," *Independent,* LIII (January, 1901), 18; Addams, *The Second Twenty Years at Hull-House,* 309, 310.

[19] Linn, *Jane Addams,* 143, 187; Addams, *The Second Twenty Years at Hull-House,* 304–306; Addams *Twenty Years at Hull-House,* 180, 181; Addams, 'Juvenile-Adult' Offender," 24.

[20] Harry Elmer Barnes, "Criminology," *Encyclopedia of the Social Sciences,* IV, 584–592; Ruth S. Cavan, *Criminology* (New York, 1948), 313–348; Fred E. Haynes, *Criminology* (New York, 1930), 23–41; Mark H. Haller, *Eugenics: Hereditarian Attitudes in American Thought* (New Brunswick, 1963), 95–96, 100–102.

[21] Addams, *et al., The Child, the Clinic and the Court,* especially Julia C. Lathrop, "The Background of the Juvenile Court in Illinois," 290–298; Mrs. Joseph T. Bowen, "The Early days of the Juvenile Court," 290–310; and Timothy D. Hurley, "Origin of the Illinois Juvenile Court Law," 320–331. The law itself appears in Abbott, *The Child and the State,* II, 392–401. See also Grace Abbott's excellent introductory essay in *ibid.,* 323–340. For a discussion of the legal theory behind the court see Herbert H. Lou, *Juvenile Courts in the United States* (Chapel Hill, 1927), 1–9; and Julian W. Mack, "The Chancery Procedures in the Juvenile Court," *The Child, the Clinic and the Court,* 310–320. The committee of the Bar Association

is quoted in Miriam Van Waters, "Juvenile Delinquency and Juvenile Courts," *Encyclopedia of the Social Sciences,* III, 528–533. Jane Addams' account of the founding of the court is in *The Second Twenty Years at Hull-House,* 304–314.

[22] William Healy, *The Individual Delinquent: A Textbook of Diagnosis and Prognosis* (Boston, 1924), 282–284 *et passim*; Francis A. Huber, "The Progressive Career of Ben B. Lindsey, 1900–1920," Ph.D. dissertation, University of Michigan, 1963; Ben B. Lindsey, "Colorado's Contribution to the Juvenile Court," *The Child, the Clinic and the Court,* 288. In this article Lindsey insists on the priority of the Colorado over the Illinois law. They were, in fact, almost contemporaneous, and independently conceived, showing the degree to which the idea was in the air. See also Ben B. Lindsey, "The Boy and the Court," *Charities and the Commons,* XIII (January 7, 1905).

[23] Frederic M. Thrasher, *The Gang: A Study of 1,313 Gangs in Chicago* (Chicago, 1927); Sheldon and Eleanor T. Glueck, *One Thousand Juvenile Delinquents: Their* Treatment by Court and Clinic, Vol. I of the *Survey of Crime and Criminal Justice in Boston* (Cambridge, 1934); Sheldon and Eleanor T. Glueck, *Predicting Delinquency and Crime* (Cambridge, 1959), especially 114–127. Recent validation of the Gluecks' prediction tests is discussed in Julius Horowitz, "The Arithmetic of Delinquency," *New York Times Magazine* (January 31, 1965), 13; and in a news story in the *New York Times,* November 10, 1964.

[24] Although this idea is expressed in many places in Jane Addams' writing, its most forceful exposition is in *Spirit of Youth and the City Streets,* 139–162.

Chapter 10: Environmentalism: The Culture of Poverty

[1] National Conference of Charities and Correction, *Proceedings* (1897), 329–338.

[2] Addams, *Spirit of Youth and the City Streets,* 18.

[3] Addams, *Democracy and Social Ethics,* 45.

[4] *Ibid.,* 53.

[5] Jane Addams, "Charity Visitor's Perplexities," *Outlook,* LXI (March, 1899), 598–600.

[6] G. H. Hubbard, "The Why of Poverty," *New Englander,* L (March, 1889), 180–188; Andrew Carnegie, "The Advantages of Poverty," *Nineteenth Century,* XXIX (March, 1891), 365–385.

[7] Bremner, *From the Depths,* 35–38.

[8] *Ibid.,* 38–41.

[9] *Ibid.,* 16–17.

[10] *Ibid.,* 140–163; National Conference of Charities and Correction, *Proceedings* (1885), 316–321.

[11] *Ibid.,* 321–383.

[12] F. G. Peabody, "How Should a City Care for Its Poor?," *Forum,* XIV (1892), 474–475; Robert A. Woods, "The Social Awakening in London," *Scribner's* XI (April, 1892), 401–424; Oscar Craig, "The Prevention of Pauperism," *Scribner's,* XIV (July, 1893), 121–132. See also the entire series in *Scribner's* for April–July, 1893.

[13] Jacob A. Riis, *How the Other Half Lives: Studies Among the Tenements of New York* (New York, 1890).

[14] Compare, for example, the series of papers debating the question of outdoor relief in National Conference of Charities and Corrections, *Proceedings* (1891), 38–50, with the later series: Charles D. Kellog, "The Situation in New York in the Winter of 1893–1894," *ibid.* (1894), 21–30; R. D. M'Gonnigle, "The Winter in Pittsburgh," 36–42; William P. Fowler, "The Emergency Work in Boston," 45–49; and Joseph G. Rosengarten, "A Successful Experiment in Utilizing Unemployed Labor," 58–62. In 1891 the speakers were 6–3 against outdoor relief; in 1894 outdoor relief was described, but opposition to it was not even mentioned.

[15] National Conference of Charities and Correction, *Proceedings* (1896), 4–5.

[16] Jane Addams, *Philanthropy and Social Progress* (New York, 1893), 2.

[17] Jane Addams to Henry Demarest Lloyd, October 18, 1898, in the Lloyd Manuscripts.

[18] Addams, *Democracy and Social Ethics,* Chapter I.

[19] Addams, *Newer Ideals of Peace,* 84.

[20] Graham Taylor, "The New View," *Charities,* XVIII (August 3, 1907), 463.

[21] Mary Richmond, "The Social Case Worker in a Changing World," *The Long View* (New York, 1930), 374.

[22] Mary Richmond, *Social Diagnosis* (New York, 1917), 357.

[23] Addams, *Newer Ideals of Peace,* 159–160.

[24] Jane Addams, "A Function of the Social Settlement," *Annals of the American Academy of Political and Social Sciences,* XIII (May, 1899), 342.

[25] Jane Addams, "Charity and Social Justice," National Conference of Charities and Correction, *Proceedings* (1910), 1–18; Addams, "The Child at the Point of Greatest Pressure," 26–30.

[26] Roy Lubove, *The Professional Altruist: The Emergence of Social Work as a Career, 1880–1930* (Cambridge, 1965); Frank J. Bruno, *Trends in Social Work* (New York, 1957); Bremner, *From the Depths, passim.*

[27] Clarke A. Chambers, *Seedtime of Reform: American Social Service and Social Action, 1918–1933* (Minneapolis, 1965) 165.

[28] Lyndon B. Johnson, State of the Union address, January 8, 1964.

Chapter 11: Community: Immigrant and Native American

[1] Jane Addams, "Chicago Settlements and Social Unrest," *Charities,* XX (May, 1908), 115.

[2] Addams, *Twenty Years at Hull-House,* 172–177.

[3] Addams, "Humanizing Tendency of Industrial Education," 266–272; M. M. Buck, "Hull House Labor Museum," *Craftsman,* XIII (November, 1907), 229–230; Anonymous, "Hull House Labor Museum," *Chautauquan,* XXXVIII (September, 1903), 60–61.

[4] Wilfred S. Reynolds to Sophonisba Breckinridge, January 14, 1926.

[5] *Chicago Inter-Ocean,* March 3, 1908; *Chicago Evening Post,* March 4, 1908.

[6] Jane Addams, "Chicago Settlements and Social Unrest," *Charities,* XX (May 2, 1908), 155–166; Harold Ickes to Jane Addams, October 12, 1908; Helen Culver to Jane Addams, March 10, 1908; Olga Averbuch to Harold Ickes [from Cerovitz, Russia, undated].

[7] J. W. Morgan to Jane Addams, May 24, 1908.

[8] John Higham, *Strangers in the Land: Patterns of American Nativism, 1860–1925* (New Brunswick, 1955); Thomas F. Gossett, *Race: The History of an Idea in America* (Dallas, 1963); Haller, *Eugenics, passim.*

[9] Jane Addams, "Work and Play as Factors in Education," *Chautauquan,* XLII (November, 1905), 251.

[10] National Conference of Charities and Corrections, *Proceedings* (1909), 213–266.

[11] National Conference of Charities and Corrections, *Proceedings* (1919), 729.

[12] Addams, *Newer Ideals of Peace,* 96–97.

[13] *Ibid.,* 14–15.

[14] *Ibid.,* 18.

[15] *Ibid.,* 70, 90–91.

[16] Addams, *Philanthropy and Social Progress,* 35–36; Addams, *Twenty Years at Hull-House,* 170.

[17] Addams, *Democracy and Social Ethics,* 232.

[18] Ernest Poole, "A Mixing Bowl for Nations," *Everybody's* XXIII (October, 1910). 554–564. The quote is from Herbert A. Miller, "The Rising National Individu-

alism," *American Journal of Sociology,* XIX (March, 1912), 604.

[19] Jane Addams, "The Immigrant and Social Unrest," National Conference of Social Work, *Proceedings* (1920), 59–62. (For earlier expression of the same idea, see the *Chicago Examiner,* April 23, 1908).

[20] Donald O. Johnson, *The Challenge to American Freedoms: World War I and the Rise of the American Civil Liberties Union* (Lexington, 1963), 119–148; William Preston, Jr., *Aliens and Dissenters: Federal Suppression of Radicals, 1903–1933* (Cambridge, 1963), 180–237.

[21] Addams, *The Second Twenty Years at Hull-House,* 288, 289, 287.

[22] *Ibid.,* 303, 304.

Chapter 12: Community: Labor and Management

[1] Hamilton, *Exploring the Dangerous Trades,* 80.

[2] Ben Tillett [of the British Dockers' Union] to Jane Addams, June 6, 1896; *Chicago Tribune,* December 2, 1900; *Chicago Journal,* August 31, 1901; *Chicago Inter-Ocean,* November 9, 1902; *Chicago Chronicle,* December 7, 1902; *Chicago News,* April 29, 1903; *Chicago Tribune,* April 30, 1903.

[3] Allen F. Davis, "The Women's Trade Union League: Origins and Organization," *Labor History* (Winter, 1964), 3–17; Jane Addams, "The Settlement as a Factor in the Labor Movement," *Hull House Maps and Papers,* 184–186.

[4] The stockyards strike: Jane Addams to Mary McDowell, July 26, 1904; Jane Addams to Mary Rozet Smith, August 13, 1904; and the *Chicago Inter-Ocean,* February 15, 1913, in which Mary McDowell recalls the strike. For the story of the waitresses' strike and Ellen Gates Starr's arrest and acquittal see the following Chicago newspapers: *Record-Herald,* February 23, March 7, March 14, 1914; *Inter-Ocean,* March 1, 1914; *Tribune,* March 8, March 12, March 22, 1914; *Examiner,* March 22, 1914.

[5] Matthew Josephson, *Sidney Hillman, Statesman of American Labor* (New York, 1952), 47–58.

[6] The Donors Book for Hull House, 1908, shows that Hart, Schaffner, and Marx each contributed substantial amounts to the settlement. For the strike: Ellen Gates Starr to Robert A. Woods, March 28, 1910; Jane Addams to Mary Rozet Smith, November 8, November 28, December 1, 1910; and February 6, 1911. See also *Chicago Evening Post,* December 21, 1910; January 13, 1911.

[7] *Chicago Chronicle,* September 14, 1903.

[8] Addams, "The Settlement as a Factor in the Labor Movement," in *Hull House Maps and Papers.*

[9] Jane Addams, "A Modern Lear: The Strike at Pullman," *Survey,* XXIX (November, 1912), 131–134.

[10] *Ibid.,* 137, uses "fleshpots"; *Newer Ideals of Peace,* 131, uses "sordid."

[11] Jane Addams, "Trade Unions and Public Duty," *American Journal of Sociology,* IV (January, 1899), 448–462.

[12] Addams, *Newer Ideals of Peace,* 36; "Larger Aspects of the Woman's Movement," *Annals of the American Academy of Political and Social Science,* LVI (November, 1914), 4.

[13] Addams, *Newer Ideals of Peace,* 33.

[14] *Chicago Chronicle,* September 14, 1903.

[15] Addams, *Democracy and Social Ethics,* 1, 2, 3.

[16] *Chicago Times-Herald,* November 1, 1897; *Boston Evening Transcript,* November 5, 1897.

[17] Addams, "Trade Unions and Public Duty," 459.

[18] Feuer, "John Dewey and the 'Back to the People Movement' in American Thought," 545–568.

[19] John C. Burnham, "Psychiatry, Psychology and the Progressive Movement,"

American Quarterly, 457–465; Samuel Haber, *Efficiency and Uplift: Scientific Management in the Progressive Era, 1890–1920* (Chicago, 1964).

[20] This redefinition of the role of government has received an enormous amount of attention from scholars; therefore I treat it here in only a cursory manner. For the general reader the entrée to this literature can be through Sidney Fine, *Laissez-Faire and the General Welfare State: A Study of Conflict in American Thought, 1865–1901* (Ann Arbor, 1956); Eric F. Goldman, *Rendezvous with Destiny* (New York, 1952); Joseph Dorfman, *The Economic Mind in American Civilization* (New York, 1946); and Morton G. White, *Social Thought in America: The Revolt Against Formalism* (New York, 1949).

Chapter 13: Suffrage and the Bull Moose

[1] The outline of the woman's movement is from Eleanor Flexner, *Century of Struggle: The Woman's Rights Movement in the United States* (Cambridge, 1959); and Aileen S. Kraditor, *The Ideas of the Woman Suffrage Movement, 1890–1920* (New York, 1965). Useful insights are in Christopher Lasch, *The New Radicalism in America, 1889–1963: The Intellectual as a Social Type* (New York, 1965), 38–68; and Jill Conway, "Jane Addams: An American Heroine," *Daedalus*, LIXIII (Spring, 1964), 761–780.

[2] Addams, *Newer Ideals of Peace*, 184–185.

[3] *Ibid.*, 188–189.

[4] *Chicago Journal*, June 1, 1912.

[5] William Loeb to Jane Addams, October 7, 1905; S. N. D. North [director of the census] to Jane Addams, December 9, 1905; *Woman's Journal*, December 30, 1905; Theodore Roosevelt to Jane Addams, January 24, 1906. Theodore Roosevelt's urging of the commission is in *Congressional Record*, 59 Congress, 1 Session, (December 5, 1905), Vol. 40, p. 94.

[6] Ida Husted Harper, *History of Woman Suffrage* (New York, 1922), VI, 274; *Boston Herald*, March 21, 1908; Jane Addams to Agnes Nestor, March 29, 1909 in the Nestor Manuscripts, Chicago Historical Society; *Chicago Examiner*, April 10, 1909.

[7] Circular letter of Illinois Equal Suffrage Association, February 20, 1911, in the Ada James Manuscripts, State Historical Society of Wisconsin; *Chicago Record-Herald*, March 7, 1911; *Chicago Tribune*, March 9, 1911; *Illinois News* [Springfield], April 20, 1911.

[8] Harper, *History of Woman Suffrage*, V, 343–390.

[9] *Ibid.*, V, 254–263; *Washington Times*, March 13, 1912; House Committee on Judiciary, *Hearings*, March 13, 1912, 62 Congress, 2 Session, House Document 762.

[10] Harper, *History of Woman Suffrage*, V, 667–668.

[11] *New York Morning Telegraph*, March 31, 1912; *New York Evening Sun*, April 2, 1912; *New York Herald Tribune*, June 1, 1912.

[12] Mark Sullivan, *Our Times: The United States, 1900–1925* (New York, 1927–1935), IV, 512–516.

[13] Theodore Roosevelt to Owen R. Lovejoy, July 9, 1912, in the Theodore Roosevelt Manuscripts, Library of Congress.

[14] Theodore Roosevelt to Medill McCormick, July 31, 1912, in Roosevelt Manuscripts.

[15] Theodore Roosevelt to Florence Lockwood La Farge, February 13, 1908, in Elting E. Morrison, ed., *Letters of Theodore Roosevelt* (Cambridge, 1952), VI, 942–943.

[16] Harper, *History of Woman Suffrage*, V, 706–707.

[17] Theodore Roosevelt [telegram] to Jane Addams, August 9, 1912; Ida Husted Harper to Editor, *New York Times*, August 22, 1912.

[18] Addams, *The Second Twenty Years at Hull-House,* 32.

[19] *New York Tribune,* August 8, 1912; *New York Herald,* August 8, 1912; *New York Commercial,* August 8, 1912.

[20] Linn, *Jane Addams,* 277.

[21] Addams, *The Second Twenty Years at Hull-House,* 35.

[22] The story of the disputed delegates is in all the national newspapers. See, for instance, the *New York Tribune,* August 6, 1912. Theodore Roosevelt explained his position a great number of times. See Theodore Roosevelt to Ryerson W. Jennings, July 30, 1912; and Theodore Roosevelt to Julian Harris, July 30, 1912; both in the Roosevelt Manuscripts.

[23] *New York Tribune,* August 6, 1912.

[24] Addams, "Respect for Law," *Independent,* LIII (February, 1901), 18; Langston Hughes, *Fight for Freedom* (New York, 1962), 22; *New York Times,* June 2, 1909; *New York Tribune,* June 1, 2, 1909; William English Walling to Jane Addams, June 8, 1909; *Boston Evening Transcript,* March 30, 1911; *Chicago Examiner,* April 7, 1912; Addams, *New Conscience and an Ancient Evil,* 118–119, 169; Jane Addams, "Has the Emancipation Act Been Nullified by National Indifference?," *Survey,* XXIX (February, 1913), 565–566.

[25] August Meier, *Negro Thought: America, 1880–1895. Racial Ideologies in the Age of Booker T. Washington* (Ann Arbor, 1963).

[26] Theodore Roosevelt [telegram] to Jane Addams, August 8, 1912.

[27] George William Cook to Jane Addams, August 17, 1912; May Childs Nerney to Jane Addams, August 13, 1912; Ernest C. Jones [telegram] to Jane Addams, August 7, 1912; William A. Trotter to Jane Addams, August 6, 1912; J. F. Ransom to Jane Addams, August 6, 1912; Colored Woman's Club of Indianapolis to Jane Addams, August 6, 1912; Robert A. Woods to Jane Addams, August 7, 1912.

[28] *New York Call,* August 13, 1912; Charles B. Tigner to Jane Addams, August 10, 1912.

[29] *Chicago Journal,* August 17, 1912; Irving Winslow to Jane Addams, August 7, August 12, 1912.

[30] *Baltimore Evening Sun,* August 19, 1912, contains a letter of Jane Addams disagreeing with Miss Boardman and defending her own position; Anna H. Shaw to Jane Addams, August 16, 1912.

[31] Eleanor Garrison to Jane Addams, August 24, 1912.

[32] *Chicago Examiner,* August 13, 1912; Francis A. Kellor to Jane Addams, August 19, August 20, September 10, September 11, 1912; *Chicago Tribune,* September 28, 1912; McNitt to Jane Addams, September 21, 1912; Edward Bok to Jane Addams, September 27, 1912; Norman Hapgood to Jane Addams, September 23, 1912; *New York Tribune,* August 21, 1912; *Kansas City Star,* October 20, 1912.

[33] Byres H. Gitchell to Jane Addams, September 13, 1912; *Wisconsin State Journal* [Madison], October 1; *New York Sun,* October 12; *Worcester Post* [Massachusetts], October 12; *Oklahoman* [Oklahoma City], October 13; *Saginaw News* [Michigan], October 16; *Wichita Eagle,* October 23; *St. Paul Dispatch,* October 25; *Minneapolis Journal,* October 25; *Fargo Courier News,* October 25; *Guthrie Leader* [Oklahoma], October 25; *St. Paul Pioneer Press,* October 27, October 28; *Sioux Falls Press,* October 31; *Denver Times,* November 1; *Denver Post,* November 2; *Colorado Springs Gazette,* November 3; *Pueblo Star Journal* [Colorado], November 3; *Kansas City Star,* November 3; all 1912.

[34] Addams, *The Second Twenty Years at Hull-House,* 38–39.

[35] *Elgin Courier* [Illinois], October 25; *Washington Times,* October 25; *Los Angeles Examiner,* September 29; *Chicago Music News,* September 27; *Kansas City Times,* September 11; *Indianapolis Star,* September 8; all in 1912. See also Jane Addams salute in *Kansas City Star,* October 30, 1912.

[36] Jane Addams to Mary Rozet Smith, November 22, 24, 1912.

[37] *Chicago American,* November 6, 1912.

[38] Theodore Roosevelt to Jane Addams, November 5, 1912.

[39] William Kent to Jane Addams, November 15, 1912; Jane Addams to Theodore Roosevelt, November 20, 1912; *Chicago Tribune,* November 11, 1912; *Chicago Inter-Ocean,* November 8, 1912.

[40] Efforts to continue the party program and denials of its death are in the *Chicago Examiner,* December 19, 1912. See also *New York Sun,* December 11, 1912; Francis Perkins [telegram] to Jane Addams, December 19, 1912; Gifford Pinchot to Jane Addams, February 12, 1913; Amos Pinchot to Hiram Johnson, December 5, 1912 (the latter two in the Pinchot Papers, Library of Congress). For the Progressive Service Committee, see Francis A. Kellor to Jane Addams, December 28, 1912; Madeline J. Doty to Jane Addams, January 15, 1912; minutes, January 9, 1913; and "Report of the Progressive Service Committee, May 1913"; all in the Swarthmore College Peace Collection.

[41] *Philadelphia Press,* November 25, 1912; *Chicago Evening Post,* November 25, 1912; *Boston Morning Journal,* November 30, 1912; *Woman's Journal,* January 18, 1913. Her travels in 1913 can be followed in: *New York American,* June 13; *New York Evening Sun,* July 2; *New York Tribune,* August 11; *Washington Times,* August 14; *New York Evening Mail,* August 15; *Staunton News* [Virginia], August 19; *Brooklyn Citizen,* September 24; *Columbus Journal* [Ohio], October 22; *Chicago Inter-Ocean,* November 4; *New York Evening Globe,* December 3; *New York Tribune,* December 5; *New York Times,* December 8. Her travels in the suffrage cause in 1914 can be followed in: *Atlanta Constitution,* March 1; *Birmingham Ace Herald,* March 10; *Philadelphia Press,* March 8; *Toledo Blade,* April 16; *Boston Transcript,* September 12; *Omaha Bee,* October 12; *St. Louis Republic,* October 18; *Aberdeen American* [South Dakota], October 18; *Kansas City Journal,* October 22; *Chicago Record Herald,* October 29; *Nashville Banner,* November 16; *Baltimore American,* November 17; *Chicago Tribune,* June 10; *Springfield Republican* [Massachusetts], June 28; *Fargo Forum* [North Dakota], August 18, 1914. For the relation of the National American Woman Suffrage Association to Woodrow Wilson, see Anna H. Shaw to Woodrow Wilson, July 2, 1914, in the Wilson Manuscripts, Library of Congress. Typescript of Jane Addams' testimony before the Committee on Rules, House of Representatives, December 3–5, 1913, in the League of Women Voters Manuscripts, "Suffrage Papers," Library of Congress.

Chapter 14: Pacifism

[1] Addams, *Newer Ideals of Peace,* 18.

[2] *Ibid.,* 182.

[3] *Ibid.,* 210, 211.

[4] Addams, *The Second Twenty Years at Hull-House,* 119.

[5] Lilliam D. Wald to W. D. Howells, September 22, 1914; Paul Kellogg to George Nasmyth, September 24, 1914; Paul Kellogg to Jane Addams, October 8, 1914 (the latter in the Wald Manuscripts, New York Public Library).

[6] *Chicago Tribune,* December 6, 1914; *Chicago Record Herald,* December 6, 1914.

[7] C. C. Catt to Jane Addams, December 14, 1914, in the Suffrage Archives, Library of Congress; Jane Addams to Lucia Ames Mead, December 23, 1914; Lillian D. Wald to Jane Addams, December 24, 1914, in the Wald Manuscripts.

[8] *Washington Herald,* January 9, 1915; *Washington Post,* January 11, 1915; *New York American,* January 11, 1915. Minutes of Woman's Peace Party organizational meeting, Washington, January 9–10, 1915, in the Swarthmore College Peace Collection, Women's International League for Peace and Freedom Manuscripts.

[9] Marie Louise Degen, *The History of the Woman's Peace Party* (Johns Hopkins

Studies in Historical and Political Science, Series LVII, Number 3, Baltimore, 1968), 65; *Chicago Tribune,* March 21, 1915; *Chicago Record,* March 21, 1915; *New York Evening Post,* March 29, 1915.

[10] Jane Addams to Lillian D. Wald, March 26, 1915, in the Wald Manuscripts.

[11] *Literary Digest,* L (1915), 1022; *New York Times,* April 28, 1915.

[12] Jane Addams to Mary Rozet Smith, April 22, April 24, 1915; Alice Hamilton to Mary Rozet Smith, April 22, 1915; W. J. Bryan to Diplomatic Officers of U. S., April 17, 1915.

[13] *New York Times,* April 28, April 29, 1915; E. G. Balch, "Journey and Impressions of the Congress" in Jane Addams, *et al., Women at the Hague: The International Congress of Women and its Results* (New York, 1915), 4–6.

[14] Degan, *Woman's Peace Party,* 84–86.

[15] Jane Addams to Mary Rozet Smith, May 9, 1915.

[16] Alice Hamilton to Mrs. Bowen, May 16, 1915; Jane Addams to Mary Rozet Smith, May 16, 1915; Secretary to Walter Hines Page to Jane Addams, May 11, 1915; Secretary to Sir Edward Grey to Jane Addams, May 12, 1915; Alice Page to Jane Addams, May 12, 1915.

[17] Degan, *Woman's Peace Party,* 97; Alice Hamilton, "At the War Capitals," in *Women at the Hague,* 27–30; Dr. Suderkinn to Jane Addams, May 21, 1915; O. Montselas to Jane Addams, May 22, 1915. These correspondents were secretaries to von Jägow and Bethmann-Hollweg.

[18] Hamilton, "At the War Capitals," *Women at the Hague,* 31; Hamilton, *Exploring the Dangerous Trades,* 171.

[19] Jane Addams, "Factors in Continuing the War," in *Women at the Hague,* 95–96.

[20] Hamilton, *Exploring the Dangerous Trades,* 174–176.

[21] Bertrand Russell to Jane Addams, June 19, 1915; Viscount Haldane to Jane Addams, June 21, 1915; Edward Grey to Jane Addams, June 20, 1915; Degen, *Woman's Peace Party,* 102.

[22] *Ibid.,* 91, 92.

[23] Jane Addams, "Revolt Against War," *Survey,* XXXIV (July 17, 1915), 355–359. The event is reported in the *New York World,* July 10, 1915. The Davis letter is in the *New York Times,* July 13, 1915. Scores of metropolitan dailies covered the controversy, which can be followed in any New York paper. See also Lillian D. Wald to Jane Addams, July 14, 1915, in the Wald Manuscripts.

[24] Woodrow Wilson to Lillian D. Wald, July 3, 1915; *New York Times,* July 21, 1915; *Chicago Examiner,* July 23, 1915.

[25] Arthur S. Link, *Wilson* (5 vols., Princeton, 1947–1966), III, 568.

[26] Jane Addams to J. G. Wales, September 20, September 22, 1915, in the Wales Manuscripts, State Historical Society of Wisconsin; Jane Addams to Paul Kellogg, September 24, 1915, in the Wald Manuscripts; Jane Addams to Miss K. D. Courtney, October 14, 1915; Jane Addams to Lillian D. Wald, November 12, 1915, in the Wald Manuscripts.

[27] Jane Addams to Rosika Schwimmer, December 24, 1915, and February 18, 1916; Jane Addams [telegram] to Aletta Jacobs, December 12, 1915, Swarthmore College Peace Collection, Woman's Peace Party Manuscripts; Mrs. Bowen to Lillian D. Wald, December 1, 1915, in the Wald Manuscripts. Also *Chicago Herald,* November 29, 1915; *Chicago American,* December 1, 1915.

[28] Letters of sympathy: Woodrow Wilson to Jane Addams, December 13, 1915; April 7, 1916. See also Jane Addams to Louis P. Lochner, February 18, 1916; *Los Angeles Times,* March 23, 1916; *San Francisco Examiner,* March 30, 1916; *New York American,* April 7, 1916; *Chicago American,* April 11, 1916; *New York Call,* November 10, 1916; *Chicago Evening Journal,* February 17, 1917; Linn, *Jane Addams,* 317.

[29] Link, *Wilson,* III, 139.

[30] His address is summarized and quoted in part in the *New York Times,* November 5, 1915. Annual message: *Congressional Record,* 64 Congress, 1 Session, pp. 95–100.

[31] The preparedness controversy is analyzed with unusual thoroughness in Link, *Wilson,* III, 137–143, 588–593, and IV, 15–54. See also Merle Curti, "Bryan and World Peace," in *Smith College Studies in History,* XVI (April–July, 1931), 165–253. The tortuous thinking of one type of progressive on preparedness is analyzed in Charles Forcey, *Crossroads of Liberalism* (New York, 1961), especially 245–250. A portion of public reaction to Woodrow Wilson's program is surveyed in "Preparedness and Politics," *Literary Digest,* V (November 20, 1915), 1143–1145. See also "Preparedness: A Poll of the Metropolitan Pulpits," *Outlook,* XI (December 8, 1915), 833; "The Preparedness We Believe In," *Outlook,* CXII (February 2, 1916), 256–258; "Preparedness for What?," *New Republic,* V (June 26, 1915), 188–189; "Preparedness—A Trojan Horse," *idem.,* V (November 6, 1915), 6.

[32] The testimony before the House Committee on Foreign Relations is in Women's International League for Peace and Freedom Files, Swarthmore College Peace Collection, January 11, 1916. See also House Committee on Military Affairs, "Statement of Miss Jane Addams, of Chicago, Illinois, Representing the Woman's Peace Party," (January 13, 1916), 201, 213; William J. Bryan to Jane Addams, January 22, 1916.

[33] *Seattle Times,* January 14, 1916; *San Diego Tribune,* January 15, 1916.

[34] *New York Times,* April 12, 1916.

[35] Jane Addams' statement on voting for Woodrow Wilson appeared in many places; see, for example, the *Wisconsin State Journal* [Madison], November 5, 1916. Woodrow Wilson to Jane Addams, November 23, December 12, 1916; *New York Times,* December 13, 1916.

[36] Louis Lochner to Jane Addams, January 30, January 31, February 1, 1917; Jane Addams [telegram] to Woodrow Wilson, February 3, 1917; *Washington Times,* February 4, 1917; House of Representatives, Committee on Foreign Affairs, *Hearings,* December 12, 1916.

[37] Vachel Lindsay to Jane Addams, April 9, 1917; Helen Dudley to Jane Addams, April 10, 1917; Jane Addams to Helen Dudley, April 19, 1917; Jane Addams to Graham Taylor, June 6, 1916. As early as June, 1917, however, Vachel Lindsay was talking about stamping out Prussianism, and probably enlisting. See Vachel Lindsay to Jane Addams, June 26, 1917.

[38] House of Representatives, Committee on Judiciary, *Hearings,* April 14, 1917. Jane Addams [telegram] to Hubert Dent, May 7, 1917; *Washington Evening Star,* April 12, 1917; *New York Evening Journal,* April 12, 1917; *New York Herald,* April 15, 1917.

[39] Addams, *Peace and Bread in Time of War,* 139; *Chicago Post,* April 30; *Chicago News,* April 30; *Indianapolis Star,* May 15; *New York Times,* June 11; *New York Herald,* June 13; *Pittsburgh Chronicle Telegram,* June 12; Portland [Oregon] *Telegraph,* June 12; John Hopkins to Jane Addams, June 11; *Louisville Herald,* June 17; *Chicago Evening Post,* June 18; Robert L. Henry to Jane Addams, June 21; Alice H. Wadsworth to *Chicago Tribune,* August 29; W. S. Moore to Jane Addams, June 11; *New York Staats-Zeitung,* July 1; all 1917.

[40] Addams, *Peace and Bread in Time of War,* 143, 147–148.

[41] *Ibid.,* 107, 127–128; Edward W. Evans to Jane Addams, December 18, 1917.

[42] Addams, *Peace and Bread in Time of War,* 82–83.

[43] An itinerary of her California trip is in the Swarthmore College Peace Collection, March–April, 1918. See also *Chicago Tribune,* November 12, 1917; *Denver*

News, November 24, 1917; *Philadelphia North American,* December 10, 1917; *Baltimore Sun,* December 16, 1917; *Chicago Examiner,* January 6, 1918; *Cincinnati Times Star,* January 17, 1917; *Cleveland Plain Dealer,* March 3, 1918; *San Antonio Light,* April 19, 1918; *New Orleans Times Picayune,* April 14, 1918; *Pittsburgh Gazette Times,* July 6, 1918; *San Francisco Examiner,* March 28, 1918. Jane Addams to Mary Rozet Smith, March 23, March 29, 1918; Jane Addams to Lillian D. Wald, April 4, 1918; Herbert Hoover to Jane Addams, March 2, 1918; Arthur E. Bestor to Jane Addams, April 30, 1918. For her help in distributing the liberty loan, see Max Shulman to Jane Addams, October 22, 1918, with a certificate dated October 19, 1918.

[44] Alice Hamilton to her family, May 1, 1919; Jane Addams to Mary Rozet Smith, May 1, 1919; Hamilton, *Exploring the Dangerous Trades,* 230–233.

[45] Alice Hamilton to Mary Rozet Smith, May 12, May 17, May 19, 1919; Jane Addams to Mary Rozet Smith, May 23, 1919; Florence Kelley to Mary Rozet Smith [?], May 22, 1919. See also Jane Addams to Woodrow Wilson, May 16, 1919, and Woodrow Wilson [telegram] to Jane Addams, May 16, 1919, both in the Wilson Papers, Library of Congress. *Washington Evening Star,* May 17; *San Francisco Call,* May 15; *New York Evening Post,* May 26, 1919. Hamilton, *Exploring the Dangerous Trades,* 233–236; Addams, *Peace and Bread in Time of War,* 156–165; Gertrude Bussey and Margaret Tims, *Women's International League for Peace and Freedom, 1915–1965: A Record of Fifty Years' Work* (London, 1965), 29–33; Degen, *Woman's Peace Party,* 217–240.

[46] Alice Hamilton to Mary Rozet Smith, May 30, June 8, July 5, 1919; Jane Addams to Mary Rozet Smith, June 11, June 14, June 23, June 24, July 5, 1919; Romain Rolland to Jane Addams, June 2, 1919; Charles H. Levermore to Jane Addams, June 17, 1919; Walter Bowerman to Jane Addams, July 7, 1919; Emily Balch to Jane Addams, July 22, 1919; Colonel Edward House to Jane Addams, August 12, 1919; Lucia Ames Meade to Jane Addams, August 13, 1919. See also *Chicago American,* August 27, 1919; Hamilton, *Exploring the Dangerous Trades,* 243–251; Addams, *Peace and Bread in Time of War,* 167–177; Frank M. Surface and Raymond L. Bland, *American Food in the World War and Reconstruction Period* (Stanford, 1931), 117; "Report of Jane Addams and Dr. Hamilton to the American Friends' Service Committee on the Situation in Germany," in the Swarthmore College Peace Collection.

Chapter 15: After the War

[1] A. Mitchell Palmer, "The Case Against the 'Reds,'" *Forum,* LXIII (February, 1920), 174; quoted in Johnson, *Challenge to American Freedoms,* 119.

[2] Addams, *The Second Twenty Years at Hull-House,* 153–154; Christopher Lasch, *The American Liberals and the Russian Revolution* (New York, 1962).

[3] *Buffalo Times,* January 25, 1919; *Boston Transcript,* January 28, 1919; *Chicago Examiner,* January 31, 1919; K. A. Burket to Jane Addams, January 25, 1919; Mrs. Jay E. Adams to Jane Addams, January 25, 1919; Lillian D. Wald [telegram] to Jane Addams, January 25, 1919; Jane Addams to Lillian D. Wald, January 26, 1919 (the latter two in the Wald Manuscripts).

[4] Preston, *Aliens and Dissenters,* 221.

[5] H. Rowland Curtsy to Jane Addams, February 23, 1920.

[6] *Chicago Daily News,* February 24, 1920.

[7] Anonymous note to Jane Addams, probably February 24, 1920.

[8] Jane Addams to Edward Scott Beck, February 23, 1920.

[9] *New York Evening Sun,* February 26, 1920; R. M. MacIver to Jane Addams, March 2, 1920.

[10] New York State Senate, Joint Legislative Committee Investigating Seditious Activities, *Revolutionary Radicalism: Its History, Purpose and Tactics* (4 vols., Albany, 1920). For Lusk's major proposals, see *New York Times,* April 12, April 13, May 10, 1921.

[11] *Boston Herald,* June 7, 1926.

[12] Arthur Garfield Hays to Jane Addams, April 23, 1926; Forest Bailey to Jane Addams, June 12, 1926; *Boston Morning Globe,* March 28, 1926; *New York Commercial,* May 18, 1926; *Boston Herald,* June 14, 1926; *New York Evening World,* November 13, 1926, Rosenwald Manuscripts. Undated memorandum of Hull House residents, probably November, 1926, against being called subversive.

[13] Mrs. Joseph T. Bowen to Charles N. Fay, January 24, 1927; Emily G. Balch to George B. Lockwood, March 31, 1927; Charles N. Fay to Editor of *Boston Herald,* May 17, 1921; C. C. Catt to Jane Addams, May 26, 1927; Florence Kelley to Jane Addams, July 29, 1927, in the Catt papers, New York Public Library; typescript of open letter to Daughters of the American Revolution defending Jane Addams against charges of subversion in Swarthmore College Peace Collection summary in *New York Herald Tribune,* July 24, 1927; Jane Addams to Mrs. Helen Tufts Bailie, May 9, 1928; *Springfield Republican* [Massachusetts], March 27, 1928; *Denver News,* April 21, 1928; *San Francisco News,* April 24, 1928; *San Francisco Chronicle,* September 8, 1928.

[14] *Independence Reporter* [Kansas], March 18, 1931.

[15] List of speaking engagements in the Swarthmore College Peace Collection; *Boston Globe,* March 9, 1919; and *Chicago American,* November 29, 1920. See also Jane Addams, "Free the World and Save the League," *New Republic,* XXIV (November 24, 1920), 325–327.

[16] Fragment of typescript article about Jane Addams in the Wald Manuscripts, dated 1933, quoting Jane Addams on Russia as "largest piece of conscious social laboratory experiment that history records." On the Russian Revolution, see Addams, "Free the World and Save the League"; Addams, *The Second Twenty Years at Hull-House,* 153–163; Addams, *Peace and Bread in Time of War,* 91–107, 194. See also an absolutely brilliant piece by Lewis S. Feuer, "American Travelers to the Soviet Union, 1917–1932: The Formation of a Component of New Deal Ideology," *American Quarterly,* XIV (Summer, 1962), 119–149, for the views of other liberals.

[17] Hundreds of items in the Swarthmore College Peace Collection are the sources for these four paragraphs. The tumor is mentioned in an English-language Tokyo newspaper of June 24 [?], 1923. The quotation about the Kellogg-Briand pact is from the *Christian Science Monitor,* August 27, 1928.

[18] *New York Herald Tribune,* January 14, 1931.

[19] Horatio B. Hacket to Jane Addams, December 21, 1934; draft reply, undated, end of 1934.

[20] *Philadelphia Record,* January 16, 1931.

[21] *Ibid.,* September 7, 1930.

[22] The Swarthmore College Peace Collection contains an immense number of letters and clippings pertaining to the Nobel Prize. The conversation is from Linn, *Jane Addams,* 389. See also Continental Illinois Trust to Jane Addams, December 24, 1931, and a note by Jane Addams in the folder for January, 1932 (both in the Swarthmore College Peace Collection).

[23] Account of Jane Addams' death is from an undated memorandum, no doubt by Alice Hamilton, in the Swarthmore College Peace Collection.

[24] *New York Times,* May 3, 1931.

BIBLIOGRAPHY

MANUSCRIPTS

The basis for any study of Jane Addams must be the large collection of material in the Swarthmore College Peace Collection, Swarthmore, Pennsylvania. In addition to Miss Addams' correspondence, this collection contains much material on Hull House, typescripts of speeches, and a huge collection of newspaper clippings, collected by a clipping service to which she subscribed. The clipping collection alone is estimated at 25,000 items and is an invaluable record of her public life.

In addition, the following manuscript collections were consulted:

Library of Congress
- Ray Stannard Baker
- Albert J. Beveridge
- Sophonisba Breckinridge
- Carrie Chapmann Catt
- Clarence Darrow
- Ida Husted Harper
- Robert Lansing
- League of Women Voters
- Ben Lindsey
- Alexander McKelway
- National Child Labor Committee
- National Consumers' League
- Amos Pinchot
- Gifford Pinchot
- Louis F. Post
- Alice Thatcher Post
- Jacob Riis
- Theodore Roosevelt
- Suffrage Archives
- Woodrow Wilson

Radcliffe Women's Archives
- Catharine Waugh McCulloch
- Anna Howard Shaw

State Historical Society of Wisconsin
- Ada James
- Robert M. La Follette
- Henry Demarest Lloyd
- Raymond Robins
- E. A. Ross

Rockford College
- Archives

University of Chicago
Grace Abbott
Edith Abbott
Julius Rosenwald
Newberry Library
Graham R. Taylor
New York Public Library
Lillian D. Wald
Carrie Chapmann Catt
Smith College
Ellen Gates Starr
Stephenson County, Illinois, Historical Society
Jane Addams materials
Social Welfare History Archives
Survey Associates Papers
Paul Kellogg
Interviews
Jessie Binnford
Fola La Follette
Lea Taylor

PRINTED WORKS

The following is a list of articles and books actually cited in the notes to this study of Jane Addams and American liberalism. It is not intended as a guide to the vast literature of progressivism, nor as a complete list of Jane Addams' own writings. For the latter, see John C. Farrell, *Beloved Lady: A History of Jane Addams' Ideas on Reform and Peace* (Baltimore, 1967), 221–241.

ARTICLES:

Abbott, Edith. "Grace Abbott and Hull House," *Social Service Review,* XXIV (1950), 374–394.

Addams, Jane. "A Function of the Social Settlement," *Annals of the American Academy of Political and Social Sciences,* XIII (May, 1899), 323–345.

Addams, Jane. "A Modern Lear: The Strike at Pullman," *Survey,* XXIX (November, 1912), 131–137.

Addams, Jane. "Charity and Social Justice," National Conference of Charities and Corrections, *Proceedings* (1910), 1–18.

Addams, Jane. "Charity Visitor's Perplexities," *Outlook,* LXI (March, 1899), 598–600.

Addams, Jane. "Chicago Settlements and Social Unrest," *Charities,* XX (May, 1908), 155–166.

Addams, Jane. "The Child at the Point of Greatest Pressure," National Conference of Charities and Corrections, *Proceedings* (1912), 26–30.

Addams, Jane. "Child Labor on the Stage," *Annals of the American Academy of Political and Social Sciences,* XXXVIII (July, 1911), Supplement, 60–65.

Addams, Jane. "Child Labor and Pauperism," *Charities,* XI (October, 1903), 300–304.

Addams, Jane. "Child Labor Legislation — A Requisite for Industrial Efficiency," *Annals of the American Academy of Political and Social Sciences,* XXV (May, 1905), 542–550.

Addams, Jane. "The College Woman and the Family Claim," *The Commons,* XXIX (September, 1898), 3–9.

Addams, Jane. "Ethical Survival in Municipal Corruption," *International Journal of Ethics,* VIII (1897–1898), 273–291.

Addams, Jane. "Factors in Continuing the War," *Women at the Hague* (New York, 1915), 95–96.
Addams, Jane. "Free the World and Save the League," *New Republic,* XXIV (November 24, 1920), 325–327.
Addams, Jane. "Has the Emanicipation Act Been Nullified by National Indifference?" *Survey,* XXIX (February 1, 1913), 565–566.
Addams, Jane. "Humanizing Tendency of Industrial Education," *Chautauquan,* XXXIX (May, 1904), 266–272.
Addams, Jane. "The Immigrant and Social Unrest," National Conference of Social Work, *Proceedings* (1920), 59–62.
Addams, Jane. "Julia Lathrop at Hull-House," *Survey Graphic,* XXIX (August, 1935), 373–377.
Addams, Jane. "The 'Juvenile-Adult' Offender," *Ladies Home Journal,* XXX (October, 1913), 24.
Addams, Jane. "Larger Aspects of the Women's Movement," *Annals of the American Academy of Political and Social Sciences,* LVI (November, 1914), 1–8.
Addams, Jane. "National Protection for Children," *Annals of the American Academy of Political and Social Sciences,* XXIX (January, 1907), 57–60.
Addams, Jane. "Operation of the Illinois Child Labor Law," *Annals of the American Academy of Political and Social Sciences,* XXVII (March, 1906), 327–330.
Addams, Jane. "Problems of Municipal Administration," *American Journal of Sociology,* X (January, 1905), 425–444.
Addams, Jane. "The Public Dance Halls of Chicago," *Ladies Home Journal,* XXX (July, 1913), 19.
Addams, Jane. "Public Recreation and Social Morality," *Charities,* XVIII (October, 1903), 492–494.
Addams, Jane. "Respect for Law," *Independent,* LIII (January, 1901), 18–20.
Addams, Jane. "Revolt Against War," *Survey,* XXXIV (July 17, 1915), 355–359.
Addams, Jane. "The Settlement as a Factor in the Labor Movement," *Hull House Maps and Papers* (no date), 184–186.
Addams, Jane. "Stage Children," *Survey,* XXV (December 3, 1910), 342.
Addams, Jane. "Ten Years Experience in Illinois," *Annals of the American Academy of Political and Social Sciences,* 38 (July, 1911), Supplement, 144–148.
Addams, Jane. "Toast to John Dewey," *Survey,* LXIII (November, 1929), 203–204.
Addams, Jane. "Trade Unions and Public Duty," *American Journal of Sociology,* IV (January, 1899), 448–462.
Addams, Jane. "Why the Ward Boss Rules," *Outlook,* LVIII (April 2, 1898), 879–882.
Addams, Jane. "Work and Play as Factors in Education," *Chautauquan,* XLII (November, 1905), 251–255.
Anonymous. "Hull House Labor Museum," *Chautauquan,* XXXVIII (September, 1903), 60–61.
Anonymous. "The Most Useful Americans," *Independent,* LXXIV (May, 1913), 956–963.
Anonymous. "Preparedness: A Poll of the Metropolitan Pulpits," *Outlook,* XI (December 8, 1915), 833.
Anonymous. "Preparedness — A Trojan Horse," *New Republic,* V (November 6, 1915), 6–7.
Anonymous. "Preparedness and Politics," *Literary Digest,* V (November 20, 1915), 1143–1145.
Anonymous. "Preparedness for What?" *New Republic,* V (June 26, 1915), 188–190.
Anonymous. "The Preparedness We Believe In," *Outlook,* CXII (February 2, 1916), 256–258.

Baker, Ray S. "Hull House and the Ward Boss," *Outlook,* LVIII (1898), 769–771.

Balch, E. G. "Journey and Impressions of the Congress," *Women at the Hague* (New York, 1915), 4–6.

Barnes, Harry Elmer. "Criminology," *Encyclopedia of Social Sciences,* IV, 584–592.

Bowen, [Mrs.] Joseph T. "The Early Days of the Juvenile Court," *The Child, The Clinic and The Court* (New York, 1927), 290–310.

Buck, M. M. "Hull House Labor Museum," *Craftsman,* XIII (November, 1907), 229–230.

Burnham, John C. "Psychiatry, Psychology and the Progressive Movement," *American Quarterly,* (Winter, 1960), XII: 457–465.

Carlyle, Thomas S. *Sartor Resartus* (Boston, 1896).

Carnegie, Andrew. "The Advantages of Poverty," *Nineteenth Century,* XXIX (March, 1891), 367–385.

Conway, Jill. "Jane Addams: An American Heroine," *Daedalus,* CXIII (Spring, 1964), 761–780.

Craig, Oscar. "The Prevention of Pauperism," *Scribner's,* XIV (July, 1893), 121–128.

Curti, Merle. "Bryan and World Peace," *Smith College Studies in History,* XVI (April–July, 1931), 165–253.

Davis, Allen F. "The Women's Trade Union League: Origins and Organization," *Labor History* (Winter, 1964), 3–17.

Dewey, John. "Play," *Cyclopedia of Education,* IV, 725–727.

Feuer, Lewis. "American Travelers to the Soviet Union, 1917–1932: The Formation of a Component of New Deal Ideology," *American Quarterly,* XIV (Summer, 1962), 119–149.

Feuer, Lewis. "John Dewey and the 'Back to the People Movement' in American Thought," *Journal of the History of Ideas,* XX (October, 1959), 545–686.

Fowler, William P. "The Emergency Work in Boston," National Conference of Charities and Corrections, *Proceedings* (1894), 45–49.

Gulick, Luther H. "Play and Democracy," *Charities,* XVIII (August, 1907), 481–486.

Hall, G. Stanley. "Some of the Methods and Results of Child Study Work at Clark University," National Education Association, *Proceedings* (1896), 860–864.

Hamilton, Alice. "At the War Capitals," *Women at the Hague* (New York, 1915), 27–30.

Horowitz, Julius. "The Arithmetic of Delinquency," *New York Times Magazine* (January 31, 1965), 13.

House Committee on Military Affairs. "Statement of Miss Jane Addams, of Chicago, Illinois, Representing the Women's Peace Party" (January 13, 1916), 201, 213.

Hubbard, G. H. "The Why of Poverty," *New Englander,* L (March, 1889), 180–188.

Hurley, Timothy D. "Origin of the Illinois Juvenile Court Law," *The Child, The Clinic and the Court* (New York, 1927), 320–331.

Illinois Senate Committee on Judiciary. "Hearings in the Matter of Children on the Public Stage" (Transcript of March 8, 1911), 17–26.

Jenkins, Elizabeth. "Froebel's Disciples in America," *German-American Review,* Number 3 (1933), 15–18.

Kelley, Florence. "Hull House," *New England Magazine,* XVIII (1898), 550–566.

Kellog, Charles D. "The Situation in New York in the Winter of 1893–1894," National Conference of Charities and Corrections, *Proceedings* (1894), 21–30.

Kirkland, E. C. "The Robber Barons Revisited," *American Historical Review,* LXVI (October, 1960), 68–73.

Lathrop, Julia C. "The Background of the Juvenile Court in Illinois," *The Child, the Clinic and the Court* (New York, 1927), 290–298.

Lindsey, Ben B. "The Boy and the Court," *Charities and the Commons,* XIII (January 7, 1905), 350–357.

Lindsey, Ben B. "Colorado's Contribution to the Juvenile Court," *The Child, the Clinic and the Court* (New York, 1927), 288.

M'Gonnigle, R. D. "The Winter in Pittsburgh," National Conference of Charities and Corrections, *Proceedings* (1894), 36–42.

Mack, Julian W. "The Chancery Procedures in the Juvenile Court," *The Child, the Clinic and the Court* (New York, 1927), 310–320.

Miller, Herbert A. "The Rising National Individualism," *American Journal of Sociology,* XIX (March, 1912), 592–605.

Moore, D. "A Day at Hull House," *American Journal of Sociology* (March, 1897).

Palmer, A. Mitchell. "The Case Against the 'Reds'," *Forum,* LXIII (February, 1920), 173–185.

Peabody, F. G. "How Should a City Care for Its Poor?," *Forum,* XIV (1892), 474–491.

Poole, Ernest. "A Mixing Bowl for Nations," *Everybody's,* XXIII (October, 1910), 554–564.

Richmond, Mary. "The Social Case Worker in a Changing World," *The Long View* (New York, 1930), 374.

Riesman, David. "Thoughts on Teachers and Schools," *Anchor Review* (New York, 1955), 27–60.

Roche, John P. "Entrepreneurial Liberty and the Fourteenth Amendment," *Labor History,* IV (Winter, 1963), 3–31.

Rosengarten, Joseph G. "A Successful Experiment in Utilizing Unemployed Labor," National Conference of Charities and Corrections, *Proceedings* (1894), 58–62.

Sayles, Mary B. "Settlement Workers and Their Work," *Outlook,* LXXVIII (October, 1904), 304–311.

Smith, Margaret K. "Child Study in Connection with the Professional Training of Teachers," National Education Association, *Proceedings* (1893), 447–451.

Taylor, Graham R. "How They Played at Chicago," *Charities,* XVIII (August 3, 1907), 471–480.

Taylor, Graham R. "The New View," *Charities,* XVIII (August 3, 1907), 463.

Taylor, Graham R. "Recreation Developments in Chicago Parks," *Annals of The American Academy of Political and Social Sciences,* XXXV (1910), 304–321.

Turner, Frederick Jackson. "The Problem of the West," *Atlantic Monthly,* LXXVIII (September, 1896), 297.

Unger, Irwin. "The 'New Left' and American History: Some Recent Trends in United States Historiography," *American Historical Review,* LXII (July, 1967), 1237–1263.

Van Waters, Miriam. "Juvenile Delinquency and Juvenile Courts," *Encyclopedia of the Social Sciences,* III, 528–533.

Vandewalker, Nina C. "Kindergarten," *Cyclopedia of Education* (New York, 1912), III, 598–606.

Woods, Robert A. "The Social Awakening in London," *Scribner's,* XI (April, 1892), 401–424.

Wright, Montgomery. "Give the Children a Chance to Play," *The American City,* II (March, 1910), 115–117.

Yeich, Edwin B. "Jane Addams," *Historical Review of Berks County,* XVII (October–December, 1951), 10–13.

BOOKS

Abbott, Grace. *The Child and the State* (Chicago, 1938).

Addams, Jane, *et al. The Child, the Clinic and the Court* (New York, 1927).

Addams, Jane. *Democracy and Social Ethics* (New York, 1902).

Addams, Jane. *My Friend, Julia Lathrop* (New York, 1935).

Addams, Jane. *A New Conscience and an Ancient Evil* (New York, 1912).

Addams, Jane. *Newer Ideals of Peace* (New York, 1907).

Addams, Jane. *Peace and Bread in Time of War* (New York, 1922).

Addams, Jane. *Philanthropy and Social Progress* (New York, 1893).

Addams, Jane. *The Second Twenty Years at Hull-House; September 1909–September 1929* (New York, 1930).

Addams, Jane. *The Spirit of Youth and the City Streets* (New York, 1920).

Addams, Jane. *Twenty Years at Hull-House; with Autobiographical Notes* (New York, 1910).

Addams, Jane, *et al. Women at the Hague; the International Congress of Women and Its Results* (New York, 1915).

Anonymous. *History of Rockford and Winnebago County* (n.p., n.d.).

Boring, Edwin G. *A History of Experimental Psychology* (New York, 1950).

Bremner, Robert H. *From the Depths: The Discovery of Poverty in the United States* (New York, 1956).

Bruner, Jerome. *Toward a Theory of Instruction* (Cambridge, 1966).

Bruno, Frank J. *Trends in Social Work, 1874–1956* (New York, 1957).

Bussey, Gertrude C., and Margaret Tims. *Women's International League for Peace and Freedom, 1915–1965; A Record of Fifty Years' Work* (London, 1965).

Cavan, Ruth S. *Criminology* (New York, 1948).

Chambers, Clarke A. *Seedtime of Reform; American Social Service and Social Action, 1918–1933* (Minneapolis, 1965).

Chicago Board of Education. *Proceedings.*

Cremin, Lawrence A. *The Transformation of the School; Progressivism in American Education, 1876–1957* (New York, 1961).

Davis, Allen F. *Spearheads for Reform: The Social Settlements and the Progressive Movement, 1890–1914* (New York, 1967).

Degen, Mary Louise. *The History of the Woman's Peace Party* (Baltimore, 1939).

Donald, David. *Lincoln Reconsidered: Essays on the Civil War* (New York, 1956).

Dorfman, Joseph. *The Economic Mind in American Civilization* (New York, 1946).

Earnest, Ernest. *S. Wier Mitchell, Novelist and Physician* (Philadelphia, 1950).

Faulkner, Harold U. *Politics, Reform and Expansion, 1890–1900* (New York, 1959).

Fine, Sidney. *Laissez-Faire and the General Welfare State: A Study of Conflict in American Thought, 1865–1901* (Ann Arbor, 1956).

Flexner, Eleanor. *Century of Struggle: The Woman's Rights Movement in the United States* (Cambridge, 1959).

Forcey, Charles M. *Crossroads of Liberalism: Croly, Weyl, Lippmann and the Progressive Era, 1900–1925* (New York, 1961).

George, Henry. *Progress and Poverty: An Inquiry into the Cause of Industrial Depressions and of Increase of Want with Increase of Wealth. . .* (New York, 1880).

Glueck, Sheldon, and Eleanor T. Glueck. *Predicting Delinquency and Crime* (Cambridge, 1959).

Glueck, Sheldon, and Eleanor T. Glueck. *One Thousand Juvenile Delinquents: Their Treatment by Court and Clinic,* Vol. I of the *Survey of Crime and Criminal Justice in Boston* (Cambridge, 1959).

Goldman, Eric F. *Rendezvous with Destiny: A History of Modern American Reform* (New York, 1952).

Goldmark, Josephine. *Impatient Crusader: Florence Kelley's Life Story* (Urbana, 1953).

Gossett, Thomas F. *Race: The History of an Idea in America* (Dallas, 1963).

Haber, Samuel. *Efficiency and Uplift: Scientific Management in the Progressive Era, 1890–1920* (Chicago, 1964).

Hall, G. Stanley. *Youth: Its Education, Regimen, and Hygiene* (New York, 1912).

Haller, Mark H. *Eugenics: Hereditarian Attitudes in American Thought* (New Brunswick, 1963).

Hamilton, Alice. *Exploring the Dangerous Trades: The Autobiography of Alice Hamilton* (Boston, 1943).

Harper, Ida Husted. *History of Woman Suffrage* (6 vols., New York, 1889–1922).

Haynes, Fred E. *Criminology* (New York, 1910).

Healy, William. *The Individual Delinquent: A Textbook of Diagnosis and Prognosis for all Concerned in Understanding Offenders* (Boston, 1924).

Higham, John. *Strangers in the Land: Patterns of American Nativism, 1860–1925* (New Brunswick, 1955).

Hofstadter, Richard M. *The Age of Reform: From Bryan to F.D.R.* (New York, 1955).

Hofstadter, Richard M. *Anti-Intellectualism in American Life* (New York, 1963).

Hofstadter, Richard M. *Social Darwinism in American Thought* (Boston, 1955).

Hughes, Langston. *Fight for Freedom: The Story of the NAACP* (New York, 1962).

James, William. *Psychology* (New York, 1890).

Johnson, Donald O. *The Challenge to American Freedoms: World War I and the Rise of the American Civil Liberties Union* (Lexington, 1963).

Josephson, Matthew. *Sidney Hillman, Statesman of American Labor* (New York, 1952).

Kirkland, E. C. *Industry Comes of Age: Business, Labor and Public Policy, 1860–1897* (New York, 1961).

Kraditor, Aileen S. *The Ideas of the Woman Suffrage Movement, 1890–1920* (New York, 1965).

Lasch, Christopher. *The American Liberals and the Russian Revolution* (New York, 1962).

Lasch, Christopher. *The New Radicalism in America, 1889–1963: The Intellectual as a Social Type* (New York, 1965).

Link, Arthur S. *Wilson* (5 vols., Princeton, 1947–1966).

Levine, Daniel. *Varieties of Reform Thought* (Madison, 1964).

Linn, James W. *Jane Addams* (New York, 1935).

Lloyd, Henry Demarest. *Wealth Against Commonwealth* (New York, 1894).

Lou, Herbert H. *Juvenile Courts in the United States* (Chapel Hill, 1927).

Lubove, Roy. *The Professional Altruist: The Emergence of Social Work as a Career, 1880–1930* (Cambridge, 1965).

McKelvey, Blake. *The Urbanization of America, 1860–1915* (New Brunswick, 1963).

Meier, August. *Negro Thought: America, 1880–1895. Racial Ideologies in the Age of Booker T. Washington* (Ann Arbor, 1963).

Monroe, Paul (ed.). *Cyclopedia of Education* (5 Vols., New York, 1911–1913).

Morison, Elting E. *Letters of Theodore Roosevelt* (8 vols., Cambridge, 1951–1954).

Mowry, George E. *The California Progressives* (Berkeley, 1951).

National Conference of Charities and Correction. *Proceedings.*

New York City Youth Board. *A Manual of Procedures for the Application of the Glueck Prediction Tables* (New York, 1964).

New York State Senate, Joint Legislative Committee Investigating Seditious Activities. *Revolutionary Radicalism: Its History, Purpose and Tactics* (Albany, 1920).

Paul, Arnold M. *Conservative Crisis and the Rule of Law: Attitudes of Bar and Bench, 1887–1895* (Ithaca, 1960).

Preston, William, Jr. *Aliens and Dissenters: Federal Suppression of Radicals, 1903–1933* (Cambridge, 1963).

Richmond, Mary. *Social Diagnosis* (New York, 1917).

Richmond, Mary. *The Long View: Papers and Addresses* (New York, 1930).

Riis, Jacob A. *How the Other Half Lives: Studies Among the Tenements of New York* (New York, 1890).

Rose, Ernest. *A History of German Literature* (New York, 1960).

Ruskin, John. *Works* (London, 1905).

Steiner, Jessie F. *Americans at Play: Recent Trends in Recreation and Leisure Time Activities* (New York, 1933).

Sullivan, Mark. *Our Times: The United States, 1900–1925* (6 vols., New York, 1926–1935).

Surface, Frank M., and Raymond L. Bland. *American Food in the World War and Reconstruction Period* (Stanford, 1931).

Thrasher, Frederic M. *The Gang: A Study of 1,313 Gangs in Chicago* (Chicago, 1927).

Tuchman, Barbara. *The Zimmermann Telegram* (New York, 1958).

Vandewalker, Nina C. *Kindergarten in American Education* (New York, 1908).

Walsel, Oskar. *German Romanticism* (New York, 1932).

Werner, M. R. *Julius Rosenwald: The Life of a Practical Humanitarian* (New York, 1939).

White, Morton G., and Lucia White. *The Intellectual Versus the City: From Thomas Jefferson to Frank Lloyd Wright* (Cambridge, 1962).

White, Morton G. *Social Thought in America: The Revolt Against Formalism* (New York, 1949).

Wiebe, Robert H. *Businessmen and Reform: A Study of the Progressive Movement* (Cambridge, 1962).

Williams, Raymond. *Culture and Society* (New York, 1958).

UNPUBLISHED WRITINGS

Cedarborg, Hazel P. *History of Rockford,* in the Rockford College Archives.

Haldeman-Julius, Marcet. "The Two Mothers of Jane Addams," typescript in the Swarthmore College Peace Collection.

Huber, Francis A. "The Progressive Career of Ben B. Lindsey, 1900–1920," Ph.D. dissertation, University of Michigan, 1963.

Post, Louis. "Living a Long Life Over Again," unpublished autobiography in the Post Collection, Library of Congress.

Pottishman, Nancy P. "Jane Addams and Education," M.A. thesis, Columbia University, 1962.

Smith, Charlotte W. "Historical Sketch of Rockford College," in the Rockford College Archives.